# Production and
# Inventory Management
# in the Computer Age

# Production and Inventory Management in the Computer Age

## Oliver W. Wight
President, Oliver Wight, Inc.

**CBI Publishing Company, Inc.**
51 Sleeper Street, Boston, Massachusetts 02210

**Library of Congress Cataloging in Publication Data**

Wight, Oliver W
  Production and inventory management in the computer
age.
  Bibliography: p.
  1. Electronic data processing—Production management.
2. Electronic data processing—Inventory control.
I. Title.
TS155.W533                    658.5                    74-7127
ISBN 0-8436-0732-7


Printing (*last digit*): 10

ISBN: 0-8436-0732-7
Library of Congress Catalog Card Number: 74-7127

Printed in the United States of America
The Book Press, Brattleboro, Vermont

# Contents

# Preface

It was around 1958 that some manufacturing companies began to give serious attention to the computer. They had problems—problems of control, problems that were caused by their inability to get the right information on a *timely* enough basis to be used for control. The computer looked like it offered a solution.

These early attempts to use computers in production and inventory management failed more often than not. A few failed disastrously, and the companies took many years to recover from their experiences with their first computer system. Most failed far less dramatically. They simply failed to generate anywhere near the results management had been led to expect.

As a result, there were probably fewer manufacturing people who were optimistic about the potential for computer applications in manufacturing in 1968 than there had been in 1958. Like any new technology, there was a real "learning curve" and consequently a period of disillusionment.

About 1970, things started to come into perspective. A number of companies—most of them with very similar systems—began to report the same story over and over. Lower inventories, better customer service, better ability to respond to changes in the business level. And these reports came from the manufacturing people themselves, not from data-processing or systems people alone.

Looking back on it, there were probably three major influences that started to bring some order out of the chaos:

1. The IBM PICS approach. In July 1965, the IBM Manufacturing Industries Marketing group got together to review their attempts at developing application programs. This had been largely a disjointed

effort, and the only really useful application program to come out of a rather costly investment was the manufacturing data-base program called the *bill of material processor*. At this meeting, a strategic decision was made by IBM to develop a fairly integrated set of *basic* application programs (named PICS—Production Information and Control System) generally built around the bill of material processor, which would be applicable to most manufacturing companies.

IBM thus established a standard that had many imitators when their system was successful. The availability of software to implement production and inventory management on a computer greatly advanced the cause and encouraged many companies to install similar systems. Because they were similar, there was considerable communication from company to company about these systems.

2. As manufacturing companies began to gain experience using these systems, a whole new body of practical knowledge developed. There used to be a great many interesting—and often bizarre—theories about what the moon was like, but then we landed. A parallel situation occurred in manufacturing.

3. A number of the top professionals in the field of production and inventory management made it a point to consciously try to draw upon other users' experience and to compare their own experiences and critique each other's opinions. This was truly the scientific method: hypotheses were revised and refined through observation. As a result the conventional theory of inventory management was dramatically revised. Other techniques we thought we understood, such as machine loading, did not work in practice the way the theories said they would; newer approaches, like capacity requirements planning, were developed.

By the mid-1970s, many observers commented that "everyone is singing from the same hymn book." The leading consultants, the literature, movies, video courses, and education programs sponsored by the American Production and Inventory Control Society (APICS) were all saying same things about the same techniques. The practitioner now had a standard set of tools he could draw upon rather than the challenge of reinventing the tools. The empirical—or "let's try it and see if it works"—approach was being replaced by a sound body of *practical* knowledge.

This progress rapidly generated further progress, and, as a result

1. Significant techniques were identified and better understood.
2. The interrelationship among the techniques began to emerge clearly.
3. The experience of users was drawn upon to learn what was needed to make these types of systems really work in a manufacturing environment.

Perhaps one of the most important things that resulted was a new attitude toward computer systems. They were no longer the gee-whiz magic black boxes that were going to produce the automatic factory and eliminate the decision-making responsibility of middle management as some of the more romantically inclined writers of the early years of the computer age had suggested. Computers began to be seen as bread-and-butter tools for getting better results in manufacturing. We moved from the age of alchemy into the age of chemistry.

In the meantime, of course, production and inventory management was becoming a much more important topic for most manufacturing companies. They found themselves with inventories higher than they would like to have them, service that tended to be lower than they would like to have it, and a product line that was increasing in size and complexity. At the same time, some of the oldtimers who once held the companies together with their informal systems were retiring. Production and inventory management, which used to be looked upon as clerk work and stock-chasing, had come of age. As a result, its potential for contributing to profits and growth is now widely recognized by manufacturing executives.

This book, then, is written for people in manufacturing management who recognize that they need to know what computer-based production and inventory management systems can do for them. *It does not deal with computers or computer programs per se.* But just as a book about travel today could not ignore the airlines or their influence on travel, it is about production and inventory management *today*, when computers are widely available.

This book was also designed to be used for college-level education. It can be used as the text for a short course in production and inventory management or as a supplementary text for a manufacturing or computer systems course of broader scope. The student should find the appendixes containing the Glossary, Case Studies, and the Bibliography particularly useful. The educator will also find some thought-provoking questions for the student in the appendix.

The book is organized into seven sections that are designed to show the manager how the elements of a formal production and inventory management system fit together. Traditionally, production and inventory management books cover lot-sizing and forecasting in the early chapters. I have purposely moved them to the sixth section—out of the mainstream—because experience has shown that operations can be improved dramatically even if very approximate lot sizes are used and even if no new forecasting techniques are introduced. Parts I through V are intended to convey the essence of an integrated production and inventory management system and its interrelationships. Part VII should be of particular value to management-level people.

I have inserted miniature case studies throughout the book. These are based on actual experience—although they do not represent real companies or persons—and are intended to give illustrations of some of the major points covered. They should help the student, in particular, to understand better the real-world applications of the principles and techniques being explained.

I would like to acknowledge three people in particular who have constantly stimulated my thinking.

Dr. Joseph A. Orlicky of IBM, my long-time associate, whose experience with manufacturing companies has given him keen insights into what had to be done to really make computers pay off in manufacturing companies. No other man has had as much influence on the development of production and inventory management systems.

L. J. Burlingame, Vice President of Materials Management, Twin Disc, Inc. Jim was one of the pioneer users of the techniques that have now become very much the "national standard" in production and inventory management. Like so many practitioners, he has a very responsible, time-consuming job in his own company, yet Jim has always been able to find the time to do what he could to advance the state of the art. That willingness, combined with a keen mind and a personality that takes occasional glee from needling the "experts," has made him one of the most stimulating thinkers in the field. I have had the good fortune to work very closely with him over the years, and have learned as much as I have taught. He has always been an outstanding example of the type of prac-

᾿itioner who proved out the ideas while the educators and the consultants publicized them and received the recognition.

In 1959, I hired a young trainee out of college. I told him about the potential I saw for production and inventory management and evidently did a good sales job. Walter Goddard won his own spurs in the field as a practitioner and later as a consultant. Since 1970, he has been Executive Vice President of Oliver Wight, Inc. Walt's professional dedication and his constant sifting and resifting of experience have been a constant spur to me.

I would also like to recognize Dick Alban of Black & Decker, Professor Ed Davis of MIT's Sloan School (who has done a lot to restore my faith that there *are* educators who are concerned about the relevance of business education), and Mike Rowan, Editor and Assistant Publisher of *Modern Materials Handling* magazine who helped so much with his reviews of this book. There have been many, many others who have contributed to my knowledge—too many to mention. I hope they will take some professional satisfaction from this book as they occasionally recognize an idea we discussed being used to help others to understand.

Reduced inventories, better customer service, better response to marketing demands that can result in real growth, and increased profits—these were all the wonderful things we talked about years ago. These are the things we said computers would help us to achieve in manufacturing companies. Today it is happening.

But now that it is, we see some values beyond the material values. The ability to run a manufacturing business more successfully means better morale and a lot more personal satisfaction for the people who have to work in a manufacturing company. No matter how our standards change or our priorities evolve, for many years to come a significant number of people will have to make their livings in manufacturing companies. The day has come when that work can be a lot more satisfying, a lot less frustrating, a lot more rewarding. Perhaps that is the greatest progress of all.

February 1974

OLIVER W. WIGHT
Blodgett Landing
New Hampshire

# Part 1 | Perspective

# 1 | The New Industrial Revolution

## The Elusive Payoff

In the early years of the computer age, people began to recognize that the real payoff application for computers in a manufacturing company was *production and inventory management.*[1] To date, however, only a few companies have achieved dramatic success. Most manufacturing companies that have attempted to put some of their production and inventory management applications on the computer have fallen far short of the potential. Success, of course, has to be judged from an operational point of view. Are inventories lower? Is service better? Is the plant operating more economically? Is the company under better *control*, better able to respond methodically and economically to marketing requirements and to increases or decreases in the levels of business?

Perhaps we can understand the problem better if we think about a classical question the computer salesman frequently asks: "Why does the accountant generally seem to know what he wants on the computer, while the manufacturing people seem very confused and cannot really define their needs?"

The answer is not obvious, yet it is really quite simple: Before the computer came along, the accountant and many other members of the company had manual systems that worked. Putting them on the computer was straightforward. Manual production and inventory management systems did not really work. The "procedures" manual described a formal

1. "Unlike the average companies, whose computer systems are generally confined to routine record-keeping activities, the lead companies have also put the computer to work on the crucial decisions of the business; in sales forecasting, in manpower and production scheduling, in inventory management." John T. Garrity, *Getting the Most Out of Your Computer* (New York: McKinsey & Company, Inc., 1963), p. 7.

3

system, but the real system was an informal one, usually built around "hot lists" and expediting.

When the computer came along, the production and inventory manager was suddenly in a position to do some things that he had never been able to do before. An obvious corollary to this is that his experience with the "systems" he had used previously simply was not relevant.

Let us think about this more specifically. One of the most popular computer applications for almost any company is payroll. There was typically a well-defined manual payroll system. The number of hours a man worked was multiplied by his hourly rate; a bonus was calculated based on a formula; taxes were deducted based on a tax table; and the final result was his net pay.

It was not very difficult to transfer this manual system to a computer. Ironically, there usually was not very much payoff either. This is one of the great truths of computer applications: **Computerizing a system that works well manually will seldom generate significant improvements.**

Why couldn't the existing production and inventory management system be computerized readily? Why didn't it work manually? Because manual systems were not able to cope with the complexity of the logistics problems in a typical manufacturing company; thus the real system was largely informal.

Manufacturing and purchasing schedules start changing the moment they are established. If a vendor is going to be late delivering a component, others used in the same product should be rescheduled. An emergency order for a good customer may push others back, requiring rescheduling of the item itself as well as some of its components. Tooling that does not work as planned, new products, engineering changes, strikes, scrap, rework, absenteeism, machine breakdowns—these make up the way of life in manufacturing. And almost everything affects schedules.

Manual systems cannot handle this kind of continuous change methodically. That is why schedules are usually generated by a formal system—and then overridden by an informal expediting system. That is why, in most manufacturing companies, the production and inventory management system that they describe in the procedures manual and the system that they really use are two different systems. That is why, in those rare companies that have been able to use the new tools made practical by the computer, a revolution in manufacturing management has taken place.

### The Formal System and the Informal System

We can break production and inventory management down into two essential problems: *priorities* and *capacity*. Priorities in this context implies something more fundamental than determining which jobs are the "hottest." It means knowing *what* material is needed and *when*, and keeping this information up to date. This is what many people mean when they use the word "scheduling." Capacity means knowing how much man and/or machine time is needed to meet a schedule.

Consider the problem of priority planning in a company making an assembled product. The inventory control system orders material one way or another, and puts *due dates* or *wanted dates* on the shop orders and purchase orders. These dates usually will not be very meaningful for very long. Even if the forecast *were* perfect, and even if the customers did *not* change their schedules, *the priorities on the parts and sub-assemblies that are used to make an assembled product are dependent.*

If one part gets scrapped and cannot possibly be remade to meet the original schedule, the *real* wanted dates for all other parts have changed—unless they are needed to make other assemblies. But the formal system, if it is a manual system, is not going to be able to keep up with the massive rescheduling required. Even if there were enough people available to do the job, *the information would not be timely enough to be of any real value.*

So, in practice, an informal system tends to build up. Companies making an assembled product, for example, have a time-tested, inefficient, confusing, yet essential approach for doing this in most cases. Their *formal* priority planning system consists of an inventory control system that releases orders to vendors and the factory. This has been called the "push" system.

Out in the factory, there are expediters who are trying to get the parts through that are *really* needed. They try to find out what the *real* priorities are. Their system—the informal system—has often been called the "pull" system.

The pull system usually consists of going to the parts storeroom with a bill of material or parts list and pulling out all components needed to make an assembly ahead of the assembly schedule date. By "accumulating"—or, as it is sometimes called, "staging"—this material, the expediter finds out what the real shortages are and tries to get these parts through the shop and in from the vendors in time to meet the schedule.

This is the informal system—the one that is really used; it is the one that tells them—usually too late—what parts they need and when they really need them.

In a typical manufacturing company, the informal and the formal systems tend to be muddled into one system that is referred to as "our system." The fact that there is a formal system that does not function properly, and an informal system that tries to correct for it—expensively, ineffectively, and only partially—is not obvious to people in the midst of this situation. Yet the symptoms are common.

Look around the typical shop or purchasing department. There are many orders that are late. Some orders are several months old and *many of these are not being expedited.* The real system is "hot lists" and "shortage lists" to tell them what material is really needed.

What is wrong with having a formal system and an informal system working together? Does it really cause any serious problems?

The verdict on that question is very clear: It certainly does. The prime job of production and inventory management is to *plan*, to provide information to tell the rest of the company how to operate in order to meet overall company objectives. There is little question about the effectiveness of the planning that is done by most production and inventory management functions. It is poor, it is confusing, it certainly does not enable them to generate plans that other people can be held responsible for executing.

Consider the nagging problem of getting vendors to deliver on schedule. How can the purchasing department insist that vendors meet delivery schedules when they know very well that these delivery schedules are not valid? They know that in practice it is more important to expedite the shortages than it is to insist that vendors meet the delivery dates generated by the formal system. In fact, in many cases, they recognize that if the vendors did meet the original delivery dates, there would be far too much inventory on hand.

The same is true in the shop. Shop people know very well that the dates placed on shop orders are not really valid. Those are the dates that they work to *only* when there are no higher priorities such as shortages, back orders, and so on. How can we expect factory people, then, to get very serious about trying to run the plant "on schedule"?

We have been talking so far about priorities. What about capacity? The inability to keep priorities up to date has an insidious effect on the ability to plan and control capacity. If a particular component is scrapped, all other components should be rescheduled. If they are not, it is obvious that there will be shop orders for these components with due dates on them that are not valid. Frequently, these components will be "late" in the shop, *even though they are not really needed because one of the other vital components required to make the product is missing.*

But, of course, these "late" shop orders will be the basis for calculating capacity requirements. Typically, the orders that are out in the shop are summarized by date to find out how many hours of capacity are required. How valid will this information be *if many orders are late when they are not really needed?* The typical "load report" shows that the shop is badly overloaded. But you can be sure that shop supervisory people will not be very excited about this information when they recognize that it is a lot more important to work on shortages than to work to the dates on the schedules.

*The Earle Company makes a line of industrial drives that are noted for their quality. The company is located in a small midwestern town and there are very few other companies locally that compete with them in the labor market. Their product has been fairly stable over the years, and their typical production control man's tenure is nineteen years. Their average foreman has a seniority of twenty-three years. Their plant manager is very proud of their "system." In practice, it is actually a hodgepodge of formal and informal systems.*

*Mike, the chief expediter, is a very experienced man who could tell you from memory what important parts go into any one of the major products. Changes in the schedule do not faze him; he is able to "pull up" the parts that are needed when assembly schedules have to be met at an earlier date. He is an expediter, not an unexpediter. He does not bother to reschedule parts that are not needed on the original date. Attempts to make machine load reports from open shop orders have proved a dismal failure primarily because of the fact that these machine load reports show many late hours that plant supervisory people recognize are not really needed.*

*Al, the plant superintendent, has his own informal system for capacity planning. He "eyeballs" the critical work centers once a day. He also looks to see what is being started. He has a good idea which jobs will generate extraordinary requirements in the gear cutting department and other operations that have limited capacity. Under normal circumstances, he can respond to minor variations in capacity requirements pretty effectively.*

*The Earle Company has done rather well; their inventory turnover has been very good indeed. But in the last six months, a couple of Mike's key expediters have retired. Al has lost a general foreman he leaned on very heavily and, at the same time, the engineering department has introduced a new line of drives more dramatically different from anything that has been seen in the last twenty years.*

*Management is very conscious of shipping dollars and, until recently, the shop has been able to meet the shipping-dollar goal every month; but in the last six months, they have missed it four times. Management is concerned and is considering replacing Mike, who still contends that the problem is that the plant—and purchasing—does not really work to the schedule.*

*The real problem is much simpler. When everything is static, the informal system works reasonably well, but with the retirement of a few people and the introduction of a new product line, the informal system at the Earle Company simply cannot do the job.*

The management personnel of a great many companies today see no need to improve their systems, since they feel pretty confident that the problems are all in somebody else's area. This is an interesting aspect of the informal system: It tends to encourage buck-passing.

The production control man who is unable to respond to schedule changes effectively with his system blames the sales department, because they are unable to forecast exactly *what* they need and *when* they need it. They always seem to be changing their minds. In the same way, he typically blames the factory and the purchasing department for not working to the dates on the orders. He feels that if they only *did*, everything would be all right. The orders that he *is* expediting, of course, are often "late," and his selective interpretation of this information only bolsters his opinion that if people only worked to the original schedules, everything would be okay. He seldom recognizes that *most of the late orders in the purchasing department and the shop are not being expedited because they are not needed.*

The purchasing man, naturally, tends to feel that he is much maligned. He is always being asked to expedite things with too short a lead time. But he often contributes to the problem by overstating lead times.

The assembly foreman knows that the inventory system is not going to be very effective in getting him the parts he really needs, so he does everything possible to get these parts by hook or by crook. Frequently, he has parts taken out of the stockroom by one of the expediters who, he knows, seldom bothers with the proper paperwork. Frequently, also, he has material brought in directly from the fabricating departments without going through the stockroom and without making out the proper paperwork. Next month, when this very same part is in short supply, he will not understand why the computer system and the inventory control people cannot do a better job. It seldom occurs to him that the lack of proper transactions to update the inventory record made it impossible for the formal system to replenish the material that he had used.

This is not to indict any of these people; it simply illustrates how insidious the informal system really is. It only works when things are going very well. In fact, it only works when the company really does not need a system very much at all. It always tends to convince people that *they* are doing a pretty good job and that if they were not surrounded by a large number of *other* people who simply are not doing their job well, the company would operate pretty effectively.

> *Harvey R., the manufacturing vice president of a large company that makes a very complex product, was at his wit's end. Business had picked up; his manufacturing organization was slow to respond. The expediters worked harder and harder generating even longer shortages lists. Red tags appeared on everything in the shop; green tags had to be put on the jobs that were really needed, and pretty soon green tags were on almost every job. One day when he went into the shop to ask the foreman why a particular part was not being worked on, he was told, "It has a red tag and a green tag, but it is not on the yellow shortage sheet."*

> *More and more, Harvey was told that the problem really was a purchasing problem. Purchased material was coming in too late. So he asked for a rundown of all the open purchase orders that were late. Just as he suspected, the list was staggering. He was infuriated, but just before he charged off on a vendetta against the purchasing department, one of his accounting people called his attention to the fact that the information he was working with could not possibly be valid. They were only 10 percent behind on their assembly schedule; how could it possibly be true that 65 percent of all the open purchase orders were behind schedule?*

Production and inventory management in many companies today is really just *order launching and expediting*. The inventory control system generates orders, puts due dates on them, and then the expediting system tries to determine what material is *really* needed and when.

The computer makes it possible to have formal systems that really will generate useful information. It can keep priorities up to date, for example.

In order to develop effective systems of this type, however, we need to rethink the entire function of production and inventory management. It is not what it used to be, and when companies try to mechanize or sophisticate the existing formal systems, typically they find that these are not very effective at all. They never really worked before; there is no reason why putting them on the computer will make them work any better. The real payoff comes from developing successful formal systems that will replace the informal systems.

Is it any wonder that, in this confusing world of the formal and the informal systems, so many operating people simply do not know what good production and inventory management on a computer really is? They have never had the ability to have a formal system that worked. They are accustomed to having a formal system that does *not* work and an informal system that tries to make up for a few of its deficiencies. They have no experience to draw on in specifying what should be done to have a sound formal system. They suddenly find themselves in the computer age with little valid experience and a great deal of invalid experience. How can their prior experience guide them in moving into a world where a formal system *can* really be made to work?

This is the true irony of production and inventory management. We were not able to do it well manually; thus when it *is* done successfully on a computer, dramatic results can be achieved. Yet it is as foolish to expect the production and inventory manager and his other associates in the company to know from experience what constitutes a good production and inventory management system on the computer as it would be to expect someone without any flying lessons to be able to jump into the cockpit of an airplane and be able to fly just by pulling and pushing on a few controls and "figuring it out" for himself.

This simple point seems to have escaped the observation of most manufacturing management people. Look, for example, at the money that is spent on education. The data processing department spends a fortune teaching their people the latest programming languages. How futile to invest this amount of money to teach people "how" when the people who have to specify "what" are so busy with their day-to-day jobs that they usually have no time to learn about the brand-new ball game they are being asked to play.

### The Functions of Production and Inventory Management

When we speak of production and inventory management, we are using the term *management* in a special way. The production and inventory management man usually does not have direct authority over most of the functions in the company, such as engineering or purchasing. He is not responsible for hiring people to man the machines, nor does he usually purchase the machines themselves that provide the capacity. But the product will *not* go out the door on time if the efforts of purchasing, manufacturing, shop maintenance, and so on are not synchronized.

*The job of production and inventory management is to generate plans that other people can be held responsible for executing.* Plans are made and performance is monitored against these plans in order to manage production and inventories.

The fact that production and inventory management in most companies has been such a haphazard, ineffective function for so many years is to a great extent because there was not a formal system functioning that could generate information to develop plans that other people could be held responsible for executing. When most of the orders that the purchasing department has are late, and only some of them are being expedited, it is not possible to hold purchasing responsible for meeting delivery schedules. Manufacturing people usually run behind schedule because the schedules are obviously overstated.

Think, for example, of the traditional distinction between "inventory control" and "production control." The inventory control function traditionally launched orders and put some due dates on these orders that turned out to be not very meaningful. The production control function, in most companies, was really *expediting*. It did not seem to occur to anyone to ask why "inventory control" couldn't keep scheduled dates current to represent real needs—or why we always expedited but seldom "unexpedited."

To understand what production and inventory management *should* be, it is necessary to consider the four basic functions it tries to perform:

1. Planning priorities.
2. Planning capacities.
3. Controlling priorities.
4. Controlling capacities.

The production control/inventory control distinction becomes lost when the functions are categorized this way. In fact, the functions in practice may more logically be broken down into *planning functions* and *control functions*, since the people who plan priorities are also in a position to plan capacities. The people responsible for "controlling" capacity are in the best position to "control" priorities. Note that they control by monitoring progress against a plan and by calling significant deviations to the attention of those responsible. There will be more about this in subsequent chapters. The important thing now is to recognize the four vital functions listed above.

In looking at these functions, a few significant points emerge:

1. If we do not know what material we need and when we need it (priority planning), it will be impossible to determine what capacity will be required to make this material.
2. Planning must precede control. There can be no control without valid planning.
3. Priority planning must work well or none of the other functions can.

Priority planning in most companies is a vital function and one that is typically not handled very effectively. The priority problem tends to be a little bit different in different types of manufacturing companies. To illustrate the point, we can classify companies as:

1. One-piece product, make-to-order.
2. One-piece product, make-to-stock.
3. Assembled product, make-to-order.
4. Assembled product, make-to-stock.

In a company that makes a one-piece product *to customer order*, such as a forge shop, priorities are pretty clearcut. The customer requests a delivery date, gets a promise, and priorities only change if he requests a change.

In a company making even a simple product *to stock*, the problem of updating priorities is a significant one if there is any substantial amount of lead time. Lead time is the replenishment time that transpires from the time it is determined that more material is needed in stock to the time material is actually received in stock. The original "required date" on an order must be based on a forecast. Thus it is not likely to remain valid for very long.

When a company makes an *assembled product*, they have the problem of "dependent priorities" mentioned earlier. The priority of one part is related to the priority of all other parts going into the assembly. If one part required for the assembly cannot possibly be available for six weeks, the *real requirement date* for all other parts used on that assembly has changed, whether the formal system recognizes it or not. There is also another kind of dependent priority. Raw material used to make a component has a priority that is dependent upon the desired start date of the component using that raw material. Whenever there are dependent priorities, the priority problem becomes quite complex; and keeping priorities up to date is a major problem that the formal system, if it is a manual one, almost never addresses successfully.

Of course, the company manufacturing an assembled product to stock has the most complex priority problem. They not only need to keep their priorities *updated*, they also have priorities that are *dependent*.

The assembled-product manufacturer has been used as an example, but many other types of products have dependent priorities. Even a company making fasteners must schedule its tool shop; and the priorities for tooling are *dependent* on an ever-changing manufacturing schedule. A carpet mill must not only plan their yarn requirements, which are dependent on the manufacturing schedule, they also must regularly revise this schedule because of its dependence on yarn availability.

The important point to see here is a very simple one: The formal system for planning priorities in most companies that are not making a one-piece product to order simply does not work. Since we have previously established that the priority planning system must be effective if priority control or capacity planning and control are to be effective, this is one of the biggest problems facing the typical manufacturing company. For that reason priority planning is one of the major points to be addressed in the balance of this book.

There are, to be sure, other functions of production and inventory management than the four significant ones mentioned above. Determining proper lot sizes, for example, is a fairly significant function, but it is not usually one of primary importance. Most companies have a problem in getting their formal priority planning system to work properly, that is, determining "when" they need the material. The "how much" question is of secondary importance to them, and it really is merely a sub-function within priority planning.

Consider again a company making an assembled product. Whether or not the lot size of any individual component is "precise" is relatively insignificant compared to the importance of getting all the parts together at the right time. It is worth noting, however, that in a company that develops the right kind of inventory system that will plan to get the components together at the right time, the biggest cause for inventory *will then be* lot sizing. So, once the priority problem is solved, the lot sizing problem does become more significant. It, too, will be covered in a later section of this book.

### The Objectives of Production and Inventory Management

Before getting into the detail of the principles and techniques of production and inventory management, it is worth asking what the function is all about. It has been defined in many ways, such as "getting the product out the door at the right time with the least cost and minimum inventory investment." Unfortunately, definitions of this type do not really shed much light on the subject. We can understand the subject better by considering its three primary objectives:

1. Customer service.
2. Minimum inventory investment.
3. Maximum plant operating efficiency.

Good customer service, obviously, means either having the product on the shelf so that the customer may have immediate delivery, or making and delivering the product to the customer within an acceptable lead time. There are, of course, many other facets of customer service, such as providing information on delivery dates, and so on, but to the typical customer, product delivery is the essence of good customer service.

The second objective, maintaining minimum inventory investment, needs little or no explanation to the business manager of today. He has typically been under extreme pressure in recent years to keep his inventories under control. Interest costs have risen and the general change in management attitude about money has put increasing pressure on the inventory investment. Companies that had plenty of cash in the bank were once considered to be "healthy" companies. Today, a company that keeps cash in the bank is generally considered to be over-conservative because its management does not have the imagination to invest the money intelligently. Because of this, companies typically operate with less cash, which tends to increase the pressure to keep inventories under control.

The third objective—plant efficiency—manifests itself in different ways. The production and inventory management function is responsible for the lot sizes—the *quantities*—of goods that are manufactured. The larger the lot size, the fewer times machines must be set up and ordering costs incurred. Large lot sizes, on the other hand, require a large inventory investment. The smaller the lot sizes, the less the inventory investment, but, on the other hand, the larger the plant operating cost. Lot sizes have a real effect on plant efficiency. Another even more significant aspect of plant efficiency is keeping the plant running at a steady pace to avoid having to hire, train, and lay off people too frequently.

These three objectives are in conflict. If inventory has increased, the production and inventory manager has had a bad year. If, however, sales pick up and customer service has declined because inventory failed to increase, he has had a bad year. If, on the other hand, operating costs in the plant have increased and he is responsible, he has had a bad year.

The production and inventory manager probably has the lowest position in the company in which three primary objectives like those listed above are in direct conflict. He can meet any one objective by neglecting the other two, but over the long term, he must try to see to it that the company meets all three objectives reasonably well.

This is not to say that it is an insurmountable job, where he has no means at his disposal to meet the objectives he is facing. It does mean that no objectives can be met 100 percent without some sacrifice of the other objectives. Performance in most companies can be improved considerably; they can reduce inventory *and* increase service *and* increase plant efficiency. Nevertheless, there is going to be a limit to what can be done and, in the final analysis, there will be a limit to the reduction in inventory, improvement in service, and improvement in plant efficiency that can be obtained. This is part of the business game no matter how good production and inventory management becomes in any company. Because it must deal with conflicting objectives and an uncertain future, it is a function where no one bats a thousand. Like top management jobs, the challenge lies in using limited resources to get the best overall results.

### A New Outlook

Production and inventory management that started out as a clerical function assisted by some stock chasing has come of age today. The pressures to keep inventories down, to give better customer service, and to maintain stability in plant employment have forced management to devote some attention to a badly neglected area. In the meantime, three major influences have accelerated the development of a body of knowledge in this field:

1. The American Production and Inventory Control Society (APICS).
2. Operations research.
3. The computer

APICS was formed in 1957. By improving communications among professionals and its support of education, publications, and seminars, it has done a great deal to advance the state of the art. APICS has had a dramatic influence on the field.

Operations research—which could be described as "applying analytical and mathematical techniques to business problems"—came into vogue after World War II, and its techniques seemed well-suited to solving production and inventory management problems that frequently deal with uncertainty (like forecasts).

It seemed apparent that these techniques had great potential to help improve production and inventory management. Up to this time the function had received very little in the way of management attention and management talent. It was recognized that some serious problems existed. Solutions were needed.

It is interesting to look back now and recall how operations research tried to "quantify" business management. It is hard to think of many really significant recent applications in the area of production and inventory management. Instead, the techniques of operations research that were practical, such as the use of statistics in measuring forecast error, have been adopted as part of modern production and inventory management. It has been said humorously—although with a great deal of truth—"Any techniques that are practical and work are no longer called operations research. Those that have not yet proved practical are still operations research."

Unfortunately, operations research has fallen on bad days from a business point of view. Like so many technical areas, technicians have gotten themselves bogged down in jargon and interesting intellectual exercises. The ability to communicate with management has declined and, at the same time, management has seen little in the way of concrete results, and has often lost confidence in the dream that someone would someday develop mathematical formulae that would relieve them of the burden of decision-making.

The computer was first viewed as a way to mechanize clerical work and replace people. The management scientists usually saw it as a tool for performing the calculations of mathematical optimization. In practice, the payoff applications have been much more mundane. They fall into the category of "massive data manipulation"—much less romantic from a technical standpoint, but far more productive.

We must remember that we have not been working with computers for very long. Fifty years from now, business historians will look back on our efforts and chuckle. A classic misdirection was the MIS fad of the late sixties. The concept that a "total management information system" could—and should—be developed was enthusiastically subscribed to by a large number of computer technicians and, of course, by many of those people who were marketing computer hardware and software. The entire idea of an MIS was primarily a computer marketing gimmick. That it did not work was a lot less surprising than the fact that a lot of people took the whole idea seriously from the beginning. John Dearden, in his article "MIS Is a Mirage,"[2] says it very well, "The notion that a company can and ought to have an expert create for it a single, completely integrated super system—an 'MIS'—to help it govern every aspect of its activity is absurd."

To the business manager, MIS is a myth. He is a lot more interested in getting workable systems even if they are not "totally integrated" than he is in the technical objectives of having a "totally integrated" system.

Does the typical company need better formal systems? The answer to that is simple: yes! Very few of them would say today that their current formal systems work very well. Very few of them are able to cope with even a moderate increase in business without having to take six months to a year to recuperate from their good fortune. Yet most of them have always run this way, and a few managers still see no need to change since "we have always done it that way."

In fact, a great deal of evidence would indicate that a few managers even *enjoy* working in a firefighting mode. It gives them a great sense of significance and a real feeling of comfort, since the formal system does tend to indicate that even though things are not going right, the fault

2. *Harvard Business Review* (Jan.–Feb. 1972), p. 90.

lies in somebody else's bailiwick. Other operations managers want better systems, but they tend to be skeptical about computer systems. In many instances extravagant false starts with grandiose computer systems have only served to confirm this skepticism.

It is always well, however, to remember that a company is not playing against par. There is no par; there is only competition. As long as the competition is bumbling along in the same way, the problems are not too serious. Today a few companies are learning to use the computer effectively in production and inventory management. They *can* respond to business increases without having serious customer service problems. They *can* respond to a business decrease without having a dramatic increase in inventory that seriously threatens their financial position. Better systems of this type are not panaceas. They are only tools. *When* a particular company requires these tools depends on when the competition decides to face up to the competitive potential of these tools.

It is worth emphasizing the fact that these systems are only tools. The philosophers used to have a phrase, "necessary but not sufficient." The meaning is very simple: If you open the hood of a car that is not running and note that it does not have a battery, it is correct to state that it will require a battery in order to run. But the presence of a battery does not guarantee that it *will* run. Better production and inventory management systems are not sufficient, but they certainly are necessary. The tools themselves do not do the job, but it is impossible to do it really well without the tools.

During the past twenty years, new methods for handling material, new manufacturing methods and new tools—like numerically controlled machines—have had a dramatic impact on the manufacturing process. While all this has been going on, however, production and inventory management has remained very much as it was; an order-launching and expediting function.

Even the computer at first only created a thin veneer of "system" that did not have very much real impact on the way the factory ran. Too often the formal system, which did not work very well anyway, was computerized while the informal system was left untouched and continued to function as it always had.

Today, however, we have a new industrial revolution. A revolution in management control—the ability to have production and inventory management systems that can really generate results. One of their most significant benefits is that they free people from the never-ending drudgery of expediting and living from crisis to crisis. One company that has been very successful in using this type of system has reduced their product cost and retail price for sixteen consecutive years. One of the significant contributions to their success is manufacturing control systems that enable them to "do the routine things routinely." As a result they have the management time to do the extraordinary things, and they do these very well indeed. Another company achieved a 35 percent increase in productivity with a 5 percent increase in direct labor force. Much of this improvement was due to their ability to get the right material to the right place at the right time. But some of the improvement was due to better methods and better supervision. Even these improvements, however, are attributed to a better production and inventory management system because they point out that their foremen had been so busy expediting in the past that they had no time to implement the improved methods that could generate results. Better production and inventory management systems can almost always be justified on the basis of inventory reduction and customer service. But once these systems have been in use the managers develop a different way of doing business. And because they really have control over manufacturing, they continue to get a payback from these systems long after the initial cream has been skimmed.

One of the things that has emerged very clearly from our early years of experience with computer applications to production and inventory management is the fact that the responsibility for these better systems rests with management, not the staff or systems people. It is, therefore, the responsibility of management people to specify what these systems ought to do for them, and this means that *they* must be conversant with modern production and inventory management in the computer age.

# Part 2 | Priority Planning

# 2 | Material Requirements Planning

### The Impact of MRP

Priority planning is the key function in production and inventory management. Without effective priority planning, other functions such as scheduling, loading, purchasing, and shop floor control must limp along using largely incorrect information. Informal systems, like "shortage lists" and expediting, become the real system.

Manual systems were incapable of doing an effective job of priority planning. Most "inventory control" functions were just order-launching systems that did not even try to keep priorities up to date.

With the advent of the computer, "requirements generation" came into vogue. At first, it was used simply as a faster, less tedious method for order launching. Then it was developed into the technique that we now call MRP—material requirements planning. MRP can be used to plan priorities effectively. It is an extremely powerful technique that makes it possible to have a formal production and inventory management system that works.

The impact of MRP on a manufacturing company is profound. A workable, formal system can be used to respond better and faster to the needs of the marketplace, to reduce inventory, and improve productivity. This has recently been proven by a number of companies.

MRP is the key technique in production and inventory management. This technique has been so successful in practice that it has virtually made the traditional theory of inventory management obsolete.

### "How Much" and "When"

When companies first tried to use computers, they could only take what they knew and mechanize it. In the early days, the justification for

23

virtually every computer application was the number of clerks saved. The computer was merely being used, in most cases, to mechanize clerical work.

Similarly, when people first started to use the computer in production and inventory management, they attempted to mechanize the existing system. While some sophistication was added, it was usually the formal system that was mechanized. Consequently, the results were seldom very dramatic.

It was popular back in the early days of the computer to begin a talk or article on inventory management by addressing two fundamental questions:

1. How much?
2. When?

The "how much," of course, was concerned with lot sizing. Formulas for economic order quantities have existed for years. The literature of production and inventory management abounds with discussions on economic order quantity (EOQ). For many years, the basic EOQ formula was rediscovered regularly, and probably more articles were written on the subject of EOQs than any other subject in the field of production and inventory management.

Today the "how much" question is seen in a somewhat different perspective. Many companies with highly successful production and inventory management systems use some lot sizes set by judgment, yet they have still gotten very significant results from their systems. The most experienced practitioners today recognize that economic order quantity calculation is *not* the most significant thing to do. Very few companies can point to large inventory reductions or large savings in ordering costs that have truly been generated by EOQ.

Today, a lot more emphasis is being placed on the "when" aspect of production and inventory management. Getting the right material to the right place at the right time can generate very significant results even though the lot sizes haven't been computed "scientifically." *Getting the right quantity at the wrong time does not accomplish anything.* Timing is particularly important where priorities are dependent: where there are parts that go into assemblies, packaging material that has to meet the product, where a semifinished component must be available in order to manufacture the finished component. As a consequence, lot sizing gets much less attention today. We will discuss it later in Chapter 11 when we talk about some of the supporting functions that can be used to improve a good production and inventory management system after it is set up and working.

The "when" question, of course, was the important one in inventory management: *when to order*. And the *order point* was usually discussed as the primary technique for determining when to order. The order point is based on some forecast or estimate of demand over the replenishment lead time. The basic formula for the order point is: $OP = Dlt + SS$. An item thus might have a six-week lead time ($lt$) with an average usage of 100 units per week. The estimated demand ($D$) over lead time would thus be 600 units, and some safety stock would have to be carried. Let us assume in this case that it has been decided to carry 250 units of safety stock ($SS$); thus the order point ($OP$) would be 850 units, and when the level of inventory on hand and on order gets down to 850 units, a replenishment order would be generated.

All this says is that the order point is constructed by estimating demand over lead time and adding safety stock to it.

There is one other fundamental technique for determining *when to order*, and this is called material requirements planning (MRP). The order point approach and MRP are quite different in the way they handle ordering. The order point system assumes that each item in inventory is independent of all other items and can be ordered independently. MRP as originally used was a way to calculate parts requirements for assembled products. MRP treats items as if their priorities are dependent and it *calculates* future demands. This calculation is based on a *master schedule* that may itself be based on a forecast. It has been said, however, that when using MRP, uncertainty exists only at the master schedule level. Schedules for all supporting material will be geared to the master schedule.

The handlebars for a bicycle are a good example of a dependent demand item to which MRP would typically be applied. MRP would base the ordering of handlebars on an estimate of demand over lead time, but that demand would be calculated by taking proposed assembly schedules and using them to determine how many handlebars would be needed. MRP requires a *bill of material* in order to make these calculations. The bill of material is a type of parts list that shows what material goes into the product. A bill of material is really a "structured" parts list. It would show the bicycle itself at the highest or zero "level"; subassemblies that go directly into the final assembly would be shown at level 1, while parts such as the gears that go into the rear axle would be at a lower level in the bill of material. A bill of material is different from an ordinary parts list in that it shows the way a product is actually put together from parts into subassemblies and then into final assemblies, rather than just listing the parts. Bills of material when put on a computer file are often called product structure records.

People using MRP manually or with punch card equipment frequently did a calculation of parts requirements (often called an "explosion") without referencing inventory on hand or on order. This approach was called the "quick deck." Using this approach, if 250 bicycles are to be made, 250 handlebars will be ordered, 250 rear axles, 250 sets of gears, and so on.

The quick deck approach was simple to calculate and has some application in industries where the product is made only once. But as soon as there is any repeat production, inventories that get out of balance need to be rebalanced. There will normally be more of one part than another due to scrap, rework, orders run short, and overruns.

Table 1 shows a refinement to MRP where gross requirements are compared with the inventory already on hand and on order for a component in order to determine what the net requirements will be.

TABLE 1: HANDLEBAR REQUIREMENTS

| | | |
|---|---|---|
| Gross Requirements | = | 250 |
| On Hand | = | 50 |
| On Order | = | 150 (Due in week 3) |
| Net Requirements | = | 50 |

In Table 1 the gross requirements are 250 handlebars. This means that 250 bicycles are to be built requiring 250 handlebars, but there are already 200 handlebars on hand and on order so the net requirements are only 50 handlebars.

In the days of manual systems or punchcard systems, users of the order point system had their problems. It was very difficult to find the time in the typical busy production and inventory control department to keep order points updated. The typical inventory supervisor simply did not have the time to do it as often as he should. He frequently found that an order point needed to be recalculated *after* he discovered that the item was out of stock because sales had picked up and the order point did not reflect the increased demand.

The requirements planners also had a problem—a very serious one. The amount of computation involved in MRP is extensive, particularly when gross to net requirements are being computed down through the levels of a complex assembled product. Some companies doing it with punch card systems took six to eight weeks to make the calculations. Thus, a new master schedule would not generate purchase requisitions for raw material until eight weeks later. Ironically, this raw material is needed before production can ever begin.

When the computer came along, the order pointers greeted it enthusiastically in many companies. The computer made it possible to calculate order points far more frequently and "scientifically" than ever before. Techniques like exponential smoothing (a rather pretentious name for a weighted moving average that will be discussed further in Chapter 10) and the "scientific" calculation of safety stocks using measures of forecast error like the mean absolute deviation (MAD—also to be discussed in Chapter 10) became popular. With the computer it became possible to recompute order points monthly or even weekly, and to use far more sophisticated techniques.

The computer was a great boon to the material requirements planner also. He could put both his bills of material and inventory records on the computer files and do his gross to net requirements planning computations in a matter of hours rather than days and weeks.

Material requirements planning became even more refined with the introduction of time phasing. Figure 1 shows an MRP output report in the very standard format that is being used by many manufacturing companies today. This MRP report is for handlebars. The gross requirements of 250 units that were shown in Table 1 have been broken down into weekly time periods and are shown in the row headed "projected requirements." The amount on hand and on order ("scheduled receipts") is also shown, and a projected "available" balance has been calculated for weeks 1 through 8. Since the lead time is four weeks and the lot size is 150, a replenishment order for 150 will have to be released in week 4. Time phased MRP pins down the when to order question fairly precisely.

Companies using the computer to calculate order points or to do MRP frequently got some very substantial results by being able to do these calculations on the computer. *But they were still operating in an order-launching and expediting mode.* The expediting out in the shop and in the purchasing department continued just as before. This is not surprising since it probably did not occur to many people that things were ever going

| Handlebars Lot Size = 150 Lead Time = 4 Weeks | | Week | | | | | | | |
|---|---|---|---|---|---|---|---|---|---|
| | | 1 | 2 | 3 | 4 | 5 | 6 | 7 | 8 |
| Projected Requirements | | 40 | 30 | 0 | 0 | 0 | 70 | 0 | 110 |
| Scheduled Receipts | 150 | | | | | | | | |
| On Hand | 50 | 160 | 130 | 130 | 130 | 130 | 60 | 60 | -50 |
| Planned Order Release | | | | | 150 | | | | |

*Figure 1. Time Phased MRP—Ordering Handlebars*

to be any different, or that there ever really would be a way to have a formal system that could schedule properly.

This "order launching and expediting frame of mind" is betrayed by the very question, "when to order?" Ask any expediter and he will tell you that when we order is not half as important as when we get the material.

*The theory of inventory management was deeply concerned with WHEN to order. The practice of production control focused on trying to get material through to cover real NEEDS.*

Consider a practitioner who decided to use "scientific inventory management" and calculated more sophisticated order points with exponential smoothing, the mean absolute deviation, etc. The order point is a forecast of demand over lead time plus safety stock. Exponential smoothing will help him to forecast the demand per week and the mean absolute deviation will allow him to measure forecast error more acurately. But now he needs to know what the lead time *really* is. He goes to his inventory record to find out how long it took to get the material the last ten times it was ordered. Table 2 shows the actual lead times that he finds.

TABLE 2: ACTUAL LEAD TIME

| | |
|---|---|
| 4 weeks | 6 weeks |
| 7 weeks | 14 weeks |
| 2 weeks | 5 weeks |
| 6 weeks | 5 weeks |
| 3 weeks | 8 weeks |

*Average Lead Time = 6 weeks.*

In practice, the lead time was two weeks once *because someone expedited this item.* Once the lead time was fourteen weeks, probably because nobody expedited the item. While the theory of inventory management assumed that lead time was a constant, in practice lead time was often substantially less than average because an item was expedited, or substantially more than average because it was not. *The formal system that we were trying to use concentrated on when to order and assumed a constant lead time. The informal system concentrated on need and varied lead times according to need.*

This is not to say that the informal expediting system did this job well. In fact, it did it very poorly. It expedited, but it never unexpedited. Consider the job with a 14-week lead time. It was not needed in week 6, nor was it needed in week 7, 8, 9, 10, 11, 12, or 13. But suddenly it showed up on a shortage list in week 14. Before that, it had showed as still being needed *in week 6*. This, of course, was not true. One of the natural by-products of the formal order-launching system combined with the informal expediting system is lots of late orders in the purchasing department and in manufacturing that are not really needed.

Keeping priorities valid in a manufacturing company was beyond the capabilities of manual systems. Even if they could have established the original need date correctly—and few systems really could—there was no way for them to keep these priorities updated in the rapidly changing real world of manufacturing.

The important feature of MRP that gave it powerful capabilities was its rescheduling feature. Figure 2 shows the same information as was shown in Figure 1, except that the scheduled receipt is now shown properly time phased. The 150 now on order is due to come in in week 3. The MRP report thus shows us that some of that 150, at least, will have to be rescheduled into week 2 in order to meet the master schedule. If it cannot be rescheduled, the master schedule for 30 units will have to be moved out into week 3 or perhaps 10 units could be built in week 2 and 20 units in week 3.

| Handlebars Lot Size = 150 Lead Time = 4 Weeks | | Week | | | | | | | |
|---|---|---|---|---|---|---|---|---|---|
| | | 1 | 2 | 3 | 4 | 5 | 6 | 7 | 8 |
| Projected Requirements | | 40 | 30 | 0 | 0 | 0 | 70 | 0 | 110 |
| Scheduled Receipts | | | | 150 | | | | | |
| On Hand | 50 | 10 | -20 | 130 | 130 | 130 | 60 | 60 | -50 |
| Planned Order Release | | | | | 150 | | | | |

*Figure 2. Time Phased MRP—Rescheduling Handlebars*

So this was the deceptively simple breakthrough in our thinking. It had never occurred to us before that an *inventory ordering system could also keep the schedules on material already on order up to date.* This was the beginning of the idea of "priority planning," the very basis of sound, modern production and inventory management. Without effective priority planning, capacity planning cannot work nor can capacity control or priority control function effectively.

It was a simple idea. But it changed the entire way we could run a manufacturing company. Even today, most production and inventory control people who think of MRP think of it as a way to order the parts that go into an assembled product. In reality, it is a way to keep the complex interrelated priorities in a manufacturing company up to date and realistic. We started out using the computer to mechanize the existing system. But we stumbled on a new way to plan and control production and inventories.

### Independent versus Dependent Priority Planning

We used to think of the inventory control system as something separate from production control. Inventory control was responsible for ordering things, production control was responsible for expediting and perhaps for some primitive form of scheduling and loading. Some companies used order point systems, others used material requirements planning. But time phasing was not really a practical approach with a manual system. There was just too much writing and calculation involved to be able to handle a large number of items fast enough—or often enough —to be very meaningful. In practice, neither the order point system nor primitive forms of MRP actually planned priorities effectively. This can be seen very readily in companies using either approach (even on the computer) where the expediter spends the bulk of his time trying to determine what material is *really* needed and then trying to rush this through—usually creating chaos along the way.

With manual systems, the order point system or MRP really were "order-launching systems." There had to be an informal system that actually determined what items were needed most at the moment. Consequently, *it did not matter much* which technique was used. With the advent of the computer, it became important to use the proper technique in the proper application. In 1965, Dr. Joseph A. Orlicky of the IBM Corporation proposed the "independent/dependent demand" principle that states that the order point should be used only on independent demand items, while MRP should be used for dependent demand items.

There are far more dependent demand items in inventory than there are independent ones. Component parts, subassemblies, raw materials, semifinished items—anything used to make something else—has demand that is dependent on when and how much of its "parent" item (or items) are to be made. Only finished goods items, service items not used in current production, and supplies really tend to have an independent demand. Even those service parts or finished goods that are maintained in an inventory that is supplying branch warehouses do not have truly independent demand. Consequently, the MRP technique has a far greater application than order points.

You would hardly recognize this, however, to read the literature of production and inventory management. Book after book has been written on inventory management without ever mentioning MRP. The order point always got the attention. Undoubtedly, the biggest reason for this was the fact that during the 1960s there was a great fad for sophistication. Anything nonmathematical like MRP was looked upon as being quite pedestrian. Statistical concepts could be used with the order point technique and thus it received most attention from the college professors, most of the consultants, the operations research and management science people, and, consequently, many of the data processing systems people. It has been observed that, for many years, the amount of literature on statistical order point versus MRP and the application potential for the techniques seemed to be inversely related.

For many years, order point systems were used where MRP would have worked better, and so the results were poor. To understand this better, a brief example is worth considering. Assume that there is an item in inventory and the demand for the past six months has been 120 units. Assume that the lead time for this item is three weeks. The order point should be made up based on demand over lead time plus safety stock. If demand has averaged 20 units per month or approximately 5 per week, then demand over lead time would be 15 units. Assume also that we have chosen to use a safety stock of 8 units. Thus, the order point equals 23 units.

Yesterday, there were 70 units on hand, but there is a sudden withdrawal of 60 units from inventory. The inventory level is now below order point and a replenishment order will have to be placed. The crucial ques-

| | Month 1 | 2 | 3 | 4 | 5 | 6 |
|---|---|---|---|---|---|---|
| Bicycle Demand | 20 | 20 | 20 | 20 | 20 | 20 |
| Crank Assembly Demand | 60 | 0 | 0 | 60 | 0 | 0 |

*Figure 3. Lumpy Demand from Lot Sizing*

tion is "When?" When is this material needed? It would seem that with an average usage of 5 per week, there is only enough inventory to last for two weeks at best. If the demand is greater than average, the inventory might not even last that long. The typical inventory planner would order this material with a "Rush," "ASAP," or perhaps he would ask for delivery next week. Looking at Figure 3, it can be seen that this item, the crank assembly that goes into the bicycle, *isn't really needed for 3 months*. This demand is *dependent* on wanting to make a bicycle. This particular bicycle, even though its demand averages 20 per month, is made in lot sizes of 60. Therefore, the demand at the lower level tends to be quite lumpy and the question is not "what" the *average* demand will be but "when" the lot size at the higher level will be manufactured.

The example of an assembled product was used here, but there are many other types of items that have dependent demand. Consider a company, for example, that has a finished goods inventory at the factory location and supplies a number of company-owned branch warehouses. This makes the items in inventory at the factory warehouse "dependent demand items," and the inventory records should be structured so that the relationship between the branch warehouses inventories and the factory warehouse inventories is recognized.

Other companies make a product, often only a one-piece product, but these are frequently made from semifinished material. Consider a company making automotive brake lining, for example. This is typically a one-piece product. Because there is a long lead time process with considerable set-up time in it, a *semifinished piece* of brake lining is manufactured and put into inventory. It can then be drawn out of inventory and used to make a particular brake. One semifinished item can be made into as many as 12 to 15 different finished items by variations in drill pattern, and so on. This is not the classic assembled product, but the demand on the semifinished lining is *dependent* on wanting to make the finished piece of brake lining, and it would be far better to predict when the semifinished lining inventory will need to be replenished based on anticipating when the finished brake lining needs to be manufactured, rather than basing this on some estimate of average usage.

As the above example indicates, the order point simply will not answer the question, "When is the material *needed*?" Some have asserted that this is not the function of the order point. The order point is "supposed to keep material on hand at all times so that it will be there when it is needed." Order point inventory theory always recognizes that when we estimate demand over lead time, there is uncertainty involved and that there is very little chance that all items will be in stock all the time. Inventory management literature abounds with discussions of statistical techniques for determining how much *safety stock* should be used to give different levels of protection against "stockout." (We will discuss some simple approaches to this in Chapter 10.) It is interesting to note that this literature, which often includes elaborate statistical techniques for calculating safety stock, usually fails to observe another significant, fundamental statistical relationship. Let us look at another example.

Assume that an assembled product is made up of a number of components that we will identify as A, B, C, etc. Assume that there is a 90 percent chance that A will be available in the stockroom anytime it is wanted. B also is expected to be in the stockroom 90 percent of the time that it is needed. Elementary statistics tells us that the chances of A *and* B both being available at any time is the product of the probabilities of each of them being available. In other words, it would be 90 percent times 90 percent or 81 percent. The chance of A, B, and C being available at any given time is the product of 90 percent times 81 percent or 72.9 percent. It is easy to see that using the order point approach, an assembled product with even a reasonable number of components would have a very small chance of having all of its components available as needed. This is not to say that many companies making assembled products with dependent demand have not tried to use the order point. In fact, those companies that used order points for dependent demand items were still able to manufacture their product (although usually not as effectively as they would like to be able to) because they did it in spite of the formal system— with an informal expediting system.

There are two fundamental methods for priority planning: the order point system and MRP. The order point system applies to that small percentage of items in the typical manufacturing company's inventory that are truly independent. To use the order point technique anywhere else is lying to the system. MRP applies to the greatest number of items since it was designed to handle dependent demand and most items in inventory do have dependent demand and, therefore, priorities that are dependent.

Even today there are a few companies using order points in the wrong place. But perhaps more significant now that the independent/dependent demand principle has become widely recognized is the number of people who use substandard MRP techniques. It is important to understand what an MRP system is from a technical aspect since it must be technically correct in order to work properly.

### The Mechanics of MRP

Figure 4 illustrates the mechanics of material requirements planning. The master schedule calls for 40 bicycles in week one, 50 in week three, 60 in week six, and 60 in week eight. The bicycle itself is the top or "zero level" assembly. This master schedule would reference a bill of materials,

| Master Schedule Bicycles | Weeks | | | | | | | |
|---|---|---|---|---|---|---|---|---|
| | 1 | 2 | 3 | 4 | 5 | 6 | 7 | 8 |
| | 40 | 0 | 50 | 0 | 0 | 60 | 0 | 60 |

MRP—Handlebars

Lead Time = 4; Order Quantity = 100

| | | | | | | | | | |
|---|---|---|---|---|---|---|---|---|---|
| Projected Requirements | | 40 | 0 | 50 | 0 | 0 | 60 | 0 | 60 |
| Scheduled Receipts | | | | 120 | | | | | |
| On Hand | 60 | 20 | 20 | 90 | 90 | 90 | 30 | 30 | -30 |
| Planned Order Release | | | | | 100 | | | | |

MRP—Cut Tubing

Lead Time = 5; Order Quantity = 200

| | | | | | | | | | |
|---|---|---|---|---|---|---|---|---|---|
| Projected Requirements | | | | | 100 | | | 120* | |
| Scheduled Receipts | | | | | | | | | |
| On Hand | 140 | 140 | 140 | 140 | 40 | 40 | 40 | -80 | -80 |
| Planned Order Release | | | 200 | | | | | | |

*Requirements from another handlebar.

*Figure 4. MRP Mechanics*

and as a result, gross requirements would be posted against all of the level-one components, such as the handlebars.

The on-hand balance of 60 handlebars is projected just as one might take his current checkbook balance, deduct from it bills that he expects to have to pay, and add to it "scheduled receipts." The scheduled receipt represents material already on order and scheduled to come in (in this case in week three). A negative balance is projected for week eight. Since the lead time is four weeks, an order will have to be released in week four. The net requirement is 30 units, but the order quantity ($OQ$) or lot size has been predetermined at 100 units, so the planned order release is for 100 units. This means that a manufacturing order to make 100 handlebars is now planned to be released in week four.

This company carries an inventory of cut lengths of tubing from which the handlebars are made. One hundred lengths of tubing will be required in week four to cover the planned order release for making handlebars. *In MRP, planned order releases at one level generate requirements at the lower level.* Note that in week seven there are other requirements coming in from another handlebar.

There could well be many handlebars using this particular type of tubing in the same cut length, and all of these requirements would be accumulated before going through the netting process. There might be some independent demands, such as service parts requirements for handlebars or even for tubing. These would also be introduced and added to the dependent demand requirements before netting.

It is important to note that the scheduled receipt for handlebars in Figure 4 did not generate requirements at the lower level. It is assumed that the order to make handlebars would not have been released unless tubing were available. When a planned order moves into the current period and is released, it is converted to a "scheduled receipt." At that time, material is taken from the stockroom and issued against the order, and no more requirements will be generated. Because there is sometimes a delay in pulling material from the stockroom, some companies consider this material "allocated" until such time as it has been pulled from the stockroom. By showing that a quantity of an item is "allocated," they are able to recognize that there is an "uncashed requisition" for that quantity currently in the stockroom.

The planned order release is a very powerful part of an MRP system. It generates material requirements at the lower levels, and as requirements or inventory availability change, these planned orders will be automatically rescheduled by the computer, thus changing requirements at the lower levels. This could result in a need to reschedule a scheduled receipt or "released" order.

This rescheduling of released orders is usually done by *people*, since it involves a number of decisions that should *not* be made automatically by the computer. If a component were scrapped, for example, the computer would signal that the next released order should be rescheduled to be brought in immediately, or that a new order should be released to be brought in immediately if there were no existing released order. This might not be possible. This is where some human intervention and judgment should be used to determine just when the new order can be scheduled. If it cannot be scheduled soon enough, then the master schedule itself should be revised. Changing the master schedule would then trigger the replanning of all of the other components that are used for this particular assembly, and the planner would then be notified to reschedule each of them to meet the new assembly requirement date.

Here is another highly significant feature of time-phased MRP; it not only tells the planner when to expedite, it tells him when to "de-expedite." Most informal systems are run by expediters who discover shortages and often try to improve delivery dates. But it is assumed that anything that is not being expedited is wanted on its original date. With a formal priority planning system like MRP, need dates can be properly maintained. In practice, this is a great benefit, since anytime anything is unexpedited it is a lot easier to get other jobs through a shop or from a vendor in less time. The most powerful expediting technique of all is unexpediting.

The planned order release performs a necessary function in MRP by generating lower level material requirements. But planned orders also have another function that is extremely valuable. They can be used for capacity planning purposes. One of the most difficult problems of all for production and inventory management people has been to give manufacturing line managers sufficient advance notice so that they can change capacity economically. Most "machine loading" is based on released orders only. With MRP, the planned orders can be used with a routing file and a capacity requirements plan can be developed. The capacity requirements plan shows not only the number of released hours involved, but also the number of planned hours that are intended to be released based on the planned order releases in MRP

Today a fairly standard feature of MRP is "pegged requirements." This simply means that as the planner looks at the MRP for an item, it will specify what higher level items generated these requirements. This can be of great assistance to the planner as he evaluates the significance of a reschedule. We will discuss later how pegging can also assist the capacity planner.

There are many techniques of inventory management that can be used with MRP. It is possible, of course, to use safety stock with MRP. Generally, this should be kept to a minimum and should be planned in the master schedule. Most companies using MRP will overplan certain options, etc., in order to protect themselves against forecast errors. If, for example, the high-speed axle on the bicycle were being planned, it probably could not be forecast as accurately as the total number of bicycles for any given model. Most companies using MRP would overplan the high-speed axles somewhat in order to be sure to have parts available to meet any reasonable demand. They would not usually plan additional safety stock for the individual parts, however, since it has already been planned in the master schedule.

Safety stocks on parts might be calculated, however, when these parts are going to be used to satisfy service requirements as well as assembly requirements. It is important to remember, however, that safety stocks tend to dilute priorities. The objective of MRP is to plan priorities effectively—to tell the truth. The minute safety stocks are introduced, this truth becomes suspect.

It would not make sense, for example, to calculate different safety stocks for a number of components going into the same assemblies. The result might very well be to have a formal priority system that says that these parts are really needed at different dates, when, in fact, all of the parts are needed at the same time.

Some companies have attempted to put "safety time" into their material requirements plan, trying to get parts in before they are actually needed in order to give themselves a little "cushion." Obviously, these safety times had better be the same for all components or the due dates for components common to one assembly simply will not coincide. But even where they are the same, there is real risk involved in telling people in the shop—or vendors—that material is needed before it is really needed. People in the shop will usually discover very rapidly what the real priorities are. When it comes time to determine whether to work overtime because something is not "on schedule," no manager in his right mind will authorize overtime to make a job a week ahead of time when it can easily be finished on regular time by the middle of the following week. *The truth will out on the firing line.*

Lot sizes can also be used with MRP, as was demonstrated in the example in Figure 4. Independently calculated lot sizes sometimes have a disadvantage in that they usually will not match requirements. If the requirement happened to be for 200 or 125, it would really be more important to make that quantity than the "economic lot size." Discrete lot sizes, as discussed in Chapter 11, apply better to MRP than the regular economic lot size calculations do.

There is a "minimum standard" that MRP must meet if it is to function properly as a priority planning system. Most MRP reports have a one-year "horizon." This horizon *must* be long enough to cover the cumulative lead time down through the product structure. It must be in a *weekly* time-phased format and must be recalculated at least weekly. Some companies today use a technique called "net change," where they are able to recalculate their requirements by exception only, usually on a daily basis.

Larger than weekly time periods, such as months, and less frequent calculation, simply do not pin down *when* material is needed close enough to be of value to people out in the factory. Telling a foreman what material is needed in a given month does not tell him very much. Telling him what is needed in a given week puts him in a better position to know what material to work on first. People who use monthly time periods, for example, or recalculate their MRP monthly, are not able to plan priorities properly. This can easily be demonstrated by going into the factory and watching expediters trying to determine what the real priorities are.

Many people who use substandard MRP systems do not *expect* MRP to be an effective priority planning technique. Their experience with inventory control systems tells them that an inventory control system simply orders material. After all, that is what the manual inventory control system did. It was not *supposed* to keep priorities up to date. That was the function of "production control" or, more realistically, expediting. The problem is a very simple one: we are victims of our experience, and the significance of a formal system that really can plan priorities effectively did not become apparent until very recently.

It is important to recognize that MRP is really just a *formalization of the informal system.* Consider a company making an assembled product.

The expediter goes to the stockroom with the bill of material for the product that appears in the master schedule. He checks to see if the material is available. He frequently pulls this off the shelf and "accumulates" or "stages it," putting it on a pallet and then making up a shortage list. He will then expedite those parts that appear on the shortage list.

The computer, in effect, is simply doing the same thing using MRP. It takes a master schedule, looks up the bill of material in its own files to find out what material is required to manufacture the product in the schedule, and then checks the inventory to see if this material is on hand. If the material is not on hand, it tells the planner to order it and tells him when it will be needed. If the material is already on order, it will reevaluate the due dates on that material and tell the planner if the due dates need to be changed. MRP is really simply a formal system for predicting the shortages that simulates what the expediter was really trying to do.

The formal MRP system re-plans regularly; unfortunately, the expediter found it impractical to put the parts back on the shelf and start over again each week. The formal MRP system also predicts shortages *soon enough* so that something can be done to prevent them. The informal expediting system simply cannot keep priorities properly updated. It usually finds out about shortages too late, thus causing excessive costs, confusion and, perhaps most important, erroneous information, since the informal system is the real system—yet most of the information people try to use to manage is generated by the formal system.

Many companies have been disappointed when they tried to develop machine loading programs, for example. They took the orders in the formal system, added them up by time periods, and suddenly found out that they had huge overloads that were not at all realistic. The problem? Priorities on these orders simply had not been updated. They had an expediting system but no unexpediting system. The dates on the orders were left the same unless the expediter said, "Do them sooner!" As a result, when this information was converted into machine loading information, it was invalid.

Similarly, other companies have tried to generate purchase commitment reports to show how many dollars would be spent for material in a particular time period. To do this, they took the purchase orders with the due dates on them and costed them out. Since these purchase orders usually had due dates on them that were no longer valid, the same situation occurred. A large number of these purchase orders were "late," but they were not really needed because the due dates were generated by the inventory control system operating in "order launching" mode. The shortage lists actually told the purchasing people what material they really had to get in immediately. Consequently, when these erroneous dates in the formal system were used to generate a purchase commitment report, the result was inevitable: a lot of dollars showed due in the first month, yet much of this "late" material was very unlikely to be received in that first month—because it was not really needed—thus the expediters would not be "chasing" it. And one more piece of information that management would like to have to help run the business better becomes simply more computer-generated nonsense. There is a moral to this point: *sound manufacturing control information starts with effective priority planning.*

### The Prerequisites for MRP

When the informal system is the mainstay of company operations, slipshod habits develop. Inventory records are not very accurate, but, of course, they do not really need to be. The expediter is going to discover shortages that occur because of inaccurate inventory records about the same time that he discovers some of the other shortages that would have been there even if the records were right. Bills of material typically are not as accurate as they should be. They represent the way the engineers think the product is put together, as opposed to the way the shop people actually do it. Routings tell how the engineers think the product is manufactured, when the foremen in the factory frequently have had to adopt an entirely different manufacturing sequence because of lack of capacity on the machine the manufacturing engineers wanted to assign the job to, improper tooling, or perhaps a better method (or occasionally *worse*) that they have developed out in the shop.

When the formal system comes along, there is a new requirement for correct information. Bills of material must be accurate. Inventory records must be correct. The responsibility for maintaining the integrity of inventory transactions has to be assigned to the stockroom manager, who is on the spot and sees the material move. He must be sure that the proper transactions are reported either through a data collection terminal or through paperwork that takes place at this time. And this may be a very different type of job for him. In the past, he thought his prime responsibility was to get the material out to the assembly floor as quickly as he could; the paperwork frequently was not an important concern.

The assembly foreman, too, has a different responsibility. He is now charged with making sure that none of his people try to take material without making out the proper paperwork. This may seem like a nuisance to him and to his people, but they are the ones who will suffer when the right material is not there. Without accurate records, no planning system can function properly to help get the right material there at the right time.

Perhaps one of the biggest problems of all in moving into the era of the formal system is simply the experience of most of the people in management today. They never had formal systems that worked, and when they are told that it is important to have accurate bills of material, accurate inventory records, and a realistic master schedule, their usual response is, "That's nice and we would like to, but we've never had them before and we've always managed to muddle through." The problems of learning to get the most out of a computer in a manufacturing company have not been so much with the technical aspects of the computer, but with teaching people a whole new way to work.

There are, however, a few technical aspects of production and inventory management that are important to learn. Perhaps one of the most significant areas that should be explored before putting a technique like MRP on the computer is the bill of material. In the past, the bill of material was a *reference* document, and people could outwit its inaccuracies. If a formal system is to work, the bill of material must be correct. It is now being used for *control*.

The bill of material must represent the way the product flows. Engineers may assign part numbers to subassemblies that are actually "built on the line" or "transient" subassemblies. If these transient subassemblies are not specifically recognized, an MRP system may generate extra paperwork that is not needed. On the other hand, an MRP system requires a part number that uniquely identifies each item that must have its priorities planned; thus a casting must have one part number in its raw state, another to designate semifinished, and still other unique part numbers to recognize its machine configuration.

When real restructuring of bills of material is required it is almost always to facilitate master scheduling. Consequently, the subject will be treated in more depth in Chapter 4.

Probably the most important aspect of MRP by computer is the master schedule. Far out in the future it is usually a forecast of anticipated production. Over the near term for many companies it is a fairly precise statement of what they intend to produce, since actual customer orders were used as the basis for the master schedule. As actual customer orders do come in, actual known demand replaces forecast as the prime reference in making a master schedule.

The master schedule is the real key to MRP. If it is overstated, MRP will not provide the proper input for priority planning. If, for example, the master schedule has more units in it than are likely to be produced, there will be a lot of orders for individual components that indicate that they are needed immediately. But the truth will out, in practice. The manufacturing people will learn that these components are not really needed. Many of them will be "late" and nobody will be looking for them. The same thing happens in purchasing. Pretty soon the purchasing people and the manufacturing people know that the dates generated by the formal system do not really mean anything, and they rely on expediting to find out what material is truly needed. The master schedule will be discussed more fully in Chapter 4.

The computer age has brought us the ability to have formal systems that really work. These systems are fairly straightforward and fairly simple. They do not require any mathematical genius to understand how they work. They do require an entirely different attitude from many people in a manufacturing company—the assembly foreman, the stockroom manager, the expediter, the production control man, the plant manager, and, for that matter, the general manager himself. If he fails to learn how to live in a world where plans need to be realistic if they are to be useful, he can do as much to destroy any hopes for a successful formal system as any of the other people involved are likely to.

Keeping plans realistic takes good judgment. Certainly, if a system is just a way to say, "It can't be done," it is not very useful. There will be times when particular customer orders will have to be worked into a master schedule with far shorter than normal lead time. But there is a limit to how much that can be done in the real world. The minute the system starts to deviate from reality, it is no longer going to be used.

There is an insidious thing about the informal system. It is always lurking in the wings. It is always waiting to become the real system. Frequently, when the formal system breaks down, it does not happen dramatically. Nobody seems to know that it is no longer working. The computer printer still prints paper, people still look at the paper, all that happens is that the old informal approaches once again are the *real* system in the plant. The manufacturing executive should be able to recognize whether or not his priority planning system is functioning and should know what to do to get it back on the track again if he finds that it is merely window dressing, and that the informal system has once again encroached.

Why is the informal system so evil? Simply because it does not work well. In this day of complex manufacturing logistics problems, it is futile to wish ourselves back in a simpler day when we had a lot of good experienced old-timers who really knew the product and who had had a chance to grow up with it. Those were the days when the informal system really could work and could be a practical and economical way to do the job. For most companies, those days are gone—and they will never return.

# 3 | Distribution Requirements Planning

## Priority Planning with the Order Point

The traditional theory of so-called scientific inventory management included some serious misconceptions. It assumed the following things:

1. *All items in inventory were independent.* No book on the subject written before 1967—and few since, for that matter—recognized that dependent demand items were by far the most prevalent.
2. *Lead time was known and fixed* and the precise computation of safety stock (in order to launch the order at *exactly* the right time) was of paramount importance. This inventory theory generally assumed that the due dates placed on an order had to remain the same once the order was released. It was assumed that an inventory control system could not keep "need" dates valid.
3. *Lead time was an independent variable.* In the real world, lead time is very much *dependent* on the urgency of the *needs* that are discovered by the informal system.

The independent/dependent demand principle has become common knowledge. Far fewer people, however, recognize that priority planning is just as vital and valuable for order point items as it is for dependent items.

Time phasing really made it possible for MRP to become the invaluable technique that it is today. In Chapter 2 we saw how time phasing not only determines when an order should be placed, but also keeps rechecking to see when open orders are actually needed. It is assumed today that any material requirements planned item would be handled in a time phased format.

The order point traditionally was not handled in a time phased format, *yet this is by far the better way to do it.* Table 3 shows how an order point would be constructed for a particular item.

TABLE 3: ORDER POINT CONSTRUCTION

| | | |
|---|---|---|
| Demand | = | 100/Week |
| Lead Time | = | 5 Weeks |
| Safety Stock | = | 250 |
| Order Point | = | 750 |

Table 4 shows the current inventory position for this item. Assuming that demand materializes as forecast at 100/week, the item would break through its order point in week 2, and a replenishment order would be generated.

TABLE 4: CURRENT INVENTORY POSITION

| | | |
|---|---|---|
| On Hand | = | 200 |
| On Order | = | 700 (due week 3) |
| Order Point | = | 750 |

This same information could be shown in the time phased format. Figure 5 shows the *time phased order point.* Note that the planned order release would occur in week 2, just as the regular order point would have handled it. But note, also, that the current open order for 700 due in week 3 is actually needed immediately since the on-hand quantity of 200 has already gone below the safety stock level.

The time phased order point will signal the planner to order material just like an order point in the non-time phased format will. But, of course,

| Lead Time = 5 Weeks<br>Safety Stock = 250<br>Order Quantity = 700 | | Week | | | | | | | |
|---|---|---|---|---|---|---|---|---|---|
| | | 1 | 2 | 3 | 4 | 5 | 6 | 7 | 8 |
| Projected Requirements | | 100 | 100 | 100 | 100 | 100 | 100 | 100 | 100 |
| Scheduled Receipts | | | | 700 | | | | | |
| On Hand | 200 | 100 | — | 600 | 500 | 400 | 300 | 200 | 100 |
| Planned Order Release | | | 700 | | | | | | |

*Figure 5. Time Phased Order Point*

the time phased format will also signal when reschedules are required. Using this format for order point, inventory control on independent demand items can make the order point technique truly a priority planning technique that will *keep* priorities up to date. The only reason that the order point was not traditionally time phased is that computer file capacity used to be a scarce and expensive resource, and time periods in the inventory records added to the record length and thus the file size. Now massive direct access files are readily available. Today order point items should be handled in the time phased format, *just like* MRP items.

In fact, what I have called the "time phased order point" is really simply the MRP logic used for independent demand items. In practice, the very same MRP computer programs can be used for both dependent and independent demand items; the forecast of requirements will be entered directly at the item level rather than derived from higher level planned orders.

There are many advantages to the time phased order point. The standard order point format assumes that demands will always be equal in all periods. There are many situations where demand in the future is known and is quite lumpy. This happens when an export order, a promotion, or some other "one-shot" large order comes in for future delivery. In the traditional format, the order point system simply cannot accommodate that kind of order. There are really two choices:

1. Enter the order at once and allocate material to these future orders that really should be used for more immediate requirements. Many practitioners do this in order to generate their lower level material requirements to cover these demands.
2. Leave the order for the unusually large quantity out of the system and try to handle it on a manual basis.

Both choices are bad: inventory requirements are overstated in the first case and run the risk of being overlooked in the second. Using the time phased order point, the large order for future delivery can simply be entered into the requirements in the proper future time period. There is typically a one-year planning horizon in the system that facilitates this. Planned orders will consequently be generated in advance of the requirement, methodically alerting the planner to the additional lower level material and capacity requirements to satisfy this lumpy future demand.

The time phased order point will also very readily handle releases against blanket orders. Many companies have service parts or even finished-goods items that they order from other companies and simply stock and resell. It is not unusual to place a "blanket order" with the vendor for a year's supply and then release against this blanket order to replenish the inventory. Too often the release rate is set up and not reviewed frequently enough, and inventory either builds up or a stock-out occurs. With the time phased order point, the releases are constantly geared to the current inventory status, which would be reevaluated each week or more frequently.

So time phasing the order point puts the emphasis on keeping the priority correct on open orders, facilitates capacity and lower level materials planning, and handles lumpy known future demands. But once this type of system is seen in operation, some of the traditional inventory management concepts begin to take on a different significance.

*Safety Stock versus Rescheduling*

In any inventory replenishment technique (like the order point) there are two primary variables: lead time and demand. The classical approach to statistical order point calculation assumed that lead time was fixed and known and that demand was the variable. In practice, lead time is an approximation at best. It is certainly not always fixed. The obvious question is: Why not vary the lead time as the demand varies?

Consider the typical fabricated part. Assume that it has a normal lead time of eight weeks and usage is 100 per week. Safety stock might be 300 units. *This really says that the need for safety stock could be virtually eliminated if the item could be made in five weeks.* The fact of the matter is that if the general manager went to the production control man and said he needed it right away, *it could probably be made in five days.* Now the production control man will be quick to point out that he can expedite a few items and get them through in much shorter than normal lead time, but that he cannot do that with very many items. Of course there is a very good reason for this. The formal priority planning system tends to break down in most companies, and the name of the game is, "Do it on the original date unless we tell you we need it sooner." They have an expediting system, but no unexpediting system.

They only have half a priority system. It seldom occurs to them that the best way to get *some* jobs through in shorter than normal lead time is to reschedule some other jobs out to longer than normal lead time. Either MRP or the time phased order point facilitates that. These techniques *can be* effective formal priority planning techniques if they are managed properly.

Does that mean that safety stock is not needed any more? Not really. There are some items where lead time really is relatively fixed. Consider, for example, some material that is purchased overseas and must come by boat. There is very little that can be done to shorten the lead time for this material. In pharmaceutical companies, too, there are established "impounding" periods that really are *fixed* lead times.

But, for many fabricated items, lead time for any individual item is a function of priority. Thus there is no need to carry the amount of safety stock that was typically carried in the past. When the formal priority planning and control system works properly, much less safety stock is needed. Classical order point theory assumed that the forecast error over the "average" or "longest normal" lead time should be calculated. With a formal priority planning system that really works, the safety stock could reasonably be calculated over the *shortest reasonable lead time*. Some companies now using MRP carry virtually no safety stock, and as we said earlier, safety stock tends to distort the truth in a priority planning system. So the answer is to use it very sparingly, because with a priority planning system that really works, safety stock is not required in the large quantities that we had to use in the past. **When lead time can be varied it is more important to plan and replan priorities than to compute safety stocks "precisely."**

Now that formal priority planning systems *can* be made to work, the shortcomings in classical inventory management theory are apparent. Safety stock was calculated to protect against periods when demand exceeded the forecast. But what about periods when demand was *less* than forecast? Safety stock not only does not help, then, it represents unnecessary extra inventory investment. Priority planning, on the other hand, reacts to increases—*and decreases*—in demand by revising need dates on open replenishment orders. It is a dramatically different concept that has improved the ratio of inventory to customer service in practice far better than "scientific" calculations of safety stock ever did.

The important thing for the manager to recognize is the importance of priority planning as opposed to safety stock calculation. It would be far more important for a practitioner to be putting his emphasis on effective priority planning than on elegant computations of the safety stock. The point is very simple: *priority planning and control has become a practical reality with the advent of computers.* This dramatically reduces the need for safety stock. While the concepts of statistical inventory control still have some validity, their significance in a modern manufacturing company is dramatically reduced.

### Applications of the Time Phased Order Point

Virtually everything in inventory should be controlled using the time phased order point or MRP. For many companies a combination of these techniques will work out best. For example, the finished goods inventory should be handled using the time phased order point. The planned orders would then be used to generate the material requirements for components going into the finished goods inventory. In the event the items in finished goods were one-piece products, the planned orders would be used to generate material requirements for raw material. They would also be used to generate capacity requirements.

A company with branch warehouses would use the time phased order point at the branch warehouses. The planned orders from each of the branch warehouses would be entered as distribution requirements into the time phased order point for the finished goods at the main plant warehouse, in addition to any forecasted customer demand to be supplied out of that warehouse.

Time phasing the order point for the branch warehouse inventory offers some real advantages. Typically, branch warehouses order material from the main plant and then complain vehemently about the poor service they get. Yet they seldom do a very good job of priority planning. These warehouses simply place orders on the finished goods inventory at the main plant and then all the evidence of the breakdown of the priority planning system emerges. They expedite some orders and even enter some new orders on an expedite basis, while other orders that are late are not really needed, so they are not expedited. The problem, of course, is simply that from the time they order a product with any substantial amount of lead time until the time they receive it, there is a need to re-evaluate *when it is actually needed.*

There is another problem, too. So often we fail to recognize that inventory is a limited resource, and the name of the game is getting the biggest bang out of the buck. Frequently the inventory man back at the main plant has to decide how to allocate an item that is in short supply. He *must* know how urgently a branch warehouse order is needed. Often, branch warehouse people will say that since they represent such a large percentage of the total demand on the main plant inventory, they should be given priority service and treated like "large customers." Unfortunately, this is great in theory, but poor in practice. The truth will always out on the firing line, and the truth is very simple: the objective is to use the inventory to give all customers serviced out of all locations good service. With the time phased order point, the inventory man can have "visibility" into each branch warehouse inventory, and can determine whether or not its needs are more urgent than needs in other locations.

Beyond this, of course, the time phased order point, with its planned orders, provides a means for planning capacity requirements. No distribution facility can expect to get good service out of a manufacturing facility when the manufacturing facility has no idea of their potential future demands upon its capacity. Just placing orders and insisting on delivery within the lead time is totally unrealistic. If business is going up, the manufacturing facility will have to have a lot of orders ahead of them in order to know that they really need to add capacity. This will mean that there will be large backlogs and delivery delays before they can respond. When business is going down, they also need to have some advance notice so that they can cut back on capacity methodically rather than in a crisis mode. Nevertheless, cutting back on capacity is generally easier than adding capacity, and it is adding capacity that is most important if customer service levels are to be maintained. Thus the planned orders out of a time phased order point can provide the information for capacity planning back at the manufacturing facilities, and can help to insure a higher level of customer service.

The time phased format has great utility and virtually universal application. Consider a company making builder's hardware, such as hinges, that they ship out of their main plant facility where they maintain a finished goods inventory. They also have branch warehouses located in various parts of the country that serve these areas and maintain a finished inventory. The hinges consist of a left-hand leaf, a right-hand leaf, and a hinge pin. Some of them get more complicated and have small ballbearings in them, but basically the product consists of three parts.

There are many different finishes that can be applied to a hinge. It can be painted different colors, or be plated bronze, chrome, dull chrome, and so on. The hinges are manufactured, put into a semifinished inventory, and then withdrawn in smaller lots and put through the finishing operations to replenish the finished goods inventory at the main plant location.

The time phased order point would be used at the branch warehouses, and this would then link their inventories to the main plant warehouse inventory. Planned orders at the branch warehouse level would become requirements on the finished goods inventory.

The time phased order point would be used for finished goods at the main plant. Independent demand for customers to be supplied from this location would be forecast, and planned orders from the branches would be added to get total requirements. Planned orders from *this* inventory would become requirements against the semifinished hinge inventory where MRP would be used. Since the hinges are an assembled product, their planned replenishment orders would become requirements against the material requirements plans for the components going into the hinges, which might very well have multiple uses. In the event they did have multiple uses, the requirements—from all hinges using the same pin, for example—would be summarized in the material requirements plan for the hinge. There would also be a material requirements plan for the steel used to make the leaves and the pin, and planned orders from the semi-finished level would become requirements at this level.

A company making machine tools uses MRP for the components going into the machine tool. Frequently some of these components are also used as service parts as well as having current requirements for assembly. The MRP can accommodate both these higher-level requirements and the service requirements in one record. There are other service parts that have independent demand since they are not used in current production. The time phased order point is used in these items. Planned orders from both the material requirements plans and the time phased order points can be used to generate capacity requirements.

MRP was originally conceived as a way to plan parts requirements —that is, "order parts" for assembled products. But as it matured and eventually evolved into the time phased format, the universality of its application potential became more apparent. It applies no matter what the product configuration is as long as there are dependent priorities. The time phased order point uses the same logic and the same file format and, in fact, the same computer program as MRP. The only difference is that the "requirements" consist of a forecast rather than being posted from planned orders, or a master schedule, generated at higher levels.

Many items, of course, have *both* independent and dependent requirements. Whether we say we are using MRP or the time phased order point is just semantics. Today, now that we have had a chance to use some of these tools made possible by the computer, we recognize the basic time phased material requirements planning technique as a universal tool that can provide visibility among different *levels* of inventory.

### Controlling Low-Value Items

There are many items in the typical inventory that have a low annual consumption in terms of dollars. Their value doesn't justify a great deal of record-keeping effort or management attention. These are typically referred to as the "C items" (the concept of "separating the vital few from the trivial many" or "distribution by value" will be covered in Chapter 14). These low-value items are determined by doing what has been called either a "distribution by value" or "ABC analysis." This simply consists of taking the annual usage for an item, extending it by the cost, and then ranking the items to determine which are the "vital few" and which are the "trivial many."

One of the classical approaches for controlling low-value items is the *two bin system*. One bin contains free stock, and withdrawals are made from this supply without any formal inventory transactions taking place. When all of the free stock is gone, material must be taken from the second bin, which is sealed and has a quantity in it equivalent to the order point—with a very generous safety stock. When the seal is broken, a reorder card is sent to purchasing or inventory control personnel to tell them to replenish the inventory.

Like so many techniques, people have often picked up the two bin system and used it blindly without recognizing what they were doing. Even though an item may have low annual dollar usage, that may be the product of a high unit cost and very few units used during the year. Some of these items—like castings, for example—would be better controlled by a ledger card than by a two bin system. The ledger card would require less management attention and, of course, the castings simply would not fit in a bin.

The most frequent complaint about the two bin system is that people don't send the cards in when they break into the bin, providing one more time that if good management principles are not applied, no system can possibly work. The management principle involved is: **When everybody is responsible, nobody is responsible.**

To make two bin systems work, the second bin needs to be kept in the stockroom or somehow isolated so that responsibility can be assigned to someone who will be in charge of sending in reorder cards when the second bin is opened.

There are other techniques for handling low value items. A very simple one that sometimes works better than the two bin system is the *periodic visual review system.* Using this approach, a review sheet is set up in the same sequence as the material is stored in the stockroom or out on the shop floor. Periodically, usually once a week, floor stocks are replenished. The reviewers, usually production and inventory control people, then take the review sheets and check the inventory of each low-value item. The review sheet typically looks something like Figure 6. Note that the order point is shown not only in units but also visually. This does not imply that a physical inventory is taken at each review, but simply that experienced personnel will use their judgment to estimate whether or not the inventory is below the order point level.

In practice, the periodic visual review system tends to be more systematic and easier to administer than the two bin system. It does not require that stock be put away in separate bins and the bins be sealed. It is also much easier to assign responsibility with the periodic visual review system, and easier to follow up to see whether or not the review sheets

| Part No. | Description | Order Point (Units) | Order Point (Visual) | Order Quantity | Remarks |
|----------|-------------|---------------------|----------------------|----------------|---------|
| 17152 | Washer | 12,000 | 12 Boxes | 60,000 | |
| 18456 | Cotter Pin | 40,000 | 80 Cans | 150,000 | |
| 18507 | Detent Ball | 9,000 | 1/2 Bin | 30,000 | |

*Figure 6. Periodic Visual Review   Low-Value Items*

have been sent to inventory control or purchasing personnel each week or every other week, whenever the review is scheduled to take place.

Today, with computers readily available, and low-cost file storage, the trend is to put all productive material on a computer inventory record. Since most of the departments within a company will be working from a common bill of materials data base, the low-value components will be in the data base anyway. If the engineering department suddenly decides to standardize particular screws or washers, changing the bill of material will immediately signal a change in requirements, where a periodic review or two bin system would be unlikely to detect this until usage had picked up on these items. It would be possible, of course, to run out of them in the meantime.

As a result, a fairly common approach today is to use MRP even for low-value items. Because of large lot sizes, these items do not require as much review. They are usually issued from the stockroom to replenish floor stocks, and usually issued in bulk so that nuts, bolts and washers are not being counted out for each assembly order. MRP then overstates their requirements somewhat because it is comparing these requirements with an inventory figure that is the balance left *after* floor stocks have been replenished. Nothing wrong with that.

Running out of stock on a low-value item is ridiculous. In the past, because of the cost of computer time and file storage, low-value components were frequently handled with the two bin and visual review system. There is nothing wrong with doing this on some items that are going to have regular demand, but today a more satisfactory system can be set up—using the computer—that requires less management attention, less labor cost, and still meets the major objective for low-value items: **Have plenty, in order to give as close to perfect service as possible with the least effort.**

### Priority Planning—Its New Significance

When MRP first came along it was used by most practitioners simply as an ordering technique. Today we recognize that it can be an effective priority planning technique and virtually eliminate the primary function of expediting—to determine what a few of the *real* priorities are.

We traditionally saw the order point as a technique to tell us *when to order*, and we concentrated on safety stock calculations. Here, too, we have learned that in most real world examples, priority planning—and replanning—is far more significant.

The fundamental material requirements planning logic and the time phased format have taken on new meaning in the computer age. It has become a virtually universal format that can be used for all kinds of products in all kinds of companies, and there is much to be said for standardizing on this kind of a format rather than developing unique "home brewed systems" that address universal problems in a nonstandard way that very seldom makes sense to anyone but the system designer.

*The Pine Street Company made customized materials-handling systems. Since they specialized in the highly engineered part of the business that larger companies were not interested in, their materials-handling systems were largely made up of unique components, and only service parts were stocked.*

*They naturally quoted long lead times, since virtually all of the material had to be ordered for each job. George H., the president of Pine Street, questioned the applicability of MRP since there were almost no stocked components. He asked whether it would even be worth while to put bills of material on the computer, since they would only be active for the life of the job, and since no two customer jobs were ever alike.*

*Nevertheless he was anxious to get some kind of better system installed. The current system consisted of ordering the material for each job and then expediting to try to get needed parts to make subassemblies and assemblies. The fact that it did not work well was apparent to everyone. George was particularly concerned because inventory investment had been increasing rapidly as the business had expanded and the product had gotten more complex. The current 1.2 inventory turns per year seemed very low to him, particularly since they were making a product strictly to order and carrying only service parts in planned inventory. At the same time, Pine Street almost never met a delivery promise and was getting a bad reputation in the industry.*

*George had looked upon MRP as an inventory control technique. It seemed inappropriate to his problems since he did not stock components. As he became more familiar with MRP and recognized that it was really a priority planning technique, he realized that this was the technique that was needed at Pine Street. Excess inventories were carried in the stockroom because nobody had recognized* in time *that a particular part was not going to be available and had not rescheduled the other parts. While Pine Street did not have many items that they carried in inventory on purpose, they had a very high inventory investment because they could not plan and replan priorities correctly. As George described it later, "We had the problem and the solution was right there in front of us, but we did not recognize it. We were thinking of MRP as an inventory ordering technique. Actually, ordering all the parts the first time was never a major problem for us. Keeping priorities up to date was our big difficulty. Manufacturing people simply have to be taught to recognize MRP as a priority planning technique.* Inventory management is a by-product of priority planning."

*At the Cressy Carpet Company, Sylvia W., the production control manager, described her problem quite lucidly: "Ordering yarn is not particularly difficult. Anybody can convert carpet requirements into yarn in a few hours manually. But, unfortunately, by the time I am finished doing it, things start to change. The yarn manufacturer tells me that he cannot give me 75,000 pounds the week I want it, but can only give me 25,000 a week. This, of course, changes my master schedule and the date when I am going to be able to replenish finished goods. In the meantime, the sales manager comes down with a big order from a new customer, and suddenly we have got to turn on a dime. Do we have the yarn available? What are the other requirements for it? What might we have to reschedule? There is simply no way to tie this all together without MRP. My big job is to sell our management that we are not really* different. *They see MRP as a way to calculate our yarn requirements. I see MRP as a priority planning system that will tie together a very complex, constantly changing relationship between what we want to do and what material and machine availability will allow us to do. Using the time phased order point for finished goods inventory, and MRP for yarn requirements, we can tie together both our demand for stock items and our demand for special items, make more realistic promises, and give better customer deliveries. At the same time, I am sure we can run the plant more efficiently because frequently we are changing set-ups in the plant simply because material is not available and we discovered it too late."*

*The Bindle Stamping Company was primarily in the make-to-order business. The big job for Sam S. was scheduling the presses properly. While he had been exposed to MRP, he did not see the applicability in his business. He explained,*

*"Material requirements are not that big a problem in our business We order steel in a limited number of sizes and usually in coils I can calculate very easily by hand what our steel requirements are " Then Sam went on to explain what his real problems were. "My problems start when we do not get a delivery of steel on time, or we get it in and it is not flat enough to run properly through the coil feed and we have to send it back. Then I have to reschedule the die shop, change customer promises, try and get some other dies sharpened earlier, and find out what steel I've got that I can use to keep the presses running That is where the real complication comes in. I would like a system that would help me tie some of these problems together. The other day, for example, the lead man called. He had a shop order for 15,000 pieces of a particularly troublesome part. It is a regular runner that we ship to one of our big customers every month and we have trouble every time we go to make it. The die is extremely fussy, and sometimes we have to tear it out, regrind it, and reset it two or three times before we really get parts made to specification. The lead man wanted to know if he could run an extra 15,000 pieces since the die was running beautifully Of course I would like to, but how do I pull together all the information I need to give him a reasonable answer? How much steel is on hand? Is that steel needed for other requirements? How important are those requirements? Could some of them be pushed out? When is more steel coming in? When are the dies to blank those other parts going to be ready? Ordering steel is easy. These are the problems that give me trouble."*

*Sam failed to recognize that MRP is a priority planning system rather than an inventory control system. These are exactly the problems that MRP addresses Sam should even consider having the dies right in the bill of material so that the die shop can be scheduled—and rescheduled—properly. As in most companies, Sam's "scheduling" problem is really one of keeping dependent priorities up to date.*

The fact that so many companies have used so many unique ways to address these universal problems is a sign of the adolescence of the field of production and inventory management. It is an outgrowth of the fact that there was not a formal production and inventory management system that worked before the computer came along, and that there really was no manual system to computerize. This, of course, is the reason why the production and inventory management function took so long to learn to use the computer effectively.

To achieve the potential from priority planning systems requires a new approach by the production and inventory control man. Because his old system could not generate valid information on a timely basis for priority planning and control, he—and others in manufacturing—learned to live with a formal system that did not really do much, and an informal system that was in spite of its shortcomings—the real system.

In addition to learning the new technology, many manufacturing control people have to break some old habits. The production and inventory control man frequently tended to exaggerate and overstate his needs. He was a man on the defensive in most companies. By making sure that all of the orders he placed were typically given a due date that was somewhat earlier than necessary, at least when he went to expedite the item nobody could tell him that he did not order it soon enough. Therefore he never even wanted to unexpedite. When in doubt he always had an early due date on an order. It was difficult for him to comprehend that this destroyed the credibility of the priority system. With the availability of formal priority planning techniques that do work, like MRP and the time phased order point, he must assume the responsibility for planning priorities credibly, otherwise the formal system will function only as an "order launcher." One of the keys to this is master scheduling, the subject of Chapter 4

# 4 | The Master Schedule

### The Key to Successful MRP

The master schedule is the prime input to MRP. The master schedule is to an MRP system as a computer *program* is to a computer.

The master schedule can be thought of as a "production forecast"; it is almost never the same as the sales forecast. Most companies start with a forecast of sales in broad terms and from this generate the planned production rate (or rates) to meet sales requirements while making any adjustments to inventory or backlog and usually trying to keep production rates level. This is called a *production plan.*

The master schedule then translates the production plan into specific product—or product "module"—terms that can be used to plan material and capacity requirements. The master schedule statement of the quantity of each item required is put into the MRP system each week or more frequently The MRP program references the bills of material corresponding to the products—or product "modules"—in the master schedule, and thus material requirements are generated. The open shop orders and planned orders from MRP are used as input to a capacity requirements planning program in turn. The master schedule drives MRP and, consequently, the entire production and inventory management system.

When we were first able to use the computer to generate material requirements, little thought was given to the master schedule. Somehow it was just supposed to be there. As we slowly recognized that MRP was a priority planning system, the master schedule took on new significance.

Today we recognize that it is not a one-time statement of some production objectives; it is an ever-changing "handle" that enables us to manage a modern production and inventory management system. The design and management of the master schedule are recognized today as keys to the success—or failure—of an MRP-based system.

### The Production Plan

Whether they explicitly recognize it or not, most companies establish some kind of production plans. The production plan is usually made by product group or other broad category. It establishes the production rate, taking into account any planned increase or decrease in inventory or backlog.

Figure 7 shows the typical production plan for a given product line in a make-to-stock company. It is expressed in units, although it could be expressed in dollars. Let us assume that this company is making carpenters' wood chisels. In this production plan the "units" are chisels, and while the chisels are different in size and require different amounts of productive capacity, in many of the facilities these "units" can be used to make approximate sales, production, and inventory plans.

In this example, the starting actual inventory is 120,000 units. At the end of the thirteen-week planning period the objective is to have 185,000 units on hand. The anticipated sales rate is 30,000 units per week. In order to meet the inventory goal, the production rate has to be 35,000 units per week (the inventory increase of 65,000 units spread over a thirteen-week period).

This example shows a production plan for a make-to-stock company. In a make-to-order company, the customer order backlog ("negative inventory") rather than inventory level would be manipulated.

| Week Ending | | Sales (thousands) | Production (thousands) | Inventory (thousands) |
|---|---|---|---|---|
| 3/31 | Plan | | | |
| | Actual | | | 120 |
| 4/7 | Plan | 30 | 35 | 125 |
| | Actual | 25 | 36 | 131 |
| 4/14 | Plan | 30 | 35 | 130 |
| | Actual | 38 | 32 | 125 |
| 4/21 | Plan | 30 | 35 | 135 |
| | Actual | 32 | 37 | 130 |
| 6/30 | Plan | 30 | 35 | 185 |
| | Actual | | | |

*Figure 7 Production Plan*

The production plan precedes the master schedule. Its prime purpose is to establish a production "rate" that will raise or lower inventories or backlogs as desired, and usually keep production relatively stable. It is particularly useful for planning around plant shutdown periods or where sales are seasonal. The master schedule will break this production plan down into more specific details so that it can generate specific materials and capacity planning information.

The production plan can also be used as a rough-cut capacity plan. This is especially valuable when production plans are broken down into reasonably meaningful units such as "all hammers," "large air-conditioners," "small hospital sterilizers," or other units that may vary somewhat in work content, but nevertheless give a reasonable handle on capacity.

In a truck manufacturing company, for example, a production plan (or "program" as the automotive industries usually call it) is established by model line. The actual master schedule is expressed in modules—engines, transmissions, bodies, etc. (but *not* the combinations of these options since it would present an impossible forecasting—hence master scheduling—problem). The final assembly schedule is made when a customer order comes in and the required planning modules are pulled together for the specific order and released to the assembly department. Note that the master schedule is expressed in "modules" while the assembly schedule is for specific configurations of the finished product (i.e., a blue sport cab, with a large V-8 engine, tape deck, black vinyl top, etc.).

Frequently it is important to be able to convert the units in the production plan or master schedule directly into approximate capacity requirements before generating the MRP report, the planned orders, and the detailed capacity plans. This type of rough-cut capacity plan can be used very readily to determine whether or not the master schedule is in the ballpark. To do this, an abbreviated computer file that will convert plans into approximate capacity requirements for key areas is sometimes used. This file could also contain data to convert new product plans into approximate hours in engineering and so on. This approach is sometimes called resource requirements planning.

### The Master Schedule in a Make-to-Stock Company

The technique for priority planning make-to-stock items is the *time phased order point*. The actual master schedule is the result of planned orders that the time phased order point generates. Since the time phased order point is based on a forecast of demand, it will generate planned orders to replenish inventory without regard for any planned production rates. One of the problems that has to be addressed with the time phased order point in a make-to-stock environment is how to generate planned orders at the *required production rate.*

Normally in an MRP system, released orders must be rescheduled by the planner, but planned orders would be rescheduled automatically by the system based on current requirements. When inventory is being built ahead of a peak season, it is obviously important *not* to reschedule these planned orders, since the inventory buildup is intentional and the planned orders are being released ahead of schedule on purpose.

Many MRP and time phased order point systems consequently incorporate a technique called the *firm planned order*, which allows the planner more control over the system. The firm planned order technique lets the planner flag a particular planned order and move it into a given time period. The system will *not* reschedule it, but instead will generate a reschedule message to the planner, which he may choose to ignore if he wishes.

When working with a production plan, the planned orders for a particular product group should obviously be generated at the planned production rate. The firm planned order technique can be particularly useful to help the planner make the system do this.

As with any master schedule input, the production plan in a make-to-stock company must be realistic. If it is overstated, priorities will become distorted. This is a very difficult message to get through to many production and inventory management people. When the plant falls behind, they want to show that it *did* fall behind, and to them the traditional way of doing this is by showing a backlog. There is nothing wrong with showing this backlog *someplace*, but if it is allowed to build up in the master schedule, soon there will be more in there than the plant can possibly turn out. This will result in too many individual jobs being "late," thus destroying the validity of the priorities. While on the surface it may seem like a good idea "to keep the pressure on," in practice it results in disaster. Just at the time when capacity is tight and it is important to get the right material through, the formal priority planning system will collapse, since when everything is late, there is no priority system. The result, of course, will be to revert to the informal expediting system to find out which of the late ones are really the most important late ones. The message is very simple, very clear, yet very difficult for people to implement in practice because it is counter-intuitive: *whenever a master schedule is overstated, the formal priority planning system becomes meaningless.*

### The Master Schedule in a Make-to-Order Plant

The companies most familiar with the techniques of MRP are those that make products (like machine tools) where for many years there was a backlog of customer orders. The delivery times were typically twelve to eighteen months. This meant that the backlog of customer orders represented a very reliable master schedule, which could then be "exploded" into parts requirements. The master schedule specified how many of which machine models would be going to the assembly floor at what time. It could then easily be converted into a schedule of component requirements, since the date the components are needed at the stockroom door is the date that an assembly order is to be issued to make a particular lot of machine tools. These requirements could then be carried down through lower levels of subassemblies, parts, and raw materials.

With a backlog of customer orders, no real forecasting was required. Typically a fairly high-level management group met once a month and planned the master schedule for the future. Usually, when these companies were working from substantial backlogs, the master schedule would be firmed up eight to twelve months in advance. This then became the authorization for the material control people to place the requisitions on the factory and the vendors in order to generate the materials needed to meet the schedule.

The master schedule in a make-to-order company requiring a long delivery lead time is relatively straightforward. Most companies that make to order, however, do not have the luxury of customer order backlogs far enough out in the future to be adequate for planning material and capacity requirements. The master schedule in this type of company is derived from a forecast over the long horizon, actual customer requirements over the short horizon, and some of both in between.

Actual customer orders must be matched against the master schedule, as they materialize. This matching is a key function of master scheduling in this type of company.

The purpose of the master schedule was to generate material and capacity requirements. In a short delivery lead time make-to-order company these requirements must be planned before the actual customer order comes in. One of the most important results of the matching function will be to determine when a customer order *can be delivered* based on the availability of material and capacity. Order acknowledgement is a vital function of master scheduling.

There are three ways to do matching:

1. *In final product configuration.* Most make-to-order companies have a variety of products made up of many combinations of options. Electric motors of the same size, for example, can have different types of switches, bearings, end bells, bases, paint, cord sets, etc. The *combinations* of these options present an impossible forecasting job. Matching a customer order for a particular product configuration with a *specific* item in the master schedule is not usually practical in a make-to-order company.
2. *Part number by part number.* This is tedious and makes it very awkward to plan material and capacity requirements effectively before the customer order is received.
3. *In product modules.* Usually these would be subassemblies in a company making an assembled product. The matching would take place in the electric motor company as the customer order was converted to the required switch, end bell, bearing, base, etc. This is generally the most practical approach.

Figure 8 shows the typical master schedule of this type. It would normally be reviewed on a weekly basis. The actual customer orders have materialized reasonably well against the master schedule for the first four-week period, but the master scheduler has reduced the master schedule eight weeks out because orders do not seem to be coming in at the planned rate. Reducing the quantity in the master schedule will free up components for other assemblies that may use components that are common to product 2113.

When a new customer order comes in, it is converted into master scheduling modules and the master schedule is reviewed to see when it can

| Product ≠2113 | Week | | | | | | | |
|---|---|---|---|---|---|---|---|---|
| | 1 | 2 | 3 | 4 | 5 | 6 | 7 | 8 |
| Actual Orders (Assembly Start Date) | | | | 450 | | | | 200 |
| Old Master Schedule | | | | 500 | | | | 600 |
| New Master Schedule | | | | 500 | | | | 500 |

*Figure 8. Master Production Schedule*

be scheduled. If there are units available in the manufacturing plan, the master scheduler knows that he has planned for both material *and capacity*. When this plan was created, it was evaluated against material and capacity availability. Since then regular feedback from the shop and purchasing people should keep the master scheduler constantly informed so that he knows whether material and capacity plans are being met. It is their responsibility to tell him if any schedules *cannot* be met. As a result he is reasonably confident that if he has units in the master schedule, he can accept an order for these units.

The master scheduling module in a short delivery lead time make-to-order company is very significant. In a wire and cable company, it could be a module that was representative of a particular type of wire's material and capacity requirements. In a fabrication and assembly shop, the module is usually a subassembly. Sometimes some restructuring of these bills of material is necessary to develop useful master scheduling modules.

### Bill of Material Structuring

The major reasons for reviewing bill of material structuring revolve around the master schedule. Before discussing actual bill of material structuring, a few points about part numbering in the bill of material are worth reviewing.

As we said in Chapter 2, the product structure—or bill of material—should represent the way the product flows. An MRP system assumes that a subassembly identified by the bill of material is an item that goes into inventory after it is manufactured or purchased, and is then released from inventory to make the next higher level assembly. Some subassemblies designated by the engineers do not really do this. In reality, parts are pulled out of the stockroom, made into the subassembly, and immediately put right into the assembly.

These "self-consumed," "made on the line," or "transient" subassemblies need to be coded in an MRP system so that the system is not generating separate planned orders for these and expecting these planned orders to be released and then completed. This can be handled by the so-called "transient bill of material routine." This simply means that the lead time for a transient item is set at zero, no lot sizes calculated and, therefore, the requirements "blow through" this transient subassembly, and come out as requirements against the lower level parts. If there happen to be any pieces of this transient item on hand because of mismatched quantities from a prior run, requirements will be netted against them.

Setting the lead time to zero and not doing any lot sizing means that net requirements for the transient subassembly automatically become gross requirements at the lower level. This is not even a modification to the standard MRP technique. It does require, however, that the bills of material be examined ahead of time to be sure that these transient sub-assemblies are properly identified and coded. If they are not handled properly, useless paperwork will have to be generated to create and complete orders for these transients. It might even result in people moving these subassemblies into a storeroom for no good purpose, taking them back out of the stockroom, and again generating extra paperwork *and* handling—not to mention the longer lead time that must be allowed to put material into the stockroom and take it back out again.

There are also occasionally going to be some items that the engineers *do not* designate by a specific part number, such as a die casting that can be painted or plated in a number of varieties. The engineers may only give this a single part number. In order to plan priorities properly for the different variations of this die casting, the production and inventory management system must have separate part numbers. The point is a very simple one: engineering people generated bills of material in the past and it was not too important that these really represented the way the product flowed in the factory. With a formal system, the bills of material suddenly must represent the way the product is made.

The bill of material must also be a useful master scheduling vehicle. Since the purpose of the master schedule is to state material and capacity requirements, it must be stated in terms of available bills of material. Perhaps existing bills of material may have to be restructured to make them useful master scheduling modules.

Some products are modular, and at final assembly they take on their final configuration. The automobile, of course, is an example that is familiar to most people. There are many options available on a car—different colors, different body styles, different engines, different transmissions. It would be foolish to try to forecast out over the entire planning horizon the final configuration of an automobile. In fact, it is not important to know what the final configuration of the automobile will be any further ahead than the assembly lead time. Thus, there should not—and probably *could* not because of the endless possibilities—be a planning bill of material for the final automobile itself. Instead, there are bills of material for each of the various types of body, one for each of the various types of engine, transmission, etc. These are the units, or *modules*, that appear in the master schedule.

Many companies that have modular products tend to recognize the problem for the automobile manufacturer, but do not see that their product is very similar from a logistics point of view. For example, companies making electronic equipment like radio transmitters usually have a series of models with a great number of variations, and each individual transmitter may also have some special frequency-sensitive components. It would be foolhardy to try to forecast the final configuration of each transmitter that could possibly be sold. The frequency-sensitive components are almost impossible to forecast. Fortunately, they tend to have fairly short lead times since they are basically simple components like resistors. But even if they had long lead times, it would be a mistake to have a final configuration bill of material that had the frequency-sensitive components in it and to try to use that bill of material in the master schedule. The forecasting should be done via bills of material that represent the building blocks out of which the product is made. Trying to create bills of material for the combinations of these buildings blocks can generate an almost impossible forecasting—and consequently master scheduling—problem. In this kind of company, bills of material may have to be restructured into practical planning modules.

Many companies have indicated that they do not know how to handle MRP because forecasting is so difficult. They use this as an excuse for using order point systems where they do not really apply. A closer look at their problem indicates that they usually have a bill of materials structuring problem that has not been recognized or addressed properly.

There are other aspects to bill of material structuring. Master scheduling can frequently be facilitated by the use of nonengineering numbers that effectively reduce the number of items in the master schedule. In manufacturing a truck, for example, there are brackets, nuts, bolts, etc., that are used to fasten the subassemblies together. Rather than have all of these items appear in the master schedule, imaginary assembly or "kit" numbers are usually assigned to groups of them. One kit number would be used to call out all of these parts that are always used on a half-ton truck, another number would call out those items used only with the eight-foot step side body, and so on. The kit number is not a real assembly number—these parts could not be used by themselves to make an assembly. This nonengineering number is simply used to identify an imaginary bag of parts for master scheduling purposes.

This nonengineering number could also be used to identify other groups of items that could more conveniently be master scheduled together —not just fasteners. There are many components that are common to all half-ton four-wheel-drive trucks. They do not actually make up an assembly by themselves, and thus the engineers do not assign a part number to this group of subassemblies. A nonengineering number could be used here to facilitate translating changes in anticipated production rates for four-wheel-drive trucks into material requirements without having to manually reschedule many individual items.

Once bills of material have been set up, responsibility should be assigned to someone in engineering and production and inventory management to maintain properly structured and accurate bills of material. These same people should also be part of the group that evaluates and plans the implementation of engineering changes.

### The Master Scheduler's Job

The master schedule drives the entire production and inventory management system. At the master schedule level, the conflicting objectives of production and inventory management are brought into sharp focus. Sometimes a customer order has to be entered in less than the normal lead time, and this usually causes increased costs in the plant. At other times certain inventory is carried, anticipating a customer order that does not materialize. But this risk is borne in order to provide customer service. At still other times, the production rate is planned to be higher than the shipping rate in order to level out manpower requirements, but, of course, at the cost of building inventory.

The master scheduler's job, then, is a critical one in a modern production and inventory management system. He has the following responsibilities:

1. Check the sales forecast for reasonableness and work with marketing to resolve questions.
2. Convert the sales forecast into a production plan.
3. Be sure that the production plan correlates with the shipping budget, inventory investment planning, and marketing plans.

4. Give delivery promises on incoming orders; match actual requirements with the master schedule as they materialize.
5. Evaluate the impact of *"top down" inputs*, such as a request for the introduction of a new product in much less than the normal delivery time.
6. Evaluate the impact of *"bottom up" inputs*, such as "anticipated delay reports" from the shop or purchasing indicating that particular components will not be available as scheduled, or that planned production rates are not being attained.
7. Revise the master schedule when necessary for lack of material or capacity.
8. Call the basic conflicts, which the master schedule brings into focus, to the attention of other members of management who need to face up to the problems that the master schedule points out—*in advance*.

Marketing may come along with a request for a promotion to counter competitive pressures. A good master scheduling system will have some policy guidelines as to just when an unplanned input can be accepted. Typical policy guidelines might be as follows:

1. A "fence" is established at the *shortest* reasonable lead time. Within that lead time, no major reschedules are normally accepted from marketing. Obviously, in practice, there may be occasions when this policy will be violated, but they should be extremely rare. Only production and inventory management people can change the master schedule because of "bottom up" inputs. It is essential that *they* be able to change it in order to keep priorities valid.
2. Between this shortest reasonable lead time and the total *average* lead time to get material to make the product which, of course, would be considerably longer, is the period when it is usually wise to change the *timing* of items in the master schedule but leave the *quantity* fixed. This policy reflects the fact that orders will have been released at the lower levels of the product structure and changes in the *quantities* in the master schedule could generate unnecessary emergency releases. It would be better to pull up the next lot in the master schedule to cover the increased requirements.
3. Out beyond the total accumulated lead time down through the product structure, any change to the master schedule that is not likely to have a great impact on capacity can be accepted. If it *is* likely to have a great impact on capacity, this must be evaluated.

In the event an item has to be inserted into the master schedule within the normal time fence, the master scheduler should evaluate the feasibility of getting the product made on time. If he does not have the units planned in the master schedule, he should evaluate their impact on materials and capacity. He can then have purchasing and manufacturing personnel determine whether the materials can be produced in the shorter than normal lead time and also whether the capacity will be available. To do this, he needs to create a trial-fit material requirements plan and capacity requirements plan. He can then superimpose capacity requirements for this new program on the existing capacity plans, and if capacity is not available, he may well go to the detailed capacity requirements planning reports to see what components are causing the current loads. (Capacity requirements planning is discussed more fully in Chapter 6.) He might, consequently, show management that one of the possibilities would be to move something else that is currently in the master schedule out into the future in order to handle this new program.

One of the most important jobs the master scheduler has is determining when the master schedule itself should be revised because material or capacity is not available. This is where extremely good judgment—and a good ability to communicate the alternatives to other members of management—is required.

Some systems designers with a mistaken idea that the objective is to get everything on the computer have insisted on rescheduling open orders in MRP ("scheduled receipts") automatically. One of the shibboleths of the systems community for many years was that the objective was to "transfer the human decision to the computer." This generally does not work out well in practice. People will not use a system they do not understand, and, unless the system is going to be 100 percent automatic and free of human intervention, it should be simple and transparent. It should be designed to *support* the man rather than supplant him.

Automatic rescheduling of open orders ignores the interrelationship among the master scheduler, the material requirements planner, and the shop planner. The master scheduler tries to fit orders into the schedule where the customer wants them or where they are needed to replenish finished goods inventory. The material requirements planner tries to have the components available that are called for in the master schedule. The shop planner, of course, tries to get this material through the shop on schedule. In the event a part is scrapped and cannot *possibly* be replaced to meet the original schedule, the master scheduler must change the assembly date for the job requiring this part. Automatic rescheduling would often automatically *put an impossible due date on the replenishment order*.

In practice, a reschedule message would come to the material requirements planner as a result of scrapping the first lot of the parts. He would then check with the shop planner to see if the reschedule is possible. He might find that he cannot possibly get the replacement lot through to meet the original schedule. *He insists, however, on getting these parts through to the best schedule possible.* He and the master scheduler then determine what that best possible schedule is, and revise the assembly date in the master schedule accordingly.

It should be emphasized that the master schedule is not being used properly if, any time a problem comes up, it is used as a way to reschedule jobs into the future. This is why the master scheduler's job is so critical. Frequently, the shop planner will come to him and tell him that a job will not be coming through on the scheduled date because of some problem. He must insist that everything possible be done to get this job through to meet the original schedule. If he tries to enforce an unrealistic master schedule, he will destroy the shop priorities. On the other hand, if he does not insist on good shop performance, customer service will suffer.

The master scheduler's job is indeed a critical one, a job that would be an excellent training ground for the future production control manager, plant manager, or for that matter, general manager. Business is made up of difficult decisions. It is made up of situations where a manager has to be able to get the best possible performance just short of insisting on performance that is impossible and morale-destroying. The effectiveness of a material requirements planning or time phased order point system—or any formal priority planning system—will depend largely on the ability of the master scheduler to keep the master schedule ambitious yet realistic. His responsibility could be defined very briefly: *Maintaining credibility in the system.*

### Managing the Master Schedule

Material requirements planning (or the time phased order point) is the keystone to a good production and inventory management system. In the next few chapters, we will be discussing capacity planning, capacity control, and priority control, but it is important to recognize that *everything starts with priority planning,* and it is also important to recognize that the master schedule is the prime input to the priority plan itself. The master schedule drives the priority planning system, which in turn drives the rest of the production and inventory management system.

Figure 9 shows this. We have been talking about the time phased order point and MRP: these are the techniques for priority planning. Capacity requirements planning will be discussed in Chapter 6. Input/output control is the technique for capacity control, the subject of Chapter 7; and the dispatch list and anticipated delay report are the most common techniques for priority control in a factory. They will be the subject of Chapter 8.

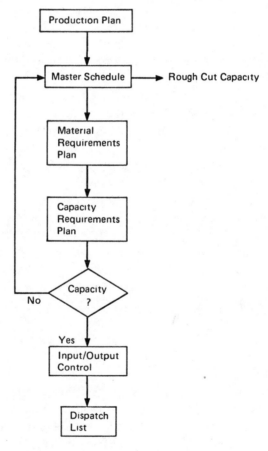

*Figure 9. Planning Sequence*

Figure 9 shows the very significant interrelationship among these techniques. The capacity planning function is particularly significant. The open shop orders are combined with planned orders from MRP to provide the input to the capacity requirements plan. This shows how much capacity is actually going to be needed at the key work centers. Once this plan has been generated, the question to be answered is whether that capacity can be made available or not. If the capacity can be made available, then the master schedule is practical and the material requirements plan can start releasing orders and generating reschedule messages. Capacity plans will be set for the significant work centers and then monitored with the input/output control technique. The dispatch list will go to the shop—usually each day—to show required schedules through each work center to meet need dates generated by MRP. Purchasing will work to MRP need dates also. The chart in Figure 9 simply shows the basic techniques that will be used for:

1. Planning priorities.
2. Planning capacity.
3. Controlling priorities.
4. Controlling capacity.

The interrelationship among the elements of a production and inventory management system is extremely important for management to understand. In particular, they must appreciate the significance of the master schedule. Frequently, the master scheduler may have to call significant problems to the attention of management and show them the impact of trying to get something like a new product into the master schedule in shorter than the normal lead time. It may be possible to put the new product in if other items can be moved out. It may be possible to get additional capacity, but at a high cost. In the event that there is a great increase in business and capacity cannot possibly be built up to handle it, it may well be significant for management to decide which products they are going to give long deliveries on and which products they are going to try to give the very best service on.

The shop planner, the material requirements planner who releases orders and reschedules orders, and even the master scheduler are really making *tactical* decisions. The master scheduler should frequently call significant conflicts to the attention of management so that they can make the *strategic* decisions necessary. With a modern production and inventory management system, the conflicts can be seen and resolved in advance.

This type of system won't keep the problems from occurring, but it will tell management what these problems are going to be and give them a choice in determining how they intend to face them.

*Martin M. was the plant manager in a medium-sized manufacturing company. He frequently commented that "a manufacturing executive can never say no." His point was a very simple one. When marketing people or the president of the company say that they want the impossible done, the man in charge of manufacturing who does not have the facts has no alternative but to say "yes" and then try to do it, knowing full well that something else is going to suffer. Martin's reaction to a material requirements planning system with capacity planning, capacity control, and a dispatch list was enthusiastic. "Sure, I'm impressed with better service, lower inventories, and lower production costs. Those are all good things, but the thing that impresses me most about this type of system is the ability to have the facts at my disposal. Now I can show management what the real alternatives are; now I can show them where we need to spend money on extra capacity or where we might want to move something out of the master schedule in order to do the 'impossible' that I know has to be done from time to time. I have known for years that there was a cost for doing the impossible. Now I can show other members of management what the costs are, what the alternatives are, and even though I hate to do it, on occasion when I have to, I can even say 'no' and make it stick."*

*Roger M., the vice president of marketing for the Theta Instrument Company, became one of the most enthusiastic supporters of their new production and inventory management system. He recognized marketing's responsibility to provide good input in order to make a master schedule, but he could also see the benefits that the system generated for him. Not only were deliveries much more reliable, not only could customer promises be given with confidence, but he could also make some strategic decisions that were significant. When a part was scrapped, the need to change the master schedule would be called to his attention. It was his choice and his responsibility to decide which customer could best accept the reschedule. Before launching a major marketing effort, he insisted that a trial fit be run through the system so that he could be assured that capacity would be available to support this program. Roger's appraisal of the system was summed up by this comment, "The realities of life in a manufacturing company often hit you pretty hard in marketing. Frequently, there are things you'd like to do and you simply can't do them. It's like trying to stop a car on slippery pavement. You'd like to hold your foot on the brake, but, unfortu-*

*nately, you would just skid out of control. The important thing to remember, though, is that if you can't stop, you had better be able to steer. By the same token, the master scheduler often tells me that there are things we can't do, but then he shows me what the realistic alternatives are and I have the option of picking them. This kind of system sure doesn't solve all of the problems in a manufacturing company, but it does give the marketing man a better way to cope with them."*

It is easy to see, then, why the master schedule is so important in a production and inventory management system. Many companies will say they do not have a master schedule, yet in one way or another they do determine how much production they are going to have. Formalizing this master schedule will help them to face up to the difficult decisions necessary in a manufacturing business.

Perhaps the essence of a formal system that really works is best demonstrated by the difficult decisions that revolve around the master schedule. Production and inventory management has always been a "getting out of trouble" function. There is nothing inherent in the modern techniques of production and inventory management that will solve the problems to which management must address themselves. All the system will do is make these problems apparent ahead of time and give management the opportunity to address these problems rationally.

Computer systems have often been unsuccessful. Too many people still expect the computer system to be an "automatic" system that will suddenly erase all of the difficulties of running a manufacturing organization. Many, for example, try to program everything they can on the computer. Some have even made the mistake of trying to generate an automatic master schedule.

The human being must control the master schedule. The foolish concept that the "manager will establish decision parameters" and these will be programmed into the system to be used from now on is obviously inappropriate when one considers that a master schedule will have to be adjusted to cope with such things as price changes, components that do not come through on schedule, dock strikes, certain customers who require preferential treatment occasionally, and all the other changing *interrelated* realities—and priorities—of the manufacturing world.

Because it is such a direct control on the system, the management of the master schedule is critical. When the informal system was the real system people frequently fell into the habit of overstating the master schedule. This was done to "motivate people." When the informal system was the real system the master schedule was like a steering wheel that was not connected. People fell into the habit of pointing it where they *wished* they were going rather than where they realistically expected to go. If they do not change their thinking about the master schedule, the formal system cannot possibly work.

*The Gindal Company manufactures a line of industrial valves. They had been using an order point system for components for years. Only Nick, the production control manager, and his crew of expediters really kept them in business. But as the valves became more complex and as experienced expediters were promoted, retired, or quit, the problem got out of hand. The backlog built up substantially and customer service deteriorated. The inventory of components increased, since they could not meet their assembly schedule because they always seemed to be short just one or two parts. When there are one or two parts missing, the inventory is going to be high, since all other parts are on hand. Of course, when this situation occurs, service is also going to be low.*

*MRP was installed at Gindal. They did almost everything right. They designed a very simple, straightforward standard type material requirements plan. But when it went on the air, the general manager insisted on putting all of the backlog—which by now amounted to about a month and a half of normal production—into the master schedule in the first month. This meant that the first month showed two and one-half times the number of valves in the master schedule as they normally would expect to produce. The general manager's argument was a very simple one: there was no real bottleneck in assembly capacity. He knew that as long as components were available, he could pick up the backlog and get it out the door immediately. What he did not understand, however, was that the integrity of priorities would be destroyed. The vendors and the manufacturing facility could not possibly react immediately. It would take them time to get cranked up to make the material that was needed. The net result of this gross overstatement of the master schedule was a long expediting list for manufacturing and a long expediting list for purchasing. Both lists were too long and too unwieldy to be useful. As a result, the informal expediting system once more became the mainstay of manufacturing operations.*

*Gindal never did manage to make MRP function well. Because the formal priority planning system was badly overstated, their expediters began pulling and accumulating parts and making up "shortage lists" again. They had started out with some good intentions about inventory transaction integrity, but the constant shortage problem overshadowed their good resolutions. Soon expediting and firefighting became the real system once again. Ironically, the management of the company believes that they are using MRP ("doesn't work as well as they say it should"), but, in fact, it is just a facade of formal system at Gindal.*

The master schedule cannot be overstated or priorities will become invalid. But overstatement is not the only problem: too few companies learn to use the master schedule to react properly to feedback. The capacity and priority control systems are designed to monitor activity to see that it is going according to plan. When a key component will not arrive on schedule, the master schedule must be revised to reflect that fact, or other component priorities will become invalid. If capacity in a key work center falls significantly behind plan, the master schedule must be revised.

It is important to emphasize: *the main job is to get the resources on time to execute the master schedule.* When this cannot be done, however, it *must be revised to reflect reality.* The master schedule is the place where what a company would *like to do* and what they *can do* must be reconciled.

A formal system that can work is a new capability. It will, by definition, be installed in an environment where people are accustomed to working primarily with informal systems. The formal system requires a different approach, and this is especially evident in watching companies learning how to manage a master schedule effectively. Few other areas can have such a direct effect on system success or failure. Few other areas are as challenging to learn to manage effectively. Few others deserve as much constant management attention.

# Part 3 | Capacity Planning

# 5 | Scheduling and Loading

## Scheduling

The term scheduling implies timing. The priority planning system—be it MRP, time phased order point, or, in a one-piece make-to-order shop, the customer's order itself—specifies when an order needs to be completed. The detailed schedule on that manufacturing order will specify when it needs to be started into production and when it needs to be worked on at each of the planned operations. We can think of scheduling as setting milestones to make sure that work is being accomplished on time.

Years ago, many factories worked strictly in an expediting mode. Nobody even looked for a shop order or did anything to check on its progress unless it was actually past due (i.e., it had not been completed on time). By assigning schedule dates to the operations required to make the product, its progress can be monitored through each of the manufacturing operations required to make it. This is the approach most companies use today.

Figure 10 shows a typical shop order with a schedule assigned. Note that for simplicity of calculation the schedule is stated in shop calendar

Shop Order No. 50043
Part No. B-4848
Quant. 300        Due: 412        Release 396

| Oper. | Dept. | Work Center | Desc. | Setup | Per Piece | Std. Hrs. | Finish |
|-------|-------|-------------|-------|-------|-----------|-----------|--------|
| 10 | 08 | 1322 | Cut Off | .5 | .010 | 3.5 | 402 |
| 20 | 32 | 1600 | Rough Turn | 1.5 | .030 | 10.5 | 406 |
| 30 | 32 | 1204 | Finish Turn | 3.3 | .048 | 17.7 | 410 |
| 40 | 11 | | Inspect | | | | 412 |

*Figure 10. Typical Shop Order*

81

days. Each of the working days is numbered consecutively—frequently out over a three- or four-year period. Since only working days—excluding weekends, holidays, and plant shutdown periods—are numbered, the scheduler can easily compute when each operation is to be scheduled, working with a set of scheduling rules and some simple arithmetic.

Typical rules would state:

1. Allow eight standard hours per day.
2. Allow two days between operations in different departments, one day between operations in the same department.
3. Allow two days to inspect, pack, and ship.
4. Release the job to the stockroom five days before it is to be started in production.

These are not intended to be ideal scheduling rules at all. They are simply presented as an example of the form the typical scheduling rules take. It is important to keep in mind that scheduling rules just put approximate benchmarks on operations. There is nothing very scientific about them. Nevertheless, if they are too loose, they can contribute to unreasonably long lead times, since the shop can be on schedule, yet still have large amounts of work in process ahead of operations.

The shop order in Figure 10 has had schedule dates applied to its operations using these scheduling rules and a shop calendar. This job is due to be completed on day 412, since two days are being allowed for inspection and it must be finished at operation 30 on day 410. Operation 30 will take three days, since eight hours per day are allowed for scheduling purposes. Operation 30 is done in the same department as operation 20, so only one day will have to be allowed between operations. Thus the job will have to be completed out of operation 20 on day 406. In this manner, each operation is scheduled until a release date has been computed.

Scheduling, then, in the strict sense of the word, does not take capacity into account. Scheduling is concerned only with establishing milestones so that a job's progress can be monitored. An engineering department can be scheduled even though it is difficult to compute its exact capacity. While scheduling per se does not imply any comparison with capacity required, loading does.

### Work Center Loading

In Figure 10 it was shown that there were three and one-half standard hours of work to be done at work center 1322. This work was to be finished on day 402. This three and one-half standard hours, then, would be put into a load report for work center 1322 in the time period that includes day 402. In this manner, the capacity requirements for all the scheduled orders will be accumulated, and a machine load report will be generated. Figure 11 shows the format of a typical machine load report for a given work center. (A work center consists of one machine in some cases, but more often it consists of a number of machines with similar capabilities.) This machine load report shows the weekly capacity that the work center is estimated to have. This capacity is typically calculated by determining the number of people who are assigned to the work center and multiplying the number of hours they are expected to work by an "efficiency factor." An efficiency factor simply relates the number of actual hours worked to the number of standard hours of output that was generated.

The production last week was 205 standard hours. Everything on the machine load report is expressed in standard hours so that the information is comparable. Note that, as with most machine load reports, there is a considerable amount of work in the past-due period and the work load out in the future is lumpy and tends to taper off rather drastically. Both of these are serious problems with a typical machine load report. In fact, there are other serious problems with a machine load report in its usual format that will be discussed below. Suffice it for now to present this as an example of the classical approach to machine loading.

This type of loading was once called "loading to *infinite* capacity." The idea behind it was to first schedule the job as was done above, and

Work Center #1600
(All Figures in Standard Hours)

| Weekly Capacity—240 hr. | | Production Last Week—205 hr. |
|---|---|---|
| Week Ending | Load | Over/Under Load |
| Past Due | 824 | + 584 |
| 396 | 286 | +  46 |
| 401 | 150 | −  90 |
| 406 | 247 | +   7 |
| 411 | 196 | −  44 |
| 416 | 90 | − 150 |
| 421 | 130 | − 110 |
| 426 | 39 | − 201 |
| 430 | 27 | − 213 |
| 435 | 68 | − 172 |
| 440 | 84 | − 156 |

*Figure 11. Machine Load Report*

then show the load in the time period when the job is really needed, whether or not capacity is available at that time. The rationale behind the infinite loading approach was that the customers, or the assembly line, for example, have specific need dates, and if the load is not shown when it is really needed, schedules will not be met. There is something to say for this rationale, but there are times when there *are* genuine capacity limitations.

So another approach to loading, called *finite* loading, has received quite a bit of attention. The idea behind *finite* loading was to load jobs to the available capacity.

### Loading to Finite Capacity

Finite capacity loading (sometimes called capacity scheduling) is considerably more complex than infinite capacity loading. Figure 12 shows the two methods graphically. In order to finite load, most companies would back schedule the shop order, just as the shop order in Figure 10 was back scheduled from its due date of day 412. Once these planned schedule dates were calculated, then they would probably have to be revised in order to fit this shop order into the available load using the finite loading approach.

In the first work center, if there were not time available to start the job on the desired date, it would have to be rescheduled to a later date. The second work center would then have to have its scheduled date recalculated based on two factors:

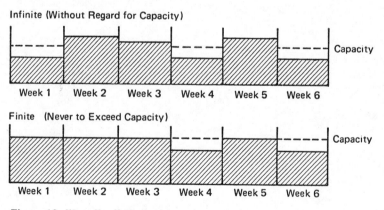

Infinite (Without Regard for Capacity)

Week 1  Week 2  Week 3  Week 4  Week 5  Week 6

Capacity

Finite (Never to Exceed Capacity)

Week 1  Week 2  Week 3  Week 4  Week 5  Week 6

Capacity

*Figure 12. "Loading" Methods*

1. When it will be completed in the preceding work center.
2. When capacity will be available in *this* work center.

MRP originally established the due date for each shop order. From this due date, the back scheduling to infinite capacity derives schedule dates for each operation, and, consequently, the load against the work centers in the time periods when it is needed. Note that the finite loading approach will now *revise* these operation schedule dates based on available capacity, and, in fact, it is quite likely, as it forwards schedules to the available capacity, that the completion date will be scheduled out beyond the desired completion time. If the schedule in question were for a component going into an assembly, *this would necessitate revising the master schedule.*

For many years, the debate has raged among production control practitioners and systems people: finite loading or infinite loading? Which is better? The infinite loaders point out that you cannot simply start with the capacity you have and work from that if you are going to give good customer service. The finite loaders point out that it is unrealistic to just dump a load into the factory if the factory cannot possibly handle it. There is something to be said for each side of the debate, but a further look at the problems involved with both approaches to loading will show that the debate, like so many, revolves primarily around semantics.

### The Problems with Classical Loading Techniques

It is only realistic to recognize that there sometimes are capacity limitations and that work cannot simply be dumped into a plant regardless of the plant's ability to handle it. The primary purpose of loading should be to show the capacity that is required. Thus, some form of infinite loading has to be a first step. Certainly no factory really has infinite capacity. It is irresponsible for production and inventory management people to dump work into a factory and throw the burden of meeting the schedule on the manufacturing people, when in some instances they could not possibly meet it—and management would not want them to.

The infinite loading technique, when properly used, is a *capacity planning* technique. Today, the term *infinite capacity loading* is obsolete. It has been superseded by the term *capacity requirements planning*, which certainly describes the function better. Capacity requirements planning will be described in greater detail in Chapter 6.

The biggest differences between infinite loading and capacity requirements planning are:

1. The capacity requirements plan picks up the *planned* orders as well as the released orders out of the MRP system. This stretches the load out further into the future to give shop people more time to react to needed changes in capacity.
2. Capacity requirements planning is an iterative technique, really a simulation. The master schedule drives MRP, and the output from MRP is used for capacity requirements planning. In the event capacity is not going to be available to meet the master schedule, then it will have to be changed.
3. *Terminology.* The term infinite loading is enough to infuriate the typical manufacturing man. He knows he does not have infinite capacity in his plant. Because the term is misleading, some production and inventory management people have misused the technique.

What about finite loading, then? Can it really be made to work? Finite loading works pretty easily when only one work center is involved. Unfortunately, when people try to apply finite loading to machine shops where many work centers are involved, complications arise. Job arrivals are not really very predictable in a work center that is being fed by a number of other work centers. Scrap, rework, absenteeism, lack of tooling, lack of a trained operator, all of these real-world problems can result in changes in the sequencing of jobs. They are not going to arrive exactly as predicted at downstream work centers. As a consequence, it seems like frivolous sophistication to go through a lot of complex scheduling calculations based on such questionable assumptions.

In the finite loading discussion above, it was observed that a component could easily have its finished date rescheduled out beyond the actual due date. In this case, the master schedule would have to be revised, *and, consequently, the due dates of all other related components would have to be revised.* This means that the loads that existed, and around which this component was rescheduled, should now be refigured. A true finite loading calculation could become an *endless* iteration.

Finite loading was once looked upon as an alternative to infinite loading. It is obvious that some leveling of load to fit into available capacity has to be done, but in the final analysis, whether a company uses infinite loading or the much more complex and sophisticated finite loading, they will wind up doing most of this load leveling via the master schedule. If finite loading has such limited practical application, why have computer programs been developed to implement it and why are many companies anxious to try it? Why have a few of them tried it, generally with disappointing results?

To understand the answers to these questions, one must recognize that these are the early years of computer application. Nobody could ever do finite loading manually for a complex factory. The computer made it possible. In fact, most companies had no chance of doing their priority effectively with a manual system, as was pointed out in earlier chapters. When the computer came along, techniques were developed out of context. Until very recently, there was little recognition of the relationship of the master schedule to MRP, to capacity planning, and so on.

Imagine the typical shop. They probably either have an order point system on dependent demand components, or they have an MRP system, but do not manage the master schedule properly. In either case, the results will be the same: a big backlog of "late" orders that are not really needed (there is some evidence of this in the machine load report shown in Figure 11). The practitioner, faced with this problem and not recognizing that his problem is in his priority planning system, is easily beguiled by the apparent logic of finite loading. It attempts to reschedule orders based on the actual capacity available, and thus gets rid of his backlog.

But, of course, it will not. It will only reschedule those orders and tell him to change the master schedule. Capacity requirements planning, a far simpler technique, could have given him the same information.

Finite loading, then, has limited application but a great deal of appeal, primarily for the following reasons:

1. *It is an apparent way to reschedule a backlog.* In fact, most of the significant backlogs ultimately have to be rescheduled via the master schedule if they cannot be eliminated.

2. *It is sophisticated.* To a great extent, this is the age of naive sophistication when many people choose the more complex technique, whether or not it will generate better results. Sophistication is expensive. It costs programming time, computer run time, and, more important, user understanding. The technician often thinks that sophistication is "good" and free. The manager recognizes that every additional bit of sophistication jeopardizes user understanding and insists that it be justified on the basis of results.

3. *It was the apparent alternative to infinite loading* and, obviously, infinite loading was unrealistic.

Finite loading *can* work for one work center, particularly if it is the starting work center. Rather significantly, those few companies that have tried finite loading by computer and claim it works generally fall into one of two categories:

1. They make a one-piece product, thus component priorities can be treated independently.
2. They make an assembled product but do not have a formal priority planning system that works (ironic—if the formal schedule has not yet become valid, why finesse it with finite loading?).

Typically, these companies are really using finite loading primarily to give delivery promises; they do not understand how to use the master schedule to determine whether material and capacity are available. Finite loading is a very complex method to use to solve a problem that a well-designed master schedule handles easily.

The real test of finite loading is not a matter of opinion, but, in fact, is quite simple to determine. Finite loading recalculates priorities based on available capacity. It then generates a dispatch list. If that dispatch list can be followed religiously without having to resort to informal systems, it can be said to work. Some of the more recent literature covering the subject of finite loading refers to it as *order release planning*. This is probably a more descriptive term that will help us to understand more realistically just what finite loading is really trying to do. It is merely trying to develop proper priorities to schedule orders to avoid *anticipated* future bottlenecks.

One last thought on the subject: even if finite loading might some-day be made to work effectively, sound priority planning and capacity planning should obviously be installed first. One of its greatest drawbacks is that in practice people who should be solving fundamental problems are distracted from them by the glamor of a sophisticated computer technique.

Neither of the classical approaches to loading, then, was very effective. Since it has only recently been possible to have priority planning systems that work properly, there was little hope of having capacity planning systems that could work properly. Attempts at capacity planning systems did not function effectively at all in most companies and, as a result, it was difficult to evaluate them and to gain a better understanding of their advantages and shortcomings until the last few years. With a number of companies quite effectively using computer systems in manufacturing today, and vastly improved communications among practitioners, far more effective—and, quite ironically, far less sophisticated —approaches have been developed.

Capacity requirements planning is really very similar to what we once called infinite loading. In practice, however, it is a far more powerful tool.

# 6 | Capacity Requirements Planning

## Planning Capacity Requirements

Since the formal priority planning system in most companies did not work, the capacity planning system could hardly have been expected to be very effective. Machine load reports in most companies simply were not significant tools as far as most operating people were concerned. Yet, one way or another, these people had to plan capacity. They had to be able to respond when there was an increase in business. They had to know that more manpower and more machines needed to be added.

Naturally, to do this they had to have an informal capacity planning system. It generally relied on visual backlogs. If the foreman and his supervisors could not see work ahead of them, they were afraid to add capacity; if visible backlogs dropped too low, even the machine operators tended to respond by slowing down the work pace. The result was an agonizingly slow reaction to increases in the business level. First the inventory system would have to generate the input. Then the backlogs would have to build up at each work center. Then, as capacity was slowly increased, the work would start to flow. Visual backlogs is the informal capacity planning system in many companies today; a slow, ineffective, laborious way to respond when capacity needs to be changed.

One of the resulting phenomena has sometimes somewhat facetiously been called galloping backlogs. The visible backlog builds up behind the first work center. Finally, capacity is increased to get rid of the backlog (usually, since there is not enough advance notice, this is done by overtime and other expensive techniques). Then this backlog moves on to downstream work centers where it is eventually worked off. If the backlog persists long enough, permanent changes to capacity by hiring and training people, for example, or subcontracting work are eventually made.

90

Some companies used to do machine loading manually, but it was quite a laborious task, and because the priority planning system did not work properly, the load reports usually did not generate very useful information. There were usually plenty of late orders that had not been rescheduled and were not really needed, thus overstating the load report.

It is interesting to observe that even when the computer came along, the basic concept of machine loading did not change. Common practice was to have an inventory system generate work and then add it up to measure how far behind the shop was. In fact, in the literature of production and inventory management, the term capacity planning is virtually absent until the late sixties when it starts to appear in some of the textbooks and computer literature. (Interestingly enough, finite loading was usually treated under the category of "capacity planning." Finite loading attempts to fit orders into the capacity that exists and is hardly a capacity *planning* technique.)

Later, when the term capacity planning did come into use, it still generated confusion among practitioners. Many of them, thinking in industrial engineering mode, conceived of capacity planning as some sort of capacity study where current man and machine capacities would be established. It is significant to know what the capacity capability and potential of a shop is, yet this information is not too hard to come by. Some simple approaches to getting this information will be discussed in the next chapter. But the important question before determining capacity availability is to determine the capacity *requirements*—how much capacity is needed.

The capacity requirements planning technique is quite similar to the old idea of infinite loading, but the application is quite different. Capacity requirements planning does not try to "plan" based on an accumulation of backlogs, but instead works from a forecast of capacity requirements based not only on released orders, but also on the planned orders that would show in a material requirements plan, or in the time phased order point format.

The practitioner's objection to infinite loading was that it did not take into account the actual capacity available, and thus usually overloaded the shop. Capacity requirements planning makes a *tentative plan* to show the capacity that is needed. This can be compared with actual capacity available to determine whether or not the master schedule can be met.

In the event the required amount of capacity is not available, the detailed capacity requirements planning report showing the individual released orders and planned orders making up the capacity requirements for a given time period will be referenced. As with any "normal distribution," a few of the part numbers are likely to be creating most of the capacity requirements. These can be traced back through the MRP system into the master schedule—using the "pegging" described in Chapter 2—to find out what the products are that are affected. The master schedule can then be revised and a new MRP and capacity requirements plan can be run. Load leveling must be done at least approximately, and this gross load leveling must ultimately take place via the master schedule.

Even after gross load leveling has been accomplished, there will be random variations in capacity requirements from week to week. A typical capacity requirements plan might look like Figure 13. The average weekly capacity requirement for the ten-week period shown is 270 hours, yet it varies quite substantially from week to week.

The important question for the planner to determine is whether these variations are truly significant. They are the accumulated hours based on the scheduled dates assigned to operations for released orders and for planned orders. Planned orders that appear in the MRP system have been scheduled by the computer, and the hours required at the proper scheduled times have been accumulated in the capacity requirements plan.

So these apparently significant variations in capacity requirements week to week are based on a number of assumptions. In particular, they assume that jobs will move according to schedule and that these schedules are quite precise and accurate. In reality, schedules are approximate, they have slack built into them, and jobs seldom move exactly according to schedule. There is tolerance built into the scheduling system in a machine-shop, as there must be. Consequently, variations even as extreme as those shown in Figure 13 are probably not terribly significant, although it might be worthwhile checking the detail load for week 9 to see if there is really

| Week | | Week | |
|------|-----|------|-----|
| 1 | 284 | 6. | 286 |
| 2 | 61 | 7 | 50 |
| 3. | 321 | 8. | 147 |
| 4. | 139 | 9. | 695 |
| 5 | 531 | 10 | 176 |

*Figure 13. Capacity Requirements*

some extraordinary requirement in there or whether this is just a random occurrence.

The important thing to know is that the capacity requirements for the next ten weeks equal 270 hours. No shop can realistically vary its output from 284 hours one week to 61 hours the next, but a shop that can maintain its output at the required average 270-hour-per-week rate is not likely to have serious problems delivering its product to its customers.

### Capacity Management

Figure 9 (p. 72) illustrates the relationships among the four vital functions of production and inventory management. The master schedule drives the priority planning system, which in turn provides the input for the capacity planning system.

Material requirements planning or the time phased order point will usually be used for priority planning in most companies. A capacity requirements plan can then be derived from the released orders and the planned orders. Before the MRP starts releasing orders, however, the validity of the master schedule must be tested against capacity. Is there capacity or is there not? If there is, production rates can be established from the capacity requirements plan and capacity control techniques like input/output control (discussed in Chapter 7) can be used to control capacity. The dispatch list is then used to control detailed priority within the factory, and purchasing follow-up is used to control priorities with vendors.

But before the system can start operating, it must first function in planning mode to show management the capacity requirements necessary to meet the master schedule and to point out to them clearly what alternatives they face. This relationship between the master schedule and capacity planning was discussed in Chapter 4, but it is so important that it is worth reemphasizing.

When the capacity requirement exceeds available capacity, there are really only two alternatives: either get more capacity or revise the master schedule. Here is where some tough management decisions have to be made, and they are not going to be made by the computer. Certainly no one is going to delegate to the computer the choice of which customers will suffer, whether to work overtime, whether to subcontract, or whether to run jobs through alternate operations that are more expensive when a numerical control machine is overloaded, for example. The power of this type of system is not that it makes decisions for management, but that it puts the alternatives into clear focus so that management can make decisions.

The problem of managing capacity is far less a technical one than a management one.

> *One of the companies that developed a very good capacity requirements planning system to go with their material requirements planning system had difficulty getting the manufacturing vice president to pay any attention to the numbers. His old approach was always to check on the total number of labor dollars being generated by the plan and to relate these to the planned output from assembly. This, of course, did nothing to insure that he was putting those labor hours into the right work centers to solve the problems. In a recent period of business increase, in spite of the availability of the numbers to help him manage the business better, he preferred to use his old comfortable "seat of the pants" techniques. As a result, inventories increased, and it took an agonizingly long time to respond to the customers' requirements. On one occasion when the materials manager was particularly concerned that the shop was not responding fast enough to marketing requirements, he could not find the vice president of manufacturing in his office. When finally tracked down, he was helping one of the millwrights repair the main steam boiler which had broken down.*

The computer has made it possible to generate the information to manage a business far differently from the way it was managed before. Many executives will welcome the ability to identify problems and alternatives ahead of time. They will take advantage of the ability to address these problems rationally and to control their manufacturing facilities better. A few will find it difficult to learn to run a business "with the numbers." The mock heroics of firefighting tend to be self-perpetuating. The value of the techniques that the computer has made possible depends on management's ability to develop the skills required to use them effectively. They are not panaceas, but they *can* provide the information that will allow management to change the focus of activities in a company away from *getting* out of trouble and toward *keeping* out of trouble.

### Using the Production Plan to Evaluate Capacity Alternatives

One of the best known approximate capacity planning techniques is the production plan discussed in Chapter 4. Another example is shown in

Figure 14. This production plan calls for an inventory buildup ahead of a peak selling season and anticipating a plant shutdown period in July. Note that the production plan then is used to monitor actual sales, production, and resulting inventory week-by-week.

This production plan is, in effect, a rough-cut capacity plan. It determines the overall production rate required. But it does not give detailed capacity planning information by work center. Instead, it is typically setting an assembly rate and even *that* might have to be broken down into more detail in many companies.

The production plan, then, establishes the rate at which work will be fed into the master schedule. The planned production rate could be the master schedule rate for a product group. The individual items in the master schedule would have to total the planned production rate.

The production plan can be an effective tool even today. It is not a detailed capacity planning technique, but it can be particularly useful for looking at alternative approaches to coping with seasonal sales activity.

Leveling production when sales are seasonal requires inventory buildups before the peak selling season. Yet level production not only reduces the direct—and indirect—costs of changing production levels, it also requires the least capacity.

Alternative production plans for coping with seasonal sales should be laid out to show management the choices they face. Approximate capacity requirements for a few critical work centers may be worth calculating along with the number and size of the capacity changes required

| Week Ending | Total Sales | Prod. | Fin. Goods Invent. | |
|---|---|---|---|---|
| 3/31 | | | (150) | |
| 4/7 | 30 (25) | 40 (41) | 160 (166) | Forecast (Actual) |
| 4/14 | 30 (38) | 40 (37) | 170 (165) | |
| 6/30 | 30 | 40 | 280 | |

*Figure 14. Quarterly Production Plan*

for each plan. This can then be compared with required inventory investment to facilitate better management policy decisions at a "gross" capacity planning level.

### Separating Priority and Capacity

It is important in addressing any problem to define the question properly. There are two major problems to be addressed in production and inventory management: priority and capacity. Time after time, in practice, manufacturing personnel simply do not seem to be able to identify which problem they are really suffering from. When business picks up, they dump more work into the factory, they get bigger backlogs, and almost inevitably someone's reaction will be to add more expediters. Expediters do not cut chips, they do not make anything; the problem they spend most of their time addressing is priority. There is no question that priority problems become more and more pressing when there is not sufficient capacity. But a capacity problem will not be solved by addressing the priority problem.

On the other hand, frequently what looks like a capacity problem is nothing more than a priority problem.

*The manufacturing vice president of the Fonsworth Company was beside himself. They had been making the same four basic models of business machines for the last three years. The total sales of business machines this year was no greater than last year and, since they were the same models, they took the same basic parts. But this year, he had a serious problem with screw machine parts. Most of the parts shortages on the assembly line were screw machine parts. The screw machine department had been working overtime, farming work out to subcontractors, yet they did not seem to be making much progress. He was particularly disturbed when he checked and found that the* total standard hours of screw machine parts *produced in the current year exceeded production in the previous year.*

*Investigation showed that a very interesting phenomenon had taken place. Screw machine output had decreased temporarily because of a flu epidemic. The production control manager immediately found his lead times in the factory getting longer. He, therefore, increased his* planning *lead times. Where he had previously planned that a screw machine part would take four weeks, he now planned that it would take six weeks. The result of this was to generate more input to the shop. The increase in input increased the backlog, which increased the lead time, and the production control manager reacted by increasing his planning lead times again. He shortly found himself with a twelve-week planning lead time, lots of work in process, and a great deal of expediting to do to try to get the right jobs through the shop.*

*But then an insidious thing started to happen. This production control manager did not have an effective MRP system. In fact, he was using order points on dependent demand screw machine parts (a big mistake!). Thus, he could not keep priorities up to date. (In fact, with the order point system, they were not even correct on the day the order was issued.) Figure 15 shows an interesting phenomenon that occurs when a formal priority planning system does not function properly. The result will be to have a system that says, "Do it on the date I told you to do it—unless I tell you I need it sooner." There is an expediting system but no unexpediting system. Consider a screw machine part that is ordered with a due date twelve weeks in the future. The chances are very remote that it will actually be needed in week twelve. If it is needed sooner, the expediter will find out about it. If it is needed later (with an order point system that is very likely to be the case), once week twelve has passed this order will show as past due! Since these orders that are not needed were not rescheduled, the machine load report at Fonsworth showed an ever-increasing number of past-due hours indicating a serious capacity problem,* when, in fact, the real problem was priority planning!

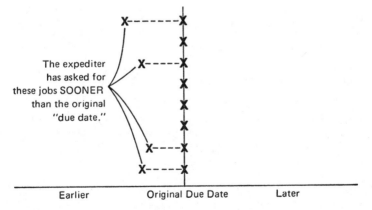

The expediter has asked for these jobs SOONER than the original "due date."

Earlier      Original Due Date      Later

*Figure 15. Formal Priority Planning System Malfunction*

Separating priority and capacity in our thinking about production and inventory management can help substantially in identifying the real problems. Traditional approaches to production and inventory management seem to want to muddle the two of them. Ask a shop foreman what he needs in order to better plan his capacity out in the future, and his answer will inevitably be, "Give me the orders."

Unfortunately, the further out into the future the orders are generated, the less accurate their priorities will be. He should really be asking for a forecast of capacity requirements.

Capacity requirements planning works well even though the forecast of planned order releases out into the future is not very accurate from a priority point of view. It *is* reasonably accurate when it is used to forecast the number of hours by work center by time period that will actually be required.

Capacity planning in most companies is the result of some kind of forecast. Forecasts are less accurate the farther out in the future they go. Capacity forecasts, by definition, have to be made fairly far into the future in order to give manufacturing people time to respond. A capacity forecast stated in machine hours—a group forecast—will, thus, be more accurate than a detailed schedule of orders.

Machine loading was an interesting concept. It was a concept built primarily around backlogs. Perhaps during the Depression years of the thirties it was a valid concept. At that time, manpower was readily available and the reaction time to change capacity was quite short. Perhaps during World War II and the ensuing Korean War, when backlogs of customer orders were stretched far out into the future, machine loading also could be used. In today's business world, the marketplace will not normally tolerate the long lead times that result from using backlogs to plan capacity.

The labor market is also considerably different from what it was during the Depression. It takes time to get good people. It takes time to train them. The company that gets the reputation for hiring and laying off erratically tends to attract the poorer performers from the labor force. Good people simply will not work for a company that does not offer them more security.

Dwindling backlogs and a longer reaction time for changing capacity have made it necessary to adopt new approaches, like capacity require-

ments planning, to replace the "loading" approaches which did not func
tion very well in most production and inventory management systems in
the past. New approaches to capacity control—which was practically nonexistent in past systems—had to be adopted also.

# Part 4 | Capacity Control

# 7 | Input/Output Control

### The Missing Element: Output Control

A control system, be it an electronic control system, a fluid control system, or an information control system, must be built around four basic elements:

1. A realistic plan or "norm."
2. Feedback to show whether the system is on plan or not.
3. Tolerance—a nervous control system that reacts too quickly is undesirable.
4. Corrective action.

It is interesting to look at the machine load report that was shown in Figure 11 (p.'83). Where is the plan? Certainly no foreman could be held responsible for producing at the erratic rate shown in that load report. Where is the feedback? It tells us what the weekly capacity is and what the production was for one week, but how indicative of performance is that?

We ought to be able to see a planned output rate smoothed out to make a realistic plan that the foreman can be held responsible for. And we ought to expect to see what his actual output has been for several weeks. Is he meeting the plan or not? One week's output is not indicative—nor is it particularly significant to know what the "theoretical capacity" of a work center is.

Figure 16 shows an output control report that was derived from the capacity requirements plan shown earlier in Figure 13 (p. 92). The output control report shows the planned output rate at 270 hours per week, the average rate over the ten-week period. The capacity requirement

103

| | W1 | W2 | W3 | W4 | W5 |
|---|---|---|---|---|---|
| Planned | 270 | 270 | 270 | 270 | 270 |
| Actual | 250 | 220 | 190 | | |
| Deviation | -20 | -70 | -150 | | |

*Figure 16. Output Control*

has been *averaged,* recognizing that work is not likely to arrive at work centers at the erratic rate shown by the capacity plan, and that even if it did, the *output* from these work centers would necessarily be quite smooth since there is a fairly stable level of manpower available.

Prior to making an output control report, people in manufacturing management should have agreed that 270 hours a week of output was a practical, attainable figure. The output control report would be unrealistic if this had not been determined during the planned phase. Only after the manufacturing management people have gone through the cycle illustrated in Figure 9 (p. 72) and agreed that the capacity required is attainable should the output control report be published.

Many practitioners seem baffled over the problem of determining how much capacity they have. In practice this is really relatively simple. It can be done on an exception basis. The capacity requirements plan shows the capacity needed. Virtually every factory has labor variance and labor efficiency reports that show what the standard hours of output were per day, week, and month. It is not too difficult to accumulate this information by work center—if it is not already available by work center—and this will show the *actual* capacity that exists today. The capacity requirements plan is not likely to show capacity requirements far in excess of this actual capacity for many work centers. Where it does, perhaps a capacity study to determine the potential capacity of that work center is justified.

It is important for the practitioner to recognize that capacity planning and control does not start with detailed capacity studies for all work centers when actual output information can be so easily obtained in so useful a format. He should also recognize that "theoretical capacity" adjusted by an "efficiency factor" does not usually allow for absenteeism and other real-world problems. By relating his actual output in standard hours to his required output he can do a better job of controlling capacity very simply.

The output control report is truly a *control* report. It shows the plan, the feedback, and then it shows the cumulative deviation of "actual" from "plan." This allows a tolerance to be established. If, for example, it is determined that no more than one half a week of deviation from the plan can be tolerated, then in the example in Figure 16, by week three it is incumbent on the manufacturing people to work overtime, add people, or do whatever is necessary to implement corrective action to get back on the plan.

There is a lot to be said for preestablishing what the "norm" and "tolerance" are. So many manufacturing meetings wind up in constant debate over whether or not corrective action needs to be taken, rather than discussions on *how* corrective action will be taken. When the plan and the tolerance are established ahead of time, discussions in manufacturing meetings tend to be far less emotional. Running a manufacturing company is just like any other game—it is a good idea to establish where the boundaries are before the game is played.

Nowhere in the classical literature of production and inventory management is capacity control discussed. Like any other subject, until it is thought of in the proper terminology it is not seen too clearly. Planning and controlling priorities, planning and controlling capacities, these are the four basic functions of production and inventory control. Yet capacity control, one of the vital ones, was never specifically defined. Certainly the machine load report was not truly a capacity control device. The output control report can be. But there is an even better approach: input/output control.

### Input/Output Control

Figure 17 shows an input/output control report. While the planned input of work to this work center is 270 hours per week the planned output is 300 hours per week for the first three weeks, since there is currently a backlog of 90 hours of work at the work center *above* the desired level of work in process. Note that in Figure 17 the input rate is very close to being on target. The output is not much below the planned rate, and it looks like the backlog in this work center will be reduced to the desired level—a little later than originally planned.

Figure 18 shows an input/output report for a downstream work center—heat treating might be a typical example. Looking first at the lower, or output, half of the report, it can be seen that output is far below plan. A serious capacity problem would seem to exist at this work center.

Work Center 0138
(All Figures in Standard Hours)

|  | Week Ending | 505 | 512 | 519 | 526 |
|---|---|---|---|---|---|
| Unreleased Backlog | Planned Input | 270 | 270 | 270 | 270 |
| | Actual Input | 270 | 265 | 270 | |
| 0 | Cumulative Deviation | | -5 | -5 | |

|  | Planned Output | 300 | 300 | 300 | 270 |
|---|---|---|---|---|---|
| Released Backlog* | Actual Output | 305 | 260 | 280 | |
| 90 | Cumulative Deviation | +5 | -35 | -55 | |

*Above desired level of work in process (standard queue) at this work
center as of start of plan.

*Figure 17. Input/Output Control Report (A)*

However, by looking at the input part of the plan it becomes apparent
that the serious capacity problem—at least for the present—exists at one
of the upstream work centers that is feeding this particular work center.
Input to the work center simply has not been up to plan.

The format of the input/output report enables the production control man to deal with the problem that always was a difficult one: knowing
that the work is *really* at the work center before he exerts pressure on the
foreman to increase capacity. The input/output control report in Figure
18 indicates very clearly that the foreman responsible for work center 0162
does not have a problem there. One of the foremen who is responsible for
a feeding work center—or centers—should be concentrating on his capacity
bottleneck to get production moving once again.

Work Center 0162
(All Figures in Standard Hours)

| Week Ending | 505 | 512 | 519 | 526 |
|---|---|---|---|---|
| Planned Input | 210 | 210 | 210 | 210 |
| Actual Input | 110 | 150 | 140 | 130 |
| Cumulative Deviation | -100 | -160 | -230 | -310 |
| Planned Output | 210 | 210 | 210 | 210 |
| Actual Output | 140 | 120 | 160 | 120 |
| Cumulative Deviation | -70 | -160 | -210 | -300 |

*Figure 18. Input/Output Control Report (B)*

Note the significant differences between the input/output approach and the machine load approach. The machine load report measures backlog. The input/output control report measures *flow* of work in and out of the work centers. The input/output control report, since it is based on a capacity requirements plan using planned orders that go well out into the future, would normally stretch out several months, giving the foreman a much longer planning horizon and much better information to base any economical changes in capacity on. The input/output control report is designed to be a *control report*, with a plan that is practical, attainable, and against which results can be measured. It shows also the feedback against the plan and the deviation from the plan. A tolerance can be introduced to determine when the system is out of control.

Input/output control reports are really quite simple to arrive at. The planned input to any work center includes the released orders that have not yet arrived at the work center, plus unreleased "planned" orders. The planned output equals the planned input plus or minus any desired change in the backlog at the work center. Actual output is the easiest figure of all to come by. It is simply standard hours of work produced. These figures are almost always available. Sometimes they need to be re-sorted into work center groups, but this is a fairly simple matter.

Actual input is a piece of information that is not usually available. This is the number of standard hours that moved into a work center—a piece of information most companies do not have. Nevertheless, this is not terribly difficult to obtain, and monitoring input this way can provide extremely valuable information for the production and inventory management group.

Note that input rate cannot really be "controlled" at any work center except a starting work center. Here, the production and inventory management people are feeding work in and, within limits, it is usually possible for them to increase or decrease the input rate. At subsequent work centers in process, *the input rate to a given work center is "controlled" by controlling the output rates at the feeding work centers. Input/output control is primarily a capacity control device.*

A backlog at a given work center can be reduced by cutting back on input or increasing output. Cutting back on input, however, will shortly result in not meeting the master schedule. The emphasis should be put on obtaining the output that is required to meet the plan or, if necessary, reducing input by cutting back the master schedule.

### Controlling Lead Time

Before discussing some of the principles of lead time control, it is worth reviewing the basic concepts. Lead time can be defined as the time that elapses between the moment it is determined that an item is needed and ordered and that moment when the item is available for use.

Lead time can include all the items of order entry time such as preparing input data for the computer, waiting for the computer to process batches of input data, review of orders for credit check, engineering, and so on. Often there is a fertile area for lead time improvement in order entry.

Among other elements in the lead time cycle that can be excessively long are backlogs in production scheduling. Particularly in make-to-order plants it is traditional to run with consistent backlogs behind starting operations in the factory. This is ostensibly because the amount of work coming in each week cannot be predicted and tends to be erratic. Most companies, however, seldom measure this incoming work rate, or know how erratic it is, and they usually carry excessive backlogs to protect themselves. An example of the application of the basic principles of lead time control to this type of situation will be given below.

But what about manufacturing lead time itself? The actual amount of elapsed lead time in the factory takes place from the moment a shop order is released to the factory until it is completed. This lead time can be broken into the following elements:

$$\text{Lead Time} = \text{Set-up Time} + \text{Running Time} + \text{Move Time} + \text{Wait Time} + \text{Queue Time}$$

*Set-up time* is the time when the job is sitting behind the machine and the machine is being set up with the proper tooling.

*Running time* is the time the job is at the machine and being worked on.

*Move time* is the actual time that a job spends in transit. In most job shops, this could be defined as the time the job actually spends on the forks of the forklift truck.

*Wait time* has been separated from the queue time so that it could be arbitrarily associated with move time, since in many factories, the dispatching job is not highly organized and the forklift truck operators usually do not get to a job as soon as it is ready to move. In some plants, an operator of a forklift truck may "clean out" one department once a day. This could mean an average wait time of half a day, and if there were ten moves in the operation sequence, five days of the time could be expended in waiting for a move.

*Queue time* is that time the job spends waiting to be worked on because another job is already being run on that machine center.

Elapsed lead times are almost always far greater than actual set-up and running time. It is hard to believe that any substantial amount of the elapsed lead time is truly spent "in transit"—on the forks of the forklift truck—in most companies. A substantial amount of time *could* be spent waiting for moves. In actual practice, most of the lead time turns out to be queue time.

A simple experiment can verify this for any company. Taking some samples from some completed shop orders, determine the date the job started in the first department and the number of elapsed working hours that took place in the first department (counting only *manned* shifts during the week). If, for example, job A takes one week to go through department 1, this amounts to forty hours of elapsed manned time. If job A has two hours of set-up and two hours of run time, then the set-up and running time are 10 percent of the elapsed time.

A continuing survey of manufacturing companies indicates that 10 percent—or less—of the total lead time in the average company is actual working time! How can that be? It would seem that queues are completely out of control. And, of course, in practice *they are.* There is overwhelming evidence in most manufacturing companies to indicate that the amount of backlog that exists is as much as the company can possibly tolerate. Backlogs on the factory floor are in evidence everywhere, and there seems to be a variation of Parkinson's Law at work in the typical manufacturing shop: **"Work-in-process normally tends to expand to fill the space available."**

What plant foreman does not feel that he is crowded for space? What shop does not occasionally run out of skids, pallets, shop boxes? What shop has open spaces out on the factory floor? In the typical job shop, work-in-process tends to be piled everywhere, and the oldest jobs always seem to get up against the wall so that the newer ones are the only ones that can be worked on. This last-in-first-out effect tends to keep customer service low, in spite of high inventories and high expediting efforts. In most shops, even a small capacity bottleneck will cause some queueing and as queues build, expediting becomes frantic.

Backlogs, of course, are the major problem, and backlogs can become excessively large either because output is not controlled properly, or input is not controlled properly. The problems of output control and techniques for controlling output (that is, capacity) have been discussed above. There is one problem of input control—lead time inflation—that is worthy of some attention.

In an example in the previous chapter we discussed a company that inflated its lead time, and because of a poor priority planning system, generated an artificial capacity problem. This type of lead time inflation is not unusual at all.

Take the example of a company that plans to have its product manufactured in a six-week lead time. As business picks up, they manage to put more into the factory than they take out. This builds up the shop backlogs and, as a result, they find that their lead times are increasing from six weeks to eight weeks.

Plant personnel always feel that if they had just a little more lead time it would be a simple matter to get jobs completed on schedule. They cite the fact that many jobs come through two weeks after their schedule date as a reason for allowing two weeks more in the lead time. When the historical "facts" show that lead time is actually closer to eight weeks, they assume that this lead time should be built back into inventory planning. Any inventory system assumes some length of lead time in its reordering mechanism. An order point system tries to forecast demand over *lead time* plus some safety stock. An MRP system tries to determine *when* requirements will fall, and then, in backing off in time to account for the *lead time*, it determines when orders should be placed. Either basic type of inventory system relies heavily on lead time estimates. Ironically, as planned lead times are increased, orders will be generated sooner, thus increasing backlogs in the shop.

An increase in the planning lead time from six weeks to eight weeks, as cited above, would immediately generate an extra two weeks worth of work for the shop—which increases the backlogs and thus increases the lead times. If the actual lead times are observed at this point, they will be longer than ever. If they are once again built back into the inventory plans, orders will be generated sooner again, thus increasing backlogs and increasing lead times once again.

This, then, is one of the most dangerous and most common misconceptions in the industry, yet many companies have even developed sophisticated computer programs to average historical lead times so that these can be built into their planning systems. Unfortunately, a computer is amoral: it can be used to do the wrong thing faster than it was ever possible to do it manually.

An even worse situation exists between vendors and their customers. It is aggravated by the fact that purchasing people often have no real understanding of the ill effects of long lead times. Some even encourage vendors to quote longer lead times in the belief that these longer lead times will be more reliable. They seldom are. Unfortunately, even if they were, the people generating the orders, usually in inventory control in the company purchasing the material, find that their ability to forecast their needs accurately goes down dramatically as they forecast further in advance. Thus they have to carry higher safety stocks and/or reschedule more frequently to protect against forecast error as vendors increase their lead times.

Many vendors quote longer lead times in the belief that this will give them a better chance to get the product out the door on time. It almost never works that way. In fact, when a vendor quotes longer lead times to his customer, he almost always winds up with a bigger backlog of orders. If, for example, a vendor has been quoting a ten-week lead time and now quotes a fifteen-week lead time, his customers will have to plan to cover all of their requirements five weeks further out than they normally did. This will result in sending the vendor an extra five weeks worth of purchase orders, thus increasing the vendor's backlog and his lead time. If he once again quotes a longer lead time, most of his customers will send him more purchase orders until they get thoroughly disgusted with him and start going to his competition.

In many industries, however, such as the gray iron foundries in the United States, capacity is often tight. As one foundry increases its lead time and customers start placing orders with competitors, the competitors wind up in a capacity squeeze and then start increasing their lead time. A small capacity problem can easily escalate lead times until they are patently absurd. It is not uncommon for gray iron foundries to be quoting lead times of 20 to 30 weeks to make castings that can easily be produced in five working days.

What happens to the vendor when this small-capacity bottleneck is finally eliminated? Under extreme pressure from his sales department, he reduces his quoted lead time from 30 weeks to 25 weeks. The salesman is delighted to convey this information to the customer's purchasing department. They convey it to production and inventory management people, who then build it back into their inventory control system. Since lead time is shorter than it was before, there is really very little they need to order right now.

Back at the vendor, the flow of incoming orders slows down. The sales department is panic stricken and decides that the competition must be getting the business. They insist upon a further reduction in lead time. When this is relayed to the customer's inventory control group, they further reduce their planned lead times. This generates fewer orders and reduces the input to the vendor which further reduces his backlog of orders!

One bearing manufacturer was quoting a forty-eight-week lead time in one product line and twelve months later could quote a three-week lead time in the same line. Three weeks is probably pretty realistic for assembling a bearing from stocked parts, but what happened to the forty-five-week backlog? It seems difficult to believe that this company could have produced fifty-two weeks of normal production and also produced enough to eliminate forty-five weeks work of backlogs. This would be equivalent to 97 normal weeks of production in a year. Of course, they really went through the lead time "deflation" cycle after having previously had their lead times inflated to forty-eight weeks (probably because of a *small* capacity bottleneck).

The role of lead time inflation has never been thoroughly explored in the study of business cycles. It certainly has made an important contribution, particularly since the increase in backlog tends to increase the real volume that a company has to handle, because as people try to forecast their requirements further and further out into the future, they are less and less accurate. They suddenly find things that they need very quickly that they were not able to anticipate. When they go to order these from their suppliers, the suppliers quote them extremely long lead times, principally because they currently have backlogs made up of other items that this customer and other customers tried to forecast far in advance of requirements—and never rescheduled.

The phenomenon of lead time inflation is a common one. Usually the people closest to it are the ones who find it most difficult to observe. Shop people tend to think that they are going to help themselves by getting more lead time. Vendors tend to think that they will help themselves by getting more lead time. But the facts of the matter are quite different if the reaction to longer lead times is to order materials farther in advance. This will only increase backlogs—and increase lead times.

Lead time, then, is a function of backlog. It can be seen in the typical manufacturing company that the lead time is equal to work-in-process level. That is to say, if there is a six-week level of work in process, the lead time will be six weeks.

Many people ask, "How much work in process *should* we have?" The answer is that queues exist in the factory primarily to absorb the fluctuations in input rates. One company, for example, sampled the backlogs behind a particular operation over a long period of time and found that the greatest number of containers of work they ever had behind that operation was 125. The smallest number they ever had was 75. This means that the fluctuation rate was approximately 50. In fact, that is what the normal allowed queue should have been. Whenever fluctuations are not measured, people tend to overcompensate for them.

Lead time is a function of backlogs; and backlogs are primarily a function of the space that is available to store work in process. Most companies' capacity planning systems rely primarily on visible backlogs.

We have dwelt on the manufacturing lead time, a very important aspect of lead time and one that is far more controllable than most manufacturing companies realize. But there are other aspects of lead time, particularly in a make-to-order company, that are just as great. Most make-to-order companies plan and control their capacity based on backlogs, using some kind of machine loading system. They would be far better off to separate priority from capacity and to forecast capacity requirements—even if they only based this forecast on the incoming order rate—rather than basing it on backlogs.

*A company that manufactures a product sold almost exclusively to customer order found that their eight-week quoted lead time consisted of four weeks for scheduling and four weeks for manufacturing. By measuring the rate of incoming orders from customers they found that there was not a very substantial variation in input rate. The random variations really tended to cancel each other over a short period of time. By monitoring the input rate, they could see trends up or down and actually plan and control capacity more effectively than by holding big backlogs of customer orders. They also found that when they needed to "make work" because incoming orders were low, they could pull ahead orders from many of their larger customers who gave them schedules well into the future. The result in this company was to reduce their lead time from eight weeks to four weeks. They found that they could operate with virtually no backlog of orders when they started using an average of weekly demand on capacity rather than basing their capacity planning on backlogs. There is an important concept here: the classical approaches to production control muddle the problems of priority and capacity. Input/output control requires that they be looked at separately, and thus does not require large backlogs of orders and consequently long lead times that simply are not justified.*

Figure 19 illustrates the concept of input/output control. Machine loading measured backlog, but input/output control measures the rate of *flow* of standard hours, as well.

The problem of backlogs and long lead times has beset manufacturing companies for some time. Before practical techniques for priority planning were made possible by the computer, long lead times caused many more problems than they need to now. When priorities could not be updated regularly, longer lead times meant more and more wrong priorities.

With modern priority planning and control systems, longer lead times do not tend to create the problems they did for the Fonsworth Company (see Chapter 6). If Fonsworth had been using MRP, the priority planning could have been properly updated and the *artificial* backlog would not have been generated.

This does not mean that lead time control has lost its importance. There is still value to keeping lead time—and the resultant work-in-process inventory—low. This reduces the investment in work-in-process inventory, reduces the materials handling problems that result from overcrowded shop floors, and avoids premature commitment of materials. In spite of

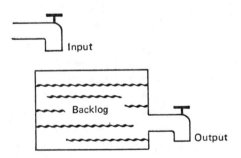

*Figure 19. Input/Output Control*

an improved ability to cope with long lead times, shorter lead times are still frequently a most important objective for production and inventory management people.

### Learning to Live with Shorter Lead Times

The informal priority planning system has become a way of life in most manufacturing companies. Large backlogs in process assure that lead times will be long. The job of getting these backlogs reduced is a most formidable one, since foremen and machine operators who have lived with the informal capacity planning system are usually deathly afraid of reductions in work-in-process.

The problem of educating machine operators so that they will not be afraid of running out of work when they see shop floor backlogs decrease is a real one. It is necessary to assure them that the work flow will continue to come, or they will tend to slow down. Even companies with an incentive pay system can have a dramatic slowdown without the employee losing much in wages (as any man who has filled out a time ticket can attest).

Some companies have fought this problem by posting on the departmental bulletin board the planned production rates as in-plant backlogs are reduced. Others have done it through education programs and by informing employees that indirect charges were going to be watched very closely as the new program was instituted. Others pay operators for idle time due to lack of material. Obviously, education is extremely important when a work-in-process reduction is contemplated. A serious work slowdown—often unconscious—can result if the education program is neglected.

This education program has to start with supervisors. If they are not convinced, no one is likely to become convinced. Most foremen are afraid that they will run out of work—and for good reason. The foreman has little or no control over the flow of work into his department. The control of input lies with other departments or with production and inventory management itself. Very few foremen have any confidence that production control will keep work flowing to them at a steady rate, and they usually are justified in believing that production and inventory management does not assume much responsibility for this. Therefore the foremen feel that the presence of physical backlogs in the factory is their only security.

Management has aggravated this problem considerably. One of the fundamental rules of management is to measure people on those functions that they truly control. The foreman feels that *he* is measured on idle time for lack of material. If a man is standing around, a great deal of pressure is exerted on the foreman to get rid of the man. On the other hand, the production and inventory management man feels that he is responsible for getting the work out the door on schedule. It would make more sense to put the responsibility for hitting the schedule on the foreman and responsibility for keeping work flowing through the shop at a steady rate on production and inventory management.

The formal capacity planning and control system in most companies is no more effective than the formal priority planning system. As a result, the reaction time for changing capacity levels is agonizingly long. Overtime and other expensive stop-gap measures have to be used excessively, and lead times tend to be more a function of the physical layout of the plant and the amount of work in process that can fit between the walls than any rational determination. The technical solutions to these problems exist. Once again, the challenge is a challenge to management in making the transition from the informal system to the formal system.

# Part 5 | Priority Control

# 8 | Shop Floor Control

### The Expediting Syndrome

The expediter has become a fixture in production and inventory management for many companies. Years ago he was called the stock chaser. The term expediter really seemed to gain in popularity during World War II. Henry Kaiser's shipbuilding feats were little less than miraculous, and according to an article in the November 1942 *Readers' Digest*, "Henry Kaiser's Secret Weapon" was the expediter. The article—undoubtedly spiced up for wartime morale-building propaganda—tells many stories about how a vital part was missing, but an expediter, through ingenuity and a determination not to take no for an answer (and frequently "damn the expense"), saved the day. Interestingly enough, in this particular article there is no attempt to explain why the missing parts were not there in the first place. Back in the days of manual systems it was normal to expect that the expediter would have to outwit the limitations of the formal system.

Expediting, however, is a disease that breeds in epidemic fashion. Most manufacturing companies have tried the red tag approach and soon find they have red tags on everything, and then they have to put green tags on the really hot jobs. Other companies have tried the color-of-the-month approach.

Some day the Smithsonian Institution should authorize a collection of expedite tags. The originality, ingenuity, and urgency of the messages is impressive. The effect of the expediting is almost always the same: the more expediting there is the less expediting results take place. Red tags on everything do not mean anything. It always seems to the expediter that if he could only do *more* expediting he would accomplish more, when in fact expediting really consists of trying to get one or more jobs done first. Unfortunately, very few jobs can be done first. Most of the others will have to be done second, third, fourth, and so on.

It is worth thinking about what the expediter spends most of his time doing. Certainly there are a few legitimate crises. These are to be expected in the best regulated factories. But in most factories, *expediting is the real production control system.* The expediter's job generally consists of one or more of the following elements:

1. *Trying to find out what the real priorities are.* He pulls materials out of the stockroom, makes up shortage lists, and tries to tell the factory and the purchasing people which of the late orders are *really* needed. This is the informal priority planning system at work.
2. *He tries to get people to do what they should have done in the first place anyway.* Frequently the expediter is the man who is telling the quality control department, "Don't just stop the job, tell us how to get it started again." Frequently he is trying to get a foreman whose boss spends most of his time with the foreman talking about budgets, to meet a schedule that his boss seldom mentions to him. When an expediter has to perform ths type of coordination function it indicates that management's objectives are not being stated very effectively to other people in the organization.
3. *Pushing hot jobs through.* This could mean hand carrying them, splitting lots, overlapping operations, and so on.

Expediting easily becomes the rule rather than the exception in a company where the formal priority planning system does not work. Shortages are discovered too late, the assembly, filling, or finishing line is going to be stopped if material is not rushed through, important customers are going to have to shut *their* production down if past-due shipments are not made at once.

When the informal system really degenerates, expediting can become fanatical. One definition of a fanatic is "a man who redoubles his efforts when all hope of reaching the goal has been lost"—a description that could apply to many expediters.

One of the first things that expediters have to understand is that just putting more rush tags out in the factory does not accomplish anything. One shop had "Do me first" tags on 90 percent of all the work on the shop floor. Obviously, 90 percent of the work cannot be done first.

It is important to understand what a priority system *should do* before discussing priority control:

1. A priority system should be relative. It should specify which jobs to do first, second, third, and so on.
2. A priority system should provide for regular updating of priorities. The priority that was put on a shop order or a purchase order when it was issued is probably going to be wrong after a very short period of time.
3. A priority system, above all, should be truthful. If it is overstated and there are a lot of jobs "late" in the shop or with vendors, an informal priority system will have to be developed to specify what jobs are *really* needed.

When properly used, the time phased order point or MRP can provide the priority planning information that meets these specifications. It is, of course, possible to overstate the master schedule in an MRP system and destroy the credibility of priorities, but the potential for telling the truth, keeping priorities updated, and keeping them relative exists in material requirements planning. It provides a company with the opportunity to have a formal priority planning system that *can* provide valid input to a priority control system.

### Sophisticated Priority Schemes

Back in the late fifties and early sixties a number of colleges, a couple of large companies, and even one of the government-sponsored think tanks got interested in priority rules. They set out to determine which priority rules would give the best results using "job shop simulators." Many rules were suggested. The *least processing time rule* says "Do the job that you can finish quickest first." If you keep using it you will get the most jobs finished (but what will ever happen to a job that has a long running time?). The *A-item rule* says "Do all the high annual dollar items first." This should minimize the work in process dollar investment. (Sounds great, but what if one of those C items is the missing part needed to get an assembly out the door?) The *oldest job first rule* requires no explanation. (How come in the real world old jobs are sitting around and nobody is looking for them, but they are expediting jobs that were started a lot later?)

For the most part, these academic studies ignored the problems of the real world. They did not recognize that priorities are dependent, particularly when a product with dependent priorities like an assembled product is being made. This, of course, means that the least processing time rule or the A-item rule are automatically eliminated. Optimizing the schedule for one component does not mean anything when all of the components are needed in order to make the product. Another real-world problem that was ignored in these academic studies was the fact that the formal priority planning system normally did not work. Doing the oldest job first, or the one with the earliest due date on it, simply would not have a great deal of impact in most manufacturing companies. They have to work to a shortage list, an informal system that tells them what at least a few of the *real priorities* are.

These studies of static priority rules have had almost no influence on manufacturing companies. Another approach to priorities, the dynamic priority approach, looked far more promising because it emphasized updating. In practice, however, even dynamic priority techniques, like critical ratio, while perfectly valid, have not worked as well as they were expected to. Before discussing why they have not, it is important to become more familiar with these techniques.

Figure 20 shows the critical ratio technique as it was originally presented. The idea behind critical ratio was to review the stock position of an item regularly and update its priority based on the latest stock position. The reviews usually take place on a weekly basis.

The example in Figure 20 shows that the stock on hand at the present time is 50 units, the order point is 100, and therefore 50 percent of the inventory is on hand. When the order was scheduled (as we did back

$$\text{Ratio } A = \frac{\text{Stock on Hand}}{\text{Order Point}} = \frac{50}{100} = 0.5$$

$$\text{Ratio } B = \frac{\text{Remaining Planned Lead Time}}{\text{Total Planned Lead Time}} = \frac{16}{20} = 0.8$$

$$\text{Critical Ratio} = \frac{\text{Ratio } A}{\text{Ratio } B} = \frac{5}{8} = 0.625$$

*Figure 20. Critical Ratio—Order Point*

in Figure 10), it was planned that it would take 20 manufacturing days. By now some of the operations have been completed and 16 manufacturing days worth of scheduled operations remain. Note that this includes planned slack time between operations, as well as actual set-up and running time. In the example, 16 days worth of unstarted operations remain, therefore 80 percent of the lead time remains. The critical ratio, then, is the combination of ratio *A* and ratio *B*, and in this case it is 0.625. A ratio of less than one is an "expedite" ratio. One is an "on schedule" ratio. A ratio greater than one is an "unexpedite" ratio.

Critical ratio was an attempt to keep priorities updated. Unfortunately, like a lot of techniques, it was picked up, used out of context, and results were disappointing.

*The Modern Scales Company had a crude material requirements planning system installed. It was not updated frequently enough and therefore they had to rely on their informal priority planning system, expediting, to get through at least some of the jobs they needed. They switched all of their dependent demand components over to an order point system so they could use critical ratio. Results were not particularly impressive, and the foremen in particular were very unhappy with critical ratio. They were especially caustic about the fact that approximately half of the shop orders being released to starting departments already had expedite ratios on them! This seemed to be quite a mystery until someone pointed out what the real situation was (depicted in Figure 21). Dependent demand components are likely to have withdrawals in fairly large quantities, thus reducing the amount on hand well below the order point. Since at that point the A ratio is going to be considerably less than 1, and the B*

On Hand      = 1100
Demand       =  600
New on Hand  =  500
Order Point  = 1000

$$\text{Ratio A} = \frac{500}{1000} = 0.5$$

$$\text{Ratio B} = \frac{\text{Remaining Lead Time}}{\text{Total Lead Time}} = 1.0$$

Critical Ratio = 0.5

*Figure 21. Critical Ratio—Misapplied*

$$CR = \frac{\text{Due Date} - \text{Today's Date}}{\text{Remaining Planned Lead Time}}$$

$$\frac{412 - 404}{6} = 1.33$$

*Figure 22. Critical Ratio — Due Date*

*ratio will be 1 (since the job is going into its first operation), the critical ratio will indicate that the job should be expedited. In many instances the component did not have another demand out in the future for some time. This caused false expediting, not due to critical ratio, but because the order point technique was being misused on dependent items.*

As originally presented, critical ratio applied only where order points were being used. This was not too surprising because back in the mid-sixties, very few people recognized MRP as a valid technique. It was assumed by many people that order point should be used for all inventory items.[1] Those companies that were erroneously using order points for dependent demand items found that adding critical ratio to the order point only compounded the confusion by making it "dynamic"! Moral: *If the priority planning system does not generate valid priorities, no amount of sophistication will improve them.*

Later, as MRP became more widely accepted, it was recognized that a different form of critical ratio would have to be used if critical ratio were to be applied very extensively. This newer type of critical ratio, based on a due date, is shown in Figure 22. As the due date is recalculated in MRP, or the time phased order point, the computation of a new critical ratio was made. This ratio was made up from the "*time remaining* between today's and the due date" compared to the "*work remaining* on unstarted operations."

In practice the due date critical ratio does not really do anything significant that cannot be done through MRP and rescheduling orders. As the MRP system changes the due date, the operation start or finish dates can be revised readily in the open shop order file. If for some reason the practitioner prefers to show these updated priorities as ratios, then

---

1. "Sometimes order points don't work. But, if so, you shouldn't even have any inventory." R. L. Van de Mark, *New Ideas in Materials Management* (Dallas: Van de Mark, Inc., 1967 [!]), p. 12

critical ratio is worth using. He should not assume that updated priorities expressed in *ratios* will give superior results to updated priorities expressed in *dates* in practice.

But what about critical ratio for order point items? One of the later approaches to order point critical ratio is shown in Figure 23. Here the ADU (average daily usage) is recalculated weekly and divided into the stock on hand to calculate a new due date. This, of course, is precisely what the time phased order point would do, and the time phased order point will handle lumpy demand, generate planned orders, and do a lot of other things that this approach to critical ratio will not do by itself.

Critical ratio has been singled out for discussion as the best-known priority technique; the comments about it apply to other priority schemes like the slack time rule, etc. Where does this type of priority technique stand today, then? When first conceived, critical ratio hit the production control practitioner like a bombshell. Most people believed up to that time that the date put on a shop order when the order was released was the *real* due date. The originators of critical ratio approaches made a significant contribution to the understanding of production and inventory control by pointing out that priorities had to be updated.

Today the time phased order point and MRP have priority updating built right into them. Whether or not these updated priorities are published in ratio form is pretty much a matter of choice on the part of the practitioner.

No one has yet proven that priority ratios have any superior operational advantages over revised operation schedule dates. Many practitioners have made the mistake of assuming that a dynamic priority system by itself would result in better priority control. Most of the companies that have tried critical ratio and have not been successful with it either used the order point critical ratio on dependent demand items or used

On Hand = 150
Average Daily Usage = 10
Run Out = 15 Days
Old Due Date = 320
Today = 312
New Due Date = 327

*Figure 23. Updating Due Date (Order Point)*

critical ratio in conjunction with MRP systems that were not properly updated or did not have properly managed master schedules. No priority scheme will work if the inventory system that plans the priorities does not generate and maintain those priorities correctly.

### Dispatching Approaches

The most popular priority control tool that the computer has made practical is the *dispatch list*. These are usually sent out on a daily basis by work center, showing the jobs in priority sequence. A sample dispatch list is shown in Figure 24. The reason the dispatch list is usually generated daily is to provide an updated "snapshot" of the current priority for the jobs that are actually in the work center on a particular day.

The dispatch list shown in Figure 24 is a very simple one. Some companies also provide a look-ahead feature in their dispatch lists. The dispatch list would show not only the jobs that are currently in the work center, but also those that are currently being worked on in preceding operations and should be in the work center very shortly. Note that priorities are communicated to the shop via the dispatch list and *do not appear on shop orders*. A modern production control system recognizes that *need* dates are always changing.

The daily dispatch list is the current form of technology. It represents a once-a-day look at what is going on. Now that computer terminals have become more economical to use, and as our expertise in the use of terminals increases, companies are replacing the daily dispatch list with terminal inquiry giving the foreman up-to-date dispatching information at any time of the day.

Some companies have instituted a type of central dispatching. The typical central dispatching system has a number of dispatchers sitting in

Work Center 1501—Day 205

| Start Date | Job # | Description | Run Time |
|---|---|---|---|
| 201 | 15131 | Shaft | 11.4 |
| 203 | 15143 | Stud | 20.6 |
| 205 | 15145 | Spindle | 4.3 |
| 205 | 15712 | Spindle | 8.6 |
| 207 | 15340 | Metering Rod | 6.5 |
| 208 | 15312 | Shaft | 4.6 |

*Figure 24. Dispatch List*

a room with timecard racks in front of them. Cards representing the operations to be done on the jobs currently in the shop are placed behind the proper work centers represented by slots in the timecard racks. These jobs are also arranged in the proper priority. The ispatchers then telephone out to the shop floor, where identical racks are maintained either by the foreman, one of his supervisors, or one of the production control men. Through telephone conversation two or three times a day, the racks on the shop floor are kept in the proper priority sequence.

When a man wants to clock on the job, he takes the card out of the rack, puts it into a data-collection terminal, and indicates that he is clocking on. Back in the central dispatch room they note that he has clocked on and that the job is now running. When he clocks off they check the count on the job against the count at the previous operation to make sure that the operator is reporting his counts properly.

People once looked upon central dispatching as an alternative to the dispatch list—but this is not true. The dispatch list really is a way to relay current priority information down to the shop floor. Today virtually every central dispatching installation uses a dispatch list, too. The most significant advantage to the central dispatching approach is its auditing feature. The dispatch list by itself does not have this.

Some companies today audit labor reports and counts on-line to the computer. As an operator reports in through a data-collection terminal, the count at the previous operation is compared with his current count, and a message is sent to an auditor to check on it if the count exceeds the count at the previous operation, for example. As on-line systems become more common, this will undoubtedly become a popular approach to auditing. In the meantime, the prime justification for the central dispatching approach described above is that it provides the potential for good auditing of counts.

One of the lessons learned through hard expeience in developing shop floor control systems is the fact that these systems are often the hardest to get accepted in the shop. Frequently production and inventory management people, convinced through years of operating with an informal system that nobody will work on the right jobs unless we make them, see the dispatching system as a policing function. If, indeed, foremen do not want to work on the right jobs, no dispatching system is going to cure that problem. That is a problem for management. When foremen do not seem very schedule-conscious, it may well be one more example of the fact that it is what management *inspects, not what management expects.* If they are constantly talking to a foreman about the budget, and only occasionally talking to him about the schedule, he is likely to react accordingly.

In most companies, though, the real problem is that the foreman has not had the proper information to help him do his job, and that is exactly what a dispatching system should be designed to do. It should provide him with the proper information so that he knows what jobs to run in what sequence to meet the overall goals of the business.

Following are a few suggestions in setting up a dispatching system:

1. *Keep it simple.* Do not burden it with oversophisticated priority rules. The success of the system will depend a lot more on the people's understanding of it than it will on the sophistication of the priority technique. There will always be the time when it is desirable to have a man understand that the priority sequence generated by the computer is not always exactly correct. It would be too bad to have him working on a job that could not be run on the next work center because of a machine breakdown, simply because he did not understand the priority system well enough to do anything but follow it blindly.

2. *Design the system to support the people, not to replace them.* The dispatch list should probably be given to a dispatcher so that he can make any notations on it and add any information that he knows about, such as material shortages, tooling problems, etc., before he gives the dispatch list to the foreman. No dispatching report generated by computer will be able to take into account all the things that are happening in the dynamic world of the factory. A good dispatching system is a blend of the computer's ability to keep priorities updated and the man's ability to use this information with the other information *he has* to run the factory better.

   Some companies issue the dispatch list in the morning to the dispatcher, who then goes over it with the foreman; then at midmorning gets together with the other dispatchers for a meeting to discuss their mutual activities that will interrelate to a great extent during the day. Then the dispatcher goes out to the shop with this updated information. He then comes back for a meeting with the other dispatchers before the next shift begins.

3. *A universal rule for successful systems is to have the user responsible for the development and installation of the system.* The user of a dispatching system is

the foreman. When developing a shop floor control system the best insurance that the system will succeed is to have foremen participate and even head up the system's development and installation team.

### The Role of the Shop Planner in a "Closed Loop" System

In the factory where production and inventory management was really order launching and expediting, the production control man in the shop usually was the focal point of the informal system. He worked with shortage lists, put red tags on the hot jobs, frequently spent a good deal of his time trying to locate jobs in the shop when a customer was requesting a delivery date or an improved delivery promise. Before the "overtime meeting" he used to go around and check the backlogs ahead of the work centers to determine whether overtime would be needed for Saturday.

With a formal priority planning system that works, and a formal capacity planning system that works, he is now the focal point of shop control. He is frequently called a shop planner now, since he works with the foremen to plan the sequence in which the jobs will be run behind each work center. The pure priorities are generated by the computer, but there are often circumstances in the factory that make it worthwhile to run a job out of sequence in order to combine machine set-ups or because tooling is not yet ready, or for many other legitimate reasons. A shop planner's judgment has to be used in reconciling day-to-day conflicts between running a plant efficiently and giving good customer service.

Most factories have developed a disdain for the dates on shop orders. Unless these orders were being expedited, or were promised to a specific customer, it was assumed that they were probably not needed terribly urgently. The hot list was the real scheduling device.

The dispatch list in a modern production and inventory management system must have valid schedule dates on it. The role of the shop planner changes dramatically from expediting the hot jobs to insuring that the jobs on the schedule are done *as scheduled*. Periodically, usually a couple of times a week, he makes out an *anticipated delay report* like that shown in Figure 25. The chief shop planner will review these delay reports and report any serious delays that could affect the master schedule to the master scheduler.

Dept 24
April 8

| Part # | Sched. Date | New Date | Cause of Delay | Action |
|--------|-------------|----------|----------------|--------|
| 17125 | 4/10 | 4/15 | Fixture Broke | Toolroom Will Return on 4/15 |
| 13044 | 4/11 | 5/1 | Out for Plating— Plater on Strike | New Lot Started |
| 17653 | 4/11 | 4/14 | New Part-Holes Don't Align | Engineering Laying Out New Jig |

*Figure 25. Anticipated Delay Report*

When a master scheduler accepts a customer order for an item that was forecast in the master schedule, he has every right to believe that material and capacity will be available. Both the shop planner and the purchasing follow-up people are now responsible for meeting legitimate schedules that they are given. When these schedules need to be revised, they will be notified by the material requirements planner who will get an exception message from the MRP system. When these schedules cannot be maintained, it is their responsibility to get this information up to the material requirements planner and eventually to the master scheduler if the master schedule is going to be affected.

A modern production and inventory management system is a *closed loop* system. It is often called a formal system because it is a system where everyone has his position to play on the team to see that the company's objectives are met. No longer is it every man for himself.

The shop planner also monitors the capacity control reports like those shown in Chapter 7 (Figures 16, 17, 18). When he sees that the actual output is outside the acceptable tolerance, it is his job to determine whether output can be picked up enough to insure meeting the master schedule, to suggest ways to get the output back on plan, to recommend alternate sources of capacity, and ultimately, when necessary, to convey the bad news to the master scheduler that the master schedule will have to be revised because capacity is not going to be available to meet the plan.

This is an entirely new role for production and inventory management. It is a role that some present personnel will fit into very well, because it is a much more organized approach that generates real results, and consequently it is a lot more satisfying than living from crisis to crisis. There probably will be a few people currently working in production control, however, who will find it difficult to put aside the heroic role of the firefighter who is always visibly solving problems, and play the more mature role of the shop planner who is responsible for preventing problems.

### Putting It All Together

A production and inventory management system is a very deeply interrelated system. Four primary functions of production and inventory control have been discussed throughout this book:

1. Priority planning.
2. Capacity planning.
3. Capacity control.
4. Priority control.

Priority planning in a one-piece make-to-order shop is not a big problem. Here the formal priority plan, which is usually the backlog of customers' orders, generates due dates that are valid. In a make-to-stock plant, the time phased order point should be used for priority planning. In a company making items with dependent demand components, MRP is the proper technique; however, it, by itself, does not insure that the priority plans will be valid. A master schedule must be used responsibly to keep the priorities in the formal system credible.

Capacity planning can start with something as simple as a production plan, but in most companies the detail provided by a capacity requirements plan is a necessity. A capacity requirements plan is made up based on released orders and planned orders in either the time phased order point or MRP system.

The capacity control report could be either a simple output control report or, preferably, an input/output control report. Here again the planned input and output rates are developed by the capacity requirements plan, and in the event these rates cannot be met, the master schedule ultimately will have to be changed.

Priority control in the factory will take place via the dispatch list. It conveys the plan to the shop, and monitoring performance against this dispatch list with an anticipated delay report will provide the priority control.

Priority control in a purchasing operation is just as important as priority control in the shop. It usually is not as easy to implement because it usually is not practical to use techniques like the dispatch list to convey this information readily to vendors. Good judgment should be used, then, in rescheduling vendors. Planners should filter out the reschedules to make sure that only the significant ones are conveyed to the vendors. Once valid priorities are given to vendors, their performance against the plan can be monitored to be sure that they are giving the kind of delivery that is required to meet the company's objectives.

An integrated production and inventory management system can provide manufacturing people with tools to run the business more effectively, but it must be emphasized—again—that the tools do not generate the results, the people do. The challenge is not in the technical aspects of using computers in production and inventory management. The real challenge is in teaching people to operate in a brand-new environment made possible by the computer.

# 9 | Purchasing: Controlling the Outside Factory

### Purchasing—Victim of the Informal System

The purchasing function in most manufacturing companies is much maligned. When the informal system is the real system, late orders abound, and any purchasing department that worked to the due dates on the orders would soon put manufacturing departments out of business. The real priorities come from phone calls and hot lists—the real measure of a purchasing department's worth in this type of company is how well it can fight fires. They usually find out about shortages too late, they are frequently processing requisitions that were placed well within the normal lead time, and trying to get the vendor to stand on his head to get them out of trouble one more time.

Under these circumstances, purchasing departments frequently find it more convenient to work to performance measures that are valid. They can, and should, be measured on material costs. There is no real way, however, to hold them responsible for meeting delivery dates when the formal system does not give them realistic delivery dates.

Nor do they have any way to evaluate vendor performance fairly. Vendor performance is a subject that has been talked about at great length, yet there are few companies today where vendor performance can really be measured, since the dates put on the orders by the formal system are either wrong to start with or not maintained properly. They are not *need dates*, they are due dates. The informal system attempts to supply the need dates.

A formal system should provide requisitions to the purchasing department in time for them to be placed with the vendors. It should give

133

them real need dates, and then it should maintain those need dates without a lot of nervous, overreactive rescheduling.

Once a formal system can be made to work, many of the old ideas—and a few new ones—can be implemented far more successfully. The purchasing department, like the manufacturing department, can adopt a posture of keeping out of trouble rather than spending all of its time getting out of trouble.

### Stockless Purchasing

Stockless purchasing is a catch phrase that simply means that the vendor carries the inventory for his customer. It has certainly been a trend in recent years. While the vendor frequently considers this to be a headache, in reality it has some advantages even for him. Since he has an authorized stock to carry on hand, he can manufacture ahead of requirements and thus level out his own production and perhaps manufacture in larger lot sizes. Generally, the vendor is more likely to have an opportunity to carry less inventory to give the same service level, because he is in a better position to use the inventory more flexibly. If, for example, he makes the same product for three different customers, and simply packages differently for each of them, he certainly can carry less safety stock than each of them would have to carry on an individual basis. Stockless purchasing can often be worked out to mutual advantage.

*The Bilco Corporation bought a line of fasteners from the Derby Fastener Company. Fred L., the inventory manager of Bilco, was constantly plagued by complaints from Derby Fastener that the lot sizes simply were not large enough. In return, he complained that the lead time of six to eight weeks for a simple fastener was unrealistic.*

*Fred decided to calculate distribution by value—ABC analysis. He found that while there were one-hundred different stock-keeping units—different product identities that were kept in finished goods inventory—there were only forty different fasteners. Many of the popular fasteners were available in a number of packaging varieties. He then found that five different fasteners in their various packaging configurations accounted for 60 percent of all of the activity in the product line.*

*Armed with this information, Fred went over to visit the Derby Fastener Company. He talked with their production manager. He recommended that they stock the five different most popular sizes of fastener in bulk and package them to order with a one-week maximum lead time. In return, he volunteered to order in lot sizes 25 percent larger than he had been using on all other items.*

*There was an advantage to the Derby Fastener Company in that they set up and produced the high-volume items in fairly large quantities. They no longer waited for individual orders in order to produce the actual fastener itself in quantities that were required for particular packaging variations. By the same token, they could more easily respond to variations in demand, since they carried these fasteners in bulk. A sudden upsurge in demand for a particular packaging variation would simply require them to draw some material out of bulk storage and package it to meet that demand. They further benefited by having larger lot sizes for the less active items.*

*Fred helped Bilco also. They required far less inventory of the fast-moving items because they could order them in very small packaging lot sizes rather than manufacturing lot sizes. They also required less safety stock because their lead time was far shorter. The modest increase in the lot sizes for the slower-moving items was offset by the reduced inventory—and better service—that resulted.*

One of the astute comments about this subject was made a number of years ago: *There is more to be gained from intelligent customer-vendor negotiations than from all the lot-size formulas in the world.*

### Blanket Ordering and Reduced Material Costs

One of the tools well known to most purchasing men is the blanket order. Armed with production and inventory management's estimate of their yearly requirements for a particular component or material, the purchasing man negotiates a quantity purchase from the vendor. He usually gives the vendor his estimate of the year's supply and then issues releases against this authorized quantity. The customer is responsible for ultimately buying the authorized quantity, although frequently he may find it necessary to reschedule it off into the future if the demand drops substantially below estimate.

In return, for these long-term commitments, many vendors are willing to negotiate lower prices. Obviously, the blanket order gives the vendor security, flexibility, the prerogative of manufacturing in larger lot sizes, and so on.

MRP really facilitates blanket ordering. The typical material requirements plan has a one-year horizon and can be used to show the purchasing man what his requirements will be well out into the future, giving him a good basis for placing blanket orders. Beyond that, the material requirements plan solves one of the major problems of blanket ordering. Typically, in the past, blanket orders were set up with a release schedule, and that release schedule was not reviewed frequently enough. As a result, material was coming in either too soon or too late, because requirements had dropped off or picked up. With MRP, requirements are balanced against inventory on a continuing basis, and releases against blanket orders can be kept up-to-date very conveniently.

Production and inventory management people with their knowledge of future requirements really generate the information that purchasing people use to do their job. The responsibility for reduced cost of purchased material certainly is partially born by production and inventory management people. It behooves each manager in this field who considers himself a professional to set some goals for keeping purchased material costs under control each year. Working with purchasing people, providing them the information, he will often find that he has great potential for reducing product costs while insuring better delivery performance and lower inventories.

### The Vendor Lead Time Problem

Purchasing people sometimes encourage vendors to quote long lead times in the mistaken belief that this will make deliveries more dependable. In practice, the best thing that can be done to get more dependable deliveries from vendors is to give them more dependable information and *then* measure their performance. A prerequisite to good vendor performance is a valid schedule—and few companies today are able to provide that. In its absence, encouraging longer vendor lead times not only will not improve delivery performance, it usually becomes worse. The reason is very simple: as forecasts are extended over longer periods, their accuracy deteriorates. Without a formal system for rescheduling regularly—like MRP—longer lead times simply create more expediting.

The vendor who asks for longer lead times usually believes that this will help him to plan better. The real question is, of course, plan *what*? Priorities or capacity? Giving the vendor bigger backlogs of orders to help him to plan capacity requirements almost inevitably leads to the loss of control over priorities.

The principles that apply in planning and controlling capacity within a company also apply when planning vendor capacity. The input/output control technique, discussed in Chapter 7, can be applied to purchased material, particularly one-piece products like forgings, castings, die castings, and the like.

The idea is to forecast capacity requirements *in terms of capacity* at the vendor's plant.

*Midwest Manufacturing found themselves with purchased casting lead times of twenty to twenty-four weeks. Recognizing the importance of input/output controls and the basic principle that capacity requirements on the vendor should be forecast without committing themselves to actual orders, they set up a very effective program with vendor foundries. They commit themselves to order a given number of molds worth of castings down each line in the foundry as far out as the foundry would like to have this commitment, based on their anticipated requirements. They do not specify the actual orders they want to run. Two weeks ahead of time they specify the actual orders they need.*

*In effect, they have blocked out capacity at the foundry and committed themselves to it, but they have not committed themselves to forecasting far in advance which orders they want to run within that capacity. They have had this approach working for several years. The only problem they have had with it is in selling the concept initially to their inventory control people, their purchasing people, and their vendors. Once it is in effect, it reduces expediting dramatically and gets them out of the lead time inflation syndrome. They are forecasting capacity requirements for the vendor's facility and they benefit from shorter lead times.*

It is particularly important, where vendors are concerned, to keep lead times short. Within the factory where the MRP system can be used to generate a daily dispatch list, it is easy to respond to changes in priority.

Changing the priority with vendors requires telephone calls, letters, and a great deal of personal time. The shorter the vendor lead time can be, the less need for rescheduling there will be.

The input/output control approach with vendors assumes that the vendor supplies more than one item. It is trying to take advantage of the fact that the forecast for each individual item may not be very accurate, but the forecast in terms of capacity requirements will be considerably more accurate. The input/output approach is different from blanket ordering because it is using the material requirements forecast for *many* items to predict capacity requirements. It takes advantage of the fact that the forecast error for the group of items using similar facilities will be less than the error for each item.

Since many vendors often have rather haphazard capacity planning systems themselves, they sometimes have difficulty thinking in terms of "capacity" commitments. Users of MRP have found that the long horizon of planned orders in the system can, by themselves, be a great way—as one of them expresses it—"to get into the vendor's load in advance."

Using MRP, they send future planned order releases to the vendor. They specify, however, that out in the future these are to be used for capacity planning only. On the intermediate horizon, they are to enable the vendors to plan material requirements. Short term, they are actual delivery schedules.

Using the MRP output to help a vendor plan offers many advantages:

1. It is a convenient by-product of MRP requiring no extra effort on the customer's part.
2. MRP *will reschedule* planned orders; thus even though the vendor is given a longer planning horizon, there is no problem of priority deterioration.
3. It can be used for products that are too complex to allow the customer to actually plan his requirements in simple terms like "molds per week."
4. It provides the vendor with information for long-range *material* as well as capacity planning.
5. It virtually eliminates the problem of lead time. An MRP report shows planned orders well out into the future. If the vendor changes his lead time a customer who is providing him with long-range plans like this is virtually unaffected.

Today some companies use their computer systems to go even further and actually use the vendor's routings to plan their capacity requirements on him. This is especially helpful where the vendor, or subcontractor, is small and has no computer available.

Vendor lead times will always be a problem if the vendor has nothing but order backlogs to plan from. His reaction time will always be too long. The tools of modern production and inventory management facilitate better planning. The company that uses these tools to help its vendors plan better inevitably reaps large rewards in the form of better vendor performance.

### Measuring Vendor Delivery Performance

Discussions about vendor performance have gone on for years. Many companies realize that vendor performance must be measured to keep its level high. Few, however, seem to have recognized that without an effective formal priority planning system vendor performance cannot be measured meaningfully.

When the production and inventory management system is really order launching and expediting, the most valuable vendor is not necessarily the one that delivers on schedule, it is the one that responds best to expediting. Therefore any vendor performance measure based on the dates on orders with the vendor will be invalid. One of the most insidious characteristics of the informal system is that its shortcomings are seldom obvious to those who use it. The production planner who operates in order launching and expediting mode is almost always the most outspoken critic of vendor performance.

A properly managed MRP system makes vendor delivery performance measurement straightforward. The vendor should be given adequate planning information well in advance; the old days when purchasing people saw requirements only when an item hit its order point are gone. The vendor delivery schedule will be updated regularly by MRP. Short term it should be firmed up and vendor performance measured against it.

One of the most challenging tasks of all is the rebuilding of credibility between the vendor and the customer. Invalid formal schedules result in poor vendor performance, since the vendor soon learns that they mean nothing. Consequently he works to the hot lists the customer gives him, and his performance always looks poor when measured against the formal schedules. His delivery promises on orders are violated frequently as he expedites to react to the hot list. The customer does not believe his promises—and the vendor does not believe the customer's requirements. An effective priority planning system makes it practical—and mandatory— to work hard to develop vendor/customer credibility.

There is a very high correlation between vendor performance and the effectiveness of the formal system in most companies, and there is a very good reason for this. If the formal system works, vendors rapidly get accustomed to delivering on schedule because they cannot stand the "noise" when they are late. They find out that every time they deliver late to a particular customer, he shuts his production line down. They realize that if they are going to retain this business, they simply have to ship on schedule. This customer becomes the squeaky wheel. On the other hand, when they have stacks of late orders they rapidly learn to recognize those customers who probably will not complain if material is delivered late.

When a realistic priority planning system is being used, vendor performance against it *can* be measured. Obviously, if the priority planning is not truthful—*as it is not in most companies*—it is extremely difficult to measure vendor performance. It has been proven time and again in practice that realistic priority planning systems and good vendor performance measures can substantially improve vendor deliveries.

### The Impact of the Formal System on Purchasing

In the classical organization that we are used to seeing, there is a planner in production and inventory management who generates requisitions that go to a buyer in purchasing. The planner is supposed to be in a position to really understand his material needs and priorities. The buyer, of course, is the man who contacts the vendor, places the requisition, and follows up or expedites material. In most companies, the planner is not allowed to talk directly to the vendor. There is usually some rationale for this, since the planners are usually organized in product-group sequence and many of them might be trying to contact the same vendor, giving him conflicting priorities. There is also some good reasoning behind the idea of having the buyer get his information filtered through the planner when the informal system is the one that really works. There are usually plenty of late orders, and the planner looking at an assembly, for example, that he really wants to make this week, finds out what the real shortages are and then tells the buyer to expedite those.

So there was some reason, historically, for having the planner and the buyer separate. But when a formal system like MRP can be made to work, there is no reason why this has to be perpetuated. A number of companies that use MRP have combined the job of planner and buyer quite successfully. With a formal system, where the priorities on materials are the true priorities, it is no longer as important to have the planner organized by product group. His responsibilities can be defined so that there will not be too much overlapping of vendor contact among planners/buyers.

It is important to understand how this planner/buyer would handle an MRP report. Figure 26 shows purchasing's copy of a material requirements plan. It is a good example of the type of information that would now be going to the planner/buyer. Note that there are three units of the rear panel currently on hand. There is an open order in the past-due period (the exception message calls this to his attention) for four units. There is also an order due next week for twenty units. Imagine the planner/buyer contacting the vendor and finding that he is having trouble getting the rear panels produced, but can get a few at once. Based on the MRP report, the buyer can tell him that he really needs at least two units from the past-due order to cover the projected requirements for week 2. (He has three on hand now, two from the past-due order will cover the requirement for five.) The balance of the order must be available, however, by period four.

Here is the kind of factual information that the planner used to be deciphering partly from the formal system, mainly from the informal

| Part #171250 | Name: Rear Panel | | Lot Size = 20 | | Lead Time = 4 | | | |
|---|---|---|---|---|---|---|---|---|
| | | Past Due | Week | | | | | | |
| | | | 1 | 2 | 3 | 4 | 5 | 6 | 7 | 8 |
| Projected Requirements | | | 0 | 5 | 0 | 18 | 0 | 0 | 15 | 0 |
| Scheduled Receipts | | 4 | 20 | | | | | | | |
| On Hand | 3 | 7 | 27 | 22 | 22 | 4 | 4 | 4 | -11 | |
| Planned Order Release | | | | | 20 | | | | | |

Message: Open order in past-due period.
Reschedule 20 from Week 1 to Week 4

*Figure 26. Material Requirements Plan*

system, and passing along to the buyer. MRP is a formal system that generates this information directly.

To whom should this planner/buyer report? Interestingly enough, in practice, it does not seem to matter. About half the companies that have taken this approach have him reporting to production and inventory management and contacting the vendors directly to place and follow up orders. The other half have him reporting to the purchasing department, working directly with the MRP output reports.

This is a good example of a fundamental management principle that is not as well understood as it should be: *performance to meet company objectives is a result of intelligent setting of these objectives and measurement of performance against them.* Too often, companies that are not getting performance look to reorganization as a solution to their problems. In some cases, reorganization may help, but a clear, direct statement of objectives and measurement of performance will do a lot more than any organizational changes to produce results.

Why does a working formal system, then, make the planner/buyer concept practical? Why does this type of system make it immaterial where the planner/buyer reports? For the very simple reason that purchasing performance could not be measured very effectively with the old informal system. There were plenty of late orders, but only some of them were the really critical ones. There were some new requisitions that were being placed today that were even more critical than some of the old ones. With a formal system that works, the planner/buyer—no matter where he reports—can be held responsible for getting material in on time to support the master schedule.

And with the formal system, his responsibilities change considerably. He is no longer the firefighter, the expediter constantly chasing one hot list after another. This is not to say that he will not have to do some expediting some time. It is not to say that there will not be some crises. It does mean, however, that he will spend most of his time ordering material from vendors, passing along significant reschedules to the vendors—reschedules out into future periods as well as reschedules to get materials sooner—and, above all, *assuming the responsibility for delivery on the promised date.*

The scheduled receipt in the MRP system shows when the material is supposed to come in. The planner/buyer must, through his knowledge of the vendor, through acknowledgement information he has from the vendor, and through following up with the vendor, be positive that this material is coming in at this time. In the event the material will not be coming in on schedule, he should *anticipate this delay* and pass it along to the master scheduler who may very well have to revise the master schedule if nothing can be done to insure that the material does come in on time. His responsibility has changed from expediting to insuring vendor performance to the schedule.

### Controlling the Cost of Purchased Material

While armies of industrial engineers have concentrated on improving manufacturing methods and reducing manufacturing costs, the control of the cost of purchased material has been left to the purchasing department to do in the time that they have left over from expediting. This is ironic, since the purchased material content of so many products typically exceeds the labor content by a substantial amount. This is not to say that value analysis programs and the like have not produced results. It *is* to say that there is still a great deal of potential for better control of the cost of purchased material.

Once the planner/buyer has assumed his new responsibilities of keeping out of trouble rather than getting out of trouble, a further logical step in assignment of responsibilities is worthy of consideration. For years we have recognized that an operating production control man could not assume systems development responsibilities and still handle his operations responsibilities. If he is not divorced from these operations responsibilities, they consume all of his time. Nobody goes home with an empty mail basket, and the problems of today are far more important than the systems development problems of tomorrow, which can always be postponed. The result is that the production control man never does get his *systems* work done unless he is divorced 100 percent from *operational* responsibilities for a period of time.

The same principle applies to purchasing people. In most purchasing departments, the day-to-day effort involved in placing requisitions, handling paperwork, and expediting needed material consumes most of the time. The very important jobs of negotiating and vendor selection tend to get worked into the spare time, yet as is pointed out above, there is a great deal of money to be saved in the area of purchased material costs.

It logically follows, then, that the negotiating/vendor-selection responsibility should be assigned to individuals who have no day-to-day order placement or expediting chores. They may have to choose other vendors if the vendor performance reports show that the vendors they have originally chosen are not able to give delivery or quality performance. But they do not get involved in expediting individual parts—only in solving major problems with vendors. Their main job is to keep the purchased material costs under control and reduce them if possible.

This approach has been in use for several years by companies using MRP. The resulting control over purchased material costs has been dramatic.

When a formal priority planning system replaces the informal expediting system, the delivery performance of vendors can become much more reliable. The purchasing people who now need to spend less time living from crisis to crisis now can have the time to do a professional purchasing job.

# Part 6 | Supporting Functions

# 10 | Forecasting

### Forecasting Approaches

Just as *planning* is a prerequisite to *control*, in most companies a great deal of the planning will have to be based on forecasting. Decisions to buy land to build a new plant, order machine tools, buy material, add people, set sales quotas, and establish the manufacturing budget are usually based on forecasts. Very few companies can operate with a large enough backlog of customer orders to avoid having to do *some* forecasting. Frequently, of course, these forecasts are made by different people at different times, and there is no question that a more coordinated forecasting effort could generate significant improvements in many companies.

In developing a more systematic approach toward forecasting, managers need to be realistic. In recent years, many of them have looked to new forecasting techniques to solve their forecasting problems, but, unfortunately, forecasting will always have limited accuracy. Forecasting techniques seldom seem to prove as helpful as their developers first claim. There is no such thing as a *reliable* forecasting technique. The great strides in recent years have been in the development of techniques like MRP that enable a company to react more frequently and easily. The progress has been in learning to work better with poor forecasts rather than in the development of significantly better forecasting techniques. Nevertheless, there are some practical tools that *can* be used by managers who recognize their limitations.

In order to understand forecasting methods better, it is useful to think of them in two general categories:

1. Statistical forecasts.
2. Judgment forecasts.

When used in its broadest sense, the statistical category could include such techniques as averaging. We will talk more about averaging techniques later. Generally, however, when people talk about statistical forecasting techniques, they are referring to techniques like least-squares analysis, regression analysis, and correlation analysis.

The least-squares technique is a method for determining a trend line based on past history. Trend lines can be determined using fairly simple approximate techniques also. Least squares is not really used widely in industry today primarily because the precision of the technique is really hardly justified when the answer is going to be an approximation at best.

Using regression and correlation analysis, mathematical formulas are calculated that give various degrees of weight to "indicators" that are related to the product or product groups that are being forecast. For example, housing starts *do* have some influence on the sales of builder's hardware. Probably Gross National Product (GNP) also does. It would be possible to construct a formula that would take into account housing starts GNP, and other indicators and try to use this to forecast the overall level of sales for builder's hardware. This would be particularly useful if the indicators like housing starts were "leading indicators." Leading indicators are those that trend up or down before the sales being forecast react.

Using these types of indicators can be useful as long as it is done with good judgment. Gasoline consumption and automobile registrations usually have some influence on the size of the automobile replacement parts market. But one thing must be remembered about any statistical technique—no matter how sophisticated the technique may look, *all statistical techniques assume that the future will be like the past*. They assume that the relationship that existed in the past between gasoline consumption and automotive replacement parts will stay the same. This is not necessarily so. With the introduction of smaller automobiles and reduced gasoline consumption, replacement parts demand may stay the same or even increase.

It is well to remember, too, that none of these techniques can compensate for or recognize certain other elements that can affect demand. If hardware distributors, because of a tight money supply, for example, decide to reduce their inventories, the relationship between housing starts and builder's hardware sales would not generate an accurate forecast. Increasing foreign competition, for example, might have a dramatic impact on the sales trend.

This is not to say that some of these techniques cannot be useful, but they must be used with good judgment. None of them is a panacea and, moreover, the use of forecasting techniques in business has demonstrated time and again a basic principle of sound computer applications: *unless the system is 100 percent reliable, it must be made simple enough so that the people who use it will know how to use it intelligently.* This is the principle of "systems transparency." Some misguided systems designers believe that the more sophisticated the technique, the better it is going to work. In practice, overly sophisticated techniques tend to be ignored by their intended users.

The fact that statistical techniques are not 100 percent reliable does not mean, of course, that judgment *is* a reliable forecasting technique. Typically, we have to go to the marketing or sales people for this judgment, and their enthusiasm or pessimism at the moment often depends upon their last customer call. Nevertheless, they can bring to bear their knowledge of the market, competitors' products, new pricing policies, and any knowledge they may have about distributor's plans to increase or decrease inventory.

In short, both statistical and judgment techniques have their short-comings; yet, in practice, both can be useful—particularly when they are used together. There are no really reliable forecasting methods, yet everybody has to forecast. Using some of the simpler statistical techniques in combination with judgment makes the most sense in the real world of business.

### Some Useful Forecasting Techniques

Inventory control people have always used averaging techniques. One of these techniques is the "year-to-date average." The year-to-date average at the end of January, of course, is a four-week average. If sales are particularly high in any one week, this will have a dramatic influence on the average. At the end of November, one week of high sales will have relatively little effect on the year-to-date average. Year-to-date averages were convenient when only manual techniques were available. While commonly used, the year-to-date average is not as useful as other types.

A practical form of average is the *moving average*. Assume that a company wanted to use a twelve-week moving average for forecasting item sales. They would add up the sales for the last twelve weeks and divide by twelve to get the average. A week later they would add the newest week of sales and discard the oldest so that once again they had a current total of the latest twelve weeks of sales. Again, they would divide by twelve to get their new moving average. The moving average tends to require the storage and manipulation of quite a bit of data and also is not as convenient in practice as a simple technique described below.

Figure 27 shows a sales forecast being made with a simple average. Note that a simple average is the equivalent of a 50/50 weighted average. For example, if we use the data in Figure 27 and take 50 percent of the old forecast plus 50 percent of the actual sales, our new forecast will be identical with the forecast arrived at with the simple average.

One of the obvious drawbacks to the use of this simple average is the fact that as much weight is placed on one month of actual sales as is placed on the old forecast. It usually makes more sense to put more than 50 percent of the weight on the old forecast and less on the current sales figure, since the current sales could be just a single erratic variation.

The weighting factors could more logically be split (they must equal 1.0 no matter how they are split) to 80 percent and 20 percent (0.8 and 0.2). Then the average would be calculated as shown in Figure 28. Note that the reaction to the current sales figure was less dramatic than in the previous example.

This technique is called, in the literature of inventory management, exponential smoothing. The weighting factor placed on the current sales—in this case, 0.2—is called the alpha factor. These are rather pretentious names that tend to obscure the fundamental simplicity of the technique: exponential smoothing is simply *a weighted moving average.*

What is its advantage? It makes computations simple and frequently means less data stored in live files. While most companies do save sales history figures (usually by month) for each item to facilitate analysis, the inventory management programs do not need to manipulate the data during each processing run as they would to compute a regular moving average. The exponential smoothing computation requires only the "old

Old Forecast (Monthly Sales ) = 100
Actual Sales (Last Month) = 80
New Forecast (Simple Average) = 90

*Figure 27. Simple-Average Forecast*

```
Old Forecast = 100 X 0.8     = 80
Actual Sales =  80 X 0.2     = 16
New Forecast (Weighted Average) = 96
```

*Figure 28. Weighted-Average Forecast*

forecast" and the alpha factor to be stored in the inventory master file. Current sales are entered and a "new forecast" is computed and stored.

More significant is the flexibility of the technique. If the "tracking signal" (described below) signals that a forecast is lagging actual demand, an analyst can manually insert a revised forecast figure in the system and start smoothing it. This is far more convenient than trying to revise a moving average computation.

When exponential smoothing was first presented, the burning question was, "what weighting factor is *right* for our product?" Many hours of computer time were consumed doing simulations to determine whether an alpha factor of 0.1 was better than 0.2, for example, on a given set of data. Experience showed, however, that it was the routine updating capability—not the precision—that was the real value of exponential smoothing.

Today, in practice, alpha factors are usually chosen using common sense. The exponential smoothing average approximates a moving average. An alpha of 0.1, for example, is roughly equivalent to a 19 period moving average; an alpha of 0.2 approximates a 9 period moving average. Probably the most practical approach to picking an alpha factor is to choose one that approximates a length of moving average that makes sense. In a style industry, a 0.1 alpha used to recalculate a monthly forecast would hardly seem responsive enough. Using an alpha of 0.3 with a forecast interval of one week might be more appropriate. For a more stable product, a longer-term moving average—and thus a lower alpha factor—would be more appropriate.

Two formulas that can be useful in relating the alpha to the moving average are:

$$A = \frac{2}{N+1} \qquad (1)$$

which simply says that the alpha factor which approximates a given period moving average can be determined by substituting the number of periods for $N$ in the equation. If it were desirable to approximate a 9 period moving average, for example, the alpha factor would be 0.2. The second formula is just as simple:

$$N = \frac{2 - A}{A} \tag{2}$$

which enables us to determine what length of moving average a given alpha factor approximates. If the alpha being used were 0.5, for example, the forecast would approximate a 3 period moving average.

When exponential smoothing was new, the question of how to use it for lumpy demands was frequently raised. When an item has no demand in several periods, can exponential smoothing work well? The answer is a flat *NO!* In spite of persistent attempts by the mathematicians to devise formulas that would forecast lumpy demand items, the best approach from a practical point of view is to use exponential smoothing on the faster moving items with continuous demand, and human judgment on others. An experienced person analyzing the history of demand on slow-moving items can almost always do a better job than these formulas in determining a practical stocking level.

Second-order smoothing is another approach that has generally not proved very practical. This is simply the exponential smoothing calculation described above plus a "trend" computation smoothed in. This technique has two problems:

1. It is difficult for users to understand because the calculations are more complex. In practice, the "double smoothed value" must be reconstructed for many periods in the past to try to understand why some of the ridiculous looking forecasts were generated by this technique.
2. No item is a trend item forever. Short-term trends are more the rule than the exception, and they are much easier to identify in retrospect than while they are occurring. It is thus difficult in the real world to make valid distinctions between stable and trend items. Practitioners have found that trend items can generally best be handled by using first-order smoothing in conjunction with a tracking signal (described below).

While formulas for making trend calculations have not proved particularly useful, the calculation of seasonality can be very helpful indeed. Seasonal indexes—by month typically—are developed from past history.

They are then used to adjust the forecast of an item—or more often a product group—or "seasonalize" it. If, for example, 10 percent of the year's sales normally come in March, the seasonal index is 0.1, and it would be applied against the yearly forecast to calculate a forecast for March. In practice, seasonal indexes prove more useful in making product group forecasts rather than individual forecasts, since production plans to build inventories ahead of peak seasons are typically made by the product group.

### Forecast Error

By definition, forecasts are probably going to be wrong to some degree. Whenever a decision is going to be made based on a forecast, it is useful to know how inaccurate that forecast is likely to be. Past history is the best guide to use in trying to predict forecast error.

There are some techniques for measuring forecast error that can be very useful in practice. Figure 29 shows actual demand figures for six months compared with the forecasts for the same periods. It also shows the deviations from the forecasts which are then averaged. There is a technical term for this average deviation—the MAD. This simply stands for mean absolute deviation. The *mean* is the statistician's term for average, *absolute* means that the plus or minus sign will be ignored, and *deviation* means the difference between the forecast and the actual. In the example in Figure 29, the MAD would be 60 units.

Figure 30 shows the same forecast for each of the six months, but in the example in Figure 30, the actual sales are different from those in Figure 29. The MAD is exactly the same as it was for the data in Figure 29, but here a new concept—the running sum of the forecast error (RSFE)—has been introduced. This is the algebraic sum of the forecast errors. Note that

| Months | Forecast | Actual | Deviation |
|--------|----------|--------|-----------|
| 1 | 500 | 400 | – 100 |
| 2 | 500 | 550 | + 50 |
| 3 | 500 | 610 | + 110 |
| 4 | 500 | 440 | – 60 |
| 5 | 500 | 490 | – 10 |
| 6 | 500 | 530 | + 30 |

Total = 360
Average Deviation = 60

*Figure 29. Calculating the Mean Absolute Deviation*

| Months | Forecast | Actual | Deviation | RSFE* |
|--------|----------|--------|-----------|-------|
| 1 | 500 | 600 | + 100 | + 100 |
| 2 | 500 | 550 | + 50 | + 150 |
| 3 | 500 | 610 | + 110 | + 260 |
| 4 | 500 | 560 | + 60 | + 320 |
| 5 | 500 | 510 | + 10 | + 330 |
| 6 | 500 | 530 | + 30 | + 360 |

*Running sum of the forecast errors.     Tracking Signal $= \dfrac{RSFE}{MAD} = 6$

*Figure 30. Calculating the Tracking Signal*

in Figure 30, all of the forecast error tends to be on the high side. In other words, sales are actually exceeding the forecast for each of the six months. This indicates that the forecast itself is too low, even though the MAD is exactly the same as it was in Figure 29 where the forecast was fairly good.

Using the MAD *and* the RSFE, a "tracking signal" can be computed by dividing the MAD into the RSFE. A large number indicates a high degree of bias to the forecast error.

The running sum of forecast errors is a calculation to determine whether or not the forecast has any positive or negative bias. A good forecast should have approximately as much positive as negative deviation. A forecast that is too low is going to have an accumulation of positive deviations. A forecast that is too high will have an accumulation of negative deviations. The running sum of the forecast errors for a good forecast would tend to cancel out and be very close to zero. This is easy to see by looking at Figure 29, where the plus deviations and the minus deviations do almost cancel each other out.

The tracking signal can be a very useful technique in practice. Rather than using second-order smoothing, where a fairly complex calculation tries to detect trend, it is generally more useful to use first-order smoothing and use the tracking signal to determine when the average is not keeping up with an upward or downward trend. When the tracking signal "trips," the actual sales data should be reviewed to determine whether the forecast should be raised or lowered.

A normal range of tracking signal limits would be from 3.0 MAD to about 7.0 MAD. This means that the system will generate an exception report when the calculated tracking signal exceeds the limit. If the limit had been set at 5.5, for example, the item shown in Figure 30 would be called out on an exception report and the sales data would be reviewed.

Tracking signal limits can be set scientifically[1] but in practice they are best set using common sense and experience. Higher activity items should get lower limits, which will generate more reviews. Lower-value/low-activity items can have less frequent reviews; thus, higher tracking signal limits would be appropriate. If the system generates more exceptions than can be handled, the limits can be increased to make the job of reviewing and revising forecasts more manageable. On the other hand, if more responsive forecasts are needed, limits can be set tighter.

Another tool similar to the tracking signal is the *demand filter*. This is simply a way of monitoring incoming demand—for stock items usually—to see that it is within a normal range. Using the MAD once again, the incoming demand for a period is related to it, and if demand is particularly high, it is usually reviewed to determine why.

While the simple techniques of the mean absolute deviation and the tracking signal can be very useful for measuring forecast error for the routine items, there is also forecast error—often a great deal of it—involved in forecasting new products, promotions, and the like. Here again it is worth looking at past history to try to determine how accurate a forecast is likely to be.

When the marketing department says "We are going to sell 10,000 units in our fall promotion," the only thing that is relatively certain is that the figure will be wrong. It is far more useful for them to try to estimate, based on past history, what the probable minimum and maximum are likely to be.

This is not as difficult to do as it may sound. Some new products and promotions are very similar to those that have gone before. Others are completely new and the potential forecast error is greater. At least having an estimate of this forecast error can provide a sound basis for making some good management decisions about whether or not to build up enough inventory to cover the maximum potential sales, or whether to just build enough inventory to cover the absolute minimum of sales and hope to react by producing more during the time of the promotion, thus risking lost sales, etc. These are difficult decisions, but at least having some estimate of forecast error to work with can help people to approach these decisions more rationally.

---

1. For a brief discussion, see Greene, *Production and Inventory Control Handbook* (New York: McGraw-Hill, 1970), pp. 16–40.

Unfortunately, too many companies fail today to recognize the inherent inaccuracy of forecasts for new products and promotions when they are planning, and afterwards, when forecasts do not materialize as planned, they seem surprised. In many of these companies, marketing does not give manufacturing sufficient time to plan for new products or promotions (which usually results in manufacturing asking for unreasonable lead times the next time around).

Forecasts, when they finally do come along, are not accompanied by estimates of forecast error and, of course, when the sales do not materialize as planned, there is a big game of finger pointing with manufacturing people blaming marketing people and marketing blaming manufacturing. No matter who is to blame, the company has not performed as well as it should. Educating people to understand that forecasts are always likely to be wrong and that every forecast should be accompanied by an estimate of forecast error to be used in planning can be a real stride forward.

### Forecast Characteristics

Forecasting is often belabored as the cause of all the ills in a manufacturing organization. In fact, forecasting typically can be improved in most companies, but too often an unrealistic attitude toward forecasting and an unresponsive system are the real problems.

Forecasting, by definition, is looking into the future; therefore, it never will be very accurate. Complaints heard about the inability to forecast accurately are primarily symptoms of production and inventory management systems that were developed *without* recognizing the fact that forecasts *will* usually be wrong. Most companies can improve their ability to live with poor forecasts considerably if they understand more about some fundamental characteristics of forecast error. There are two of them that are extremely important:

1. Forecasts are more accurate for larger groups of items.
2. Forecasts are more accurate over shorter periods of time.

Most people have seen these characteristics in action. Try forecasting how tall the next man who walks by will be. It takes a lot of luck to do that accurately. He could be a basketball player or a midget, but, on the average, a forecast of the height of the next 100 men who walk by could be reasonably accurate. Forecasts for groups are more accurate than forecasts for individuals in the group, primarily because the forecast errors tend to cancel. Some are high, some are low, but, on the average, they work out reasonably well.

The second characteristic is just as easy to understand. The forecast of a household budget for next month should be reasonably accurate, but the forecast of a household budget for the twelfth month out in the future is much less likely to be accurate. Forecasting is like aiming a gun; the farther away from the target one stands, the less accurate he is likely to be.

If more people understood these two forecast characteristics, production and inventory management systems could function far better in spite of all the problems that exist in the factory today. How often we hear the foreman of a manufacturing department say, "Just give us the orders as far out as you can see them and we will make them the way you want us to." The minute this is done, of course, the forecast characteristics mentioned above have been ignored. They are generating orders for individual items far in advance, and the forecast characteristics will be working against them. *By creating a detailed schedule (which is usually based on some kind of forecast) farther out into the future for individual items, the chances for forecast error are dramatically increased.*

This foreman does not really need to know what items he should be making far out into the future. He needs to know things like how much *capacity* he should be providing. A forecast that just tells how much capacity he needs could be much more accurate than the detailed schedule. The actual shop order quantities for these individual items should not be released any farther ahead than they must be unless it is convenient to revise their priorities regularly and conveniently. By forecasting capacity requirements only, the chances of generating a reasonably accurate forecast are greatly improved.

There are some principles that result from these two forecast characteristics, often ignored in production and inventory management systems today. They are:

1. Any forecast that must be made far into the future should be made for the largest possible group of items.
2. Any forecast for an individual item should be made over the shortest possible time into the future.

*The Barcus Machine Tool Company for years operated with a twelve-to eighteen-month backlog of customer orders. In fact, when the backlog got down to less than twelve months, they normally would try to reduce their labor force. In recent years, however, this has not worked out well. The tighter labor supply makes it more difficult and expensive to handle temporary layoffs. At the same time, their competition promises shorter deliveries—usually in the range of six to nine months or less—so that they have not had the luxury of a comfortable backlog of orders to work from. This, of course, has introduced the need for forecasting.*

*At Barcus, they had a technique for ordering the subassemblies and parts that went into machine tools; it worked reasonably well when they had a large backlog. Once every three months, they simply sat down and firmed up their schedule for the next nine months. They then went to their bills of material, found out what material was needed and, with some history of lead time for this material, they were able to order at approximately the right time.*

*With the reduction in the firm backlog, they had to base their material ordering on a forecast. This forecast nine months out into the future, machine model by machine model, was never very accurate, especially since the newer model machines had so many options available. The production and inventory manager blamed his problems on the marketing department's lack of ability to provide a good forecast. It never occurred to him that his inability to recalculate material requirements quickly enough to respond to the real demand as it materialized against the forecast was the real root of his problem.*

The complaint that forecasts are not accurate is, of course, usually valid. But too often it represents a very subtle form of buck-passing also. When manufacturing people assume that they do not need to make any improvements in their control systems because all of their problems stem from somebody else's lack of ability to forecast accurately, they are simply being unrealistic. There will never be *accurate* forecasts; thus, companies that design their systems to recognize this forecast error and take advantage of the forecast characteristics discussed above will be the ones most able to compete successfully.

### Using Forecast Error Measurement

The basic order point (OP) formula is Order Point equals Demand over Lead Time plus Safety Stock, or·

$$OP = DLT + SS$$

The order point calculation includes a forecast of demand over lead time and a calculation of safety stock which can sometimes be improved using statistics.

The inventory management theory that reached its pinnacle of development in the 1950s and 1960s was based on the assumptions that:

1. Lead time is fixed; or
2. Lead time is an independent variable.
3. The due date originally assigned will not change.

The computation of safety stock that would be able to compensate precisely for the variations in demand over lead time—or the interacting independent variations in lead time and demand—thus became the primary concern of inventory theoreticians.

Today we realize that lead time is highly variable and that it is shortened or lengthened—not usually very scientifically in most companies—by the expediting (or lack of expediting) of the informal system. The great breakthrough in our thinking has been the recognition that, in most cases, lead time is a reasonably controllable variable, and that priorities must be revised continually to respond to changing needs. In the real world:

1. Lead time is usually variable based on the priority a job is assigned in the queue.
2. Lead time is usually dependent, at least relatively, upon need; i.e., even if they do not come through when needed, at least the most needed are likely to come through in the shortest lead time.
3. With the advent of MRP, priorities *can* be updated regularly based on needs.

The computation of safety stock, therefore, is much less important than we once thought it to be. There are some places where these concepts still do apply, however:

1. *Where lead time is fixed.* This is possible when an overseas shipment is involved and transit time is a substantial part of lead time.
2. *At the master schedule level.* Uncertainty exists only at the master schedule level with MRP. There is some value in being able to measure the probabilities of having to produce $X$ units more than the forecast.

3. *For protection against demand variations over the shortest minimum lead time.*
Even with the powerful ability of priority planning techniques like
MRP to alter lead times, there is a minimum reasonable lead time for
most items. Safety stock for independent demand items could be computed statistically to protect against demand variations over this
shortest lead time. It is important to remember, however, that the real
results the system can produce will come from keeping priorities updated and valid.

Today, then, we attach less importance to safety stock than we once
did. Nevertheless, there is value to the manager in knowing how to rationally measure and cope with demand variations.

### Calculating Safety Stock

There are a number of reasons why the amount of safety stock should
sometimes be different for different inventory items. Safety stock requirements can be influenced by the following factors:

1. *Forecast error.* Any estimate of demand over lead time is likely to be subject to forecast error. High-volume items in inventory will generally
   tend to have a fairly smooth demand because there are so many demands. Low-volume items will have a more erratic demand, and thus
   require a higher percentage of safety stock to protect them against the
   forecast error. Frequently, items with the same total unit demand have
   a very different degree of forecast error. Consider a company that makes
   a product to be sold under their own brand name and also to be sold to
   a private brand account (like Sears or Montgomery Ward) with only a
   difference in the finish or label. Their own marketing will be through
   hundreds of distributors, and the orders coming in from these distributors will tend to smooth out because there are so many for them. The
   private brand account will place a few large orders, and this demand
   will tend to be much more erratic, requiring a higher percentage of
   safety stock. The technique for measuring forecast error is the calculation of the mean absolute deviation (MAD) described earlier. The
   MAD is used in the calculation of safety stock.
2. *Exposures to stockout.* Stockout occurs when the new supply does not
   arrive in time to cover the demand. The stockout risk is highest just

before the new supply of material is received. In fact, the number of stockout risks is a function of the number of reorders per year, and, consequently, it is an inverse function of the lot size. If the lot size were equal to a one-year supply, only one replenishment order per year would be generated, and only one exposure to stockout per year would result. If the lot size were equal to a one week supply, 50 exposures to stockout would result. As a consequence, a higher level of safety stock is usually required for items with smaller lot sizes.

3. *Lead time.* The concept that forecast error increases as lead time increases was discussed earlier in this chapter. Thus, items with long lead times will have to have higher levels of safety stock than items with short lead times. But the relationship is not linear. If, for example, an item with a four-week lead time requires two weeks worth of safety stock, an item with an eight-week lead time will *not* require as much as four weeks of safety stock. And the reason for this is very simple: it is very unlikely that a two-week period with a high level of demand will be followed back-to-back by another two-week period with a high level of demand. So safety stock increases "quantitatively" as lead time increases, but not in direct proportion to the increase in lead time.

4. *Service level requirement.* It is frequently desirable to have a higher level of service for some items in inventory than for others. A company making automotive replacement parts would certainly be more concerned about having parts for recent models of Fords, Chevrolets, and Plymouths than they would about having replacement parts in stock at all times for earlier models of less popular cars. While they might very well stock these less popular parts, they might be quite willing to accept a lower level of customer service; i.e., more frequent stockouts.

Let us look at an item that has an estimated demand over lead time of 500 units. The MAD has been calculated to be 60 units. This is the calculation that was discussed earlier in this chapter. Looking at the table of safety factors in Figure 31, a safety stock can be constructed that will give the desired level of service. If the order point is set equal to 500, there would be no safety stock included, and it could be anticipated that about 50 percent of the time demand would be greater than the average and a stockout would be likely to occur. One MAD protects for about 80 percent service. Two gives about 95 percent. Setting this up in the form of a simple table:

| Safety Stock | Order Point | Service | No. of MADs |
|---|---|---|---|
| 0 | 500 | 50% | 0 |
| 60 | 560 | 80% | 1 |
| 96 | 596 | 90% | 1.60 |
| 192 | 692 | 99.5% | 3.20 |
| 300 | 800 | 99.99% | 5.00 |

One thing the manager should note from this table is the large amounts of safety stock required to give very high service levels. Of course, no amount of safety stock can guarantee that there will be no stockouts, since an extraordinarily large unpredictable demand could occur and cause a stockout situation.

It is important to remember the concept of a stockout as used in these discussions. A stockout occurs when the new supply of material is not received soon enough, either because demand was greater than anticipated during lead time or because there was some problem with the supply, such as a longer than anticipated lead time. So, in calculating the amount of safety stock required for a given service level, the first thing that must be decided is the number of stockouts per year that can be tolerated. The number of exposures to stockout per year is a function of the lot size. It is important to recognize this because *before* choosing the safety factor from Figure 31, a desired *service percentage* must be determined.

Consider, for example, an item with a lot size equal to a six-month's supply. There are only two replenishment periods or order cycles when there is an exposure to a stockout. Thus, if one stockout per year can be

| Service Level (% Order Cycles without Stockout) | MAD* |
|---|---|
| 50% | 0.00 |
| 80% | 1.05 |
| 90% | 1.60 |
| 95% | 2.06 |
| 97% | 2.35 |
| 98% | 2.56 |
| 99% | 2.91 |
| 99.5% | 3.20 |
| 99.8% | 3.60 |
| 99.99% | 5.00 |

*Mean Absolute Deviation.

*Figure 31. Table of Safety Factors*

tolerated, no safety stock is required, since there is only a 50–50 chance of stockout without any safety stock. On the other hand, an item that is reordered in a lot size equal to a five-week's supply would have approximately *ten* exposures to stockout per year. If it were desired to have only one stockout per year, this would require 1.60 mean absolute deviations of safety stock in order to give a 90 percent service percentage. Ninety percent simply means that with ten exposures to stockout per year and one period during which a stockout will be permitted, the safety stock will be computed to cover nine out of ten exposures.

The steps in calculating an order point, then, are:

1. Determine the number of stockouts per year that can be tolerated.
2. Express the reorder cycles when no stockout is desired as a percentage of the total number of reorder cycles or exposures per year. If there are 5 exposures per year and it is desired to have one stockout per year, this service percentage would be 80 percent, for example.
3. Reference the table of safety factors to get the appropriate value to multiply by the mean absolute deviation.

The concept of stockouts and service levels is a statistical one. Service, in practice, is often measured in terms of line items shipped, the number of items on a weekly backorder list which shows which items are currently out of stock, the quantities of backorders against them, and so on. The practitioner needs to equate the statistical concept of stockouts with some real-life measure of service that is meaningful. It is always important to remember that the statistics, no matter how precise the computations may appear, represent only an approximation.

The safety stock computation should be used with great discretion. Priority planning—and replanning—is a much more vital concern. In most real-world situations, the results will be far more dependent on the skill the users can develop in managing priorities. Consequently, safety stocks can often be established approximately without impairing the results the system will generate.

It must always be recognized that safety stocks tend to dilute the validity of priorities. They should be computed at the master schedule level and then exploded into the components, rather than computed for each component. Safety stocks should be computed *only* at the independent demand—or master schedule—level to avoid mismatched quantities of components. Inconsistent need dates on components going into the same assembly can result from independently computed safety stocks on dependent demand items.

The mathematical computation of safety stocks was once considered the most important technique of inventory management. Today, we realize that "when to order" was a question of secondary importance, and that priority planning based on *need* is the important concern. The techniques for computing safety stocks are still valid, but they are no longer as significant as they were once thought to be.

### Developing a Workable Forecasting System

Most forecasts will turn out to be wrong, at least to some degree. As a consequence, the marketing and sales departments often tend to duck the responsibility for forecasting as long as they can. The production and inventory management people usually complain vigorously—and often rightfully—that they are getting little or no help from the only group that could possibly be of assistance. When management finally lends a sympathetic ear and says, "Okay, what kind of forecast do you need from marketing?" the production control manager's reply all too often is, "We have 15,000 items that we carry in inventory; have them forecast every one of them each month for the next six months out into the future," or "Tell me how many of each type of machine we will be selling nine months from now." This kind of request is, of course, patently absurd. And it is very disturbing to the executive who recognizes that marketing and sales people have better things to do than to try to forecast thousands of items every month.

What should marketing people be forecasting? Their knowledge of external events that could be used to help improve forecasts makes it reasonable to ask them to forecast:

1. Sales for product groups.
2. Sales for promotion items.
3. Sales for new products.
4. Sales for any individual items that are expected to have a significant up or down trend because of external factors.

This approach says, of course, that production and inventory management people can usually make the routine-item forecast better themselves than anyone else can. In fact, as one production control manager puts it, "Every time I ask the sales department for a forecast, they ask me for the data to make it."

These routine forecasts are typically going to be made using some kind of averaging technique, such as exponential smoothing. For most items, the best possible forecast is usually the average of recent, past sales. There is no need to have marketing people wasting their time making this kind of forecast. Obviously, if their product group forecasts *do not* come up with the same total as the individual averages for the product group, *it would be necessary to pro-rate the average figures per item to adjust them to the product group forecast* if this is assumed to be more accurate.

The principle, of course, is quite straightforward: **Production and inventory control people are best equipped to make intrinsic forecasts, and marketing people are in the best position to make extrinsic forecasts.** Intrinsic forecasts are those based on internal factors like historical demand; extrinsic are based on external factors like a competitor's price change or new product line. Frequently, the best forecasts are those using both approaches.

One of the most serious problems many companies have with forecasting is that they never clearly identify what purpose their forecasts must serve. Perhaps once a year the capital budget must be proposed. At that time, it might be useful to have some overall product-group forecasts for the next four or five years in order to estimate more accurately capital equipment needs. Other forecasts are made in order to set capacity requirements for the next few months to determine manpower needs. These forecasts do not need to be in detail, part number by part number, but need to specify instead the total number of hours required by work center over the planning period.

Other forecasts actually have to specify the individual items to be manufactured in order to provide the material needed for their manufacture. These forecasts should be updated frequently. These are the routine forecasts that are, for the most part, made on a continuing basis by the production and inventory management department.

Most companies find that when they can get production and inventory management and marketing people working together on forecasts, they get better forecasts. Once again, that hackneyed old word teamwork seems to be the key. Generally, the following assignments of responsibility seem to work best:

1. Marketing people should forecast only product groups, or promotion items and items where a definite trend is expected or has been detected. Routine items can be forecast using averages by people in production and inventory management.
2. Production and inventory management people should be responsible for tracking forecasts. They will undoubtedly want to participate in some of the forecasting activities, especially since they will normally have the historical information the forecasters will want to use. They should be responsible for reporting deviations of a significant magnitude to the marketing people so that these deviations can be properly interpreted.
3. The responsibility lies with the production and inventory management people to translate the sales forecasts into production plans. These differ from the sales forecast since companies usually do not plan to make products exactly as they will be sold because of the necessity to level the workload on the plant, etc.
4. It is the responsibility of marketing people to respond promptly when they are told that a forecast needs to be interpreted. Every moment that a forecast is not revised, it must be assumed that the forecast is valid. Manufacturing and purchasing activities will not stop while someone takes the time to be absolutely sure he will not be caught being wrong. If we wait long enough we will not need a forecast!

Perhaps the most important thing to develop in a company is a realistic attitude toward forecasts. There is nothing very romantic about forecasts; they are a normal business requirement. Even if there is no explicit organized approach to forecasting, the company is undoubtedly using forecasts today, and these have to be made one way or another. The real question is whether they will be made in a responsible, coordinated manner by the people best qualified to do the job.

It is important that management people take a responsible attitude toward forecasts. The optimistic forecast that sounds so good to the general manager when it is presented to him by the marketing department can generate a large inventory investment if the forecast is followed and does not materialize. The general manager has the responsibility for understanding the implications of forecasts. The top manager is more responsible than anyone in the company for generating a more realistic attitude toward forecasting. Developing a forecasting policy, spelling out what needs to be forecast and when, assigning the responsibility, encouraging a spirit of teamwork between production and inventory management people and marketing people, and especially developing a responsive production and inventory management system, can do more to improve a company's performance than all of the fancy mathematical forecasting techniques that have ever been developed.

# 11 | Lot Sizing

## The Concept of an Economic Order Quantity

The idea that there is an optimum or economic ordering quantity (EOQ) has been around since the early part of this century. In most manufacturing facilities the production rates exceed the usage rates, and therefore items are made in lot sizes. The larger the lot sizes the higher inventory investment will be. By the same token, large lot sizes require fewer reorders. Machine set-up cost—particularly where presses, screw machines, and other complex manufacturing equipment are concerned—can be quite substantial. Anytime a machine is being set up it cannot be producing, so from this point of view, large lot sizes are desirable. On the other hand, inventory investment needs to be kept to a minimum. Smaller lot sizes would keep the inventory down, but, of course, generate higher ordering costs. The EOQ should occur where these costs are in balance. This should be the optimum lot size.

Figure 32 shows the trial-and-error calculation of the economic ordering quantity. In this example the costs have purposely been chosen for arithmetic simplicity rather than realism. The ordering cost is $10. This is the cost incurred each time a new reorder is entered. Set-up cost, for example, would be included in ordering cost. The cost of placing a purchase order would also be an ordering cost.

The inventory carrying cost should include:

1. Obsolescence
2. Deterioration
3. Inventory Taxes
4. Inventory Insurance
5. Storage Costs
6. Cost of Capital

168

Ordering cost = $10
Annual usage = $900
Inventory carrying cost = 20%

| Order Quantity | Average Inventory | Carrying Cost | Orders per Year | Order Cost | Total Cost |
|---|---|---|---|---|---|
| $150 | $ 75 | $15 | 6 | $60 | $ 75 |
| $300 | $150 | $30 | 3 | $30 | $ 60 |
| $450 | $225 | $45 | 2 | $20 | $ 65 |
| $900 | $450 | $90 | 1 | $10 | $100 |

*Figure 32. Economic Ordering Quantity (EOQ)*

In practice, the inventory carrying cost is an estimate, and nobody has ever pinned down what it actually costs to carry inventory any more than they know what it costs to be out of stock. The concept that this cost is a specific definable cost is more appealing to the mathematician than the manager. Nevertheless, it does fit conveniently into the formula. Later we will see that the formula can be used quite effectively in spite of the problems involved in coming up with an accurate inventory carrying cost.

The example in Figure 32 shows an annual usage of $900 for the item. This might be 1800 units at 50¢ apiece.

The first order quantity tested is the $150 lot size. Since this lot size will come into inventory, get used up, and another lot quantity will come in and get used up again, the *average* lot size inventory will be $75. The carrying cost at 20 percent will be $15, and a $150 lot size will require 6 reorders per year. At $10 apiece, the ordering cost will be $60, and the total annual cost for a $150 lot size will be $75.

Note that as the order quantity increases, the average inventory will increase and carrying costs will increase proportionately, and the $300 lot size would result in the lowest total cost. Note that with the $300 lot size the carrying cost and the ordering cost are equal. This is the *economic ordering quantity*.

A very simple formula could be made up using this logic to get a direct solution to the economic ordering quantity question:
Assume that

$S$ = set-up or ordering cost
$A$ = annual usage expressed in $
$I$ = inventory carrying cost
$Q$ = quantity

The inventory cost is the product of one-half the order quantity times the inventory carrying costs percentage, thus it would be expressed:

$$\frac{QI}{2}$$

The cost of ordering would be calculated by dividing the order quantity into the annual usage $(A/Q)$ multiplied by the cost per order $(S)$. Thus this side of the equation would be:

$$\frac{AS}{Q}$$

Therefore the total equation—recognizing that the economic order quantity occurs when the ordering cost and the inventory cost are balanced—would be:

$$\frac{QI}{2} = \frac{AS}{Q}$$

An equation of this type can be cross multiplied, and the result would be:

$$Q^2 I = 2AS$$

$$Q^2 = \frac{2AS}{I}$$

$$Q = \sqrt{\frac{2AS}{I}}$$

This formula is the basis for practically every economic ordering quantity formula ever used by hand, slide rule, or in a computer. It can be modified and refined, but essentially it always does the same thing and it can be used to solve directly the problem that was done by trial-and-error above:

$$EOQ = \sqrt{\frac{2 \times 900 \times 10}{0.2}}$$

$$= \sqrt{90,000}$$

$$= \$300$$

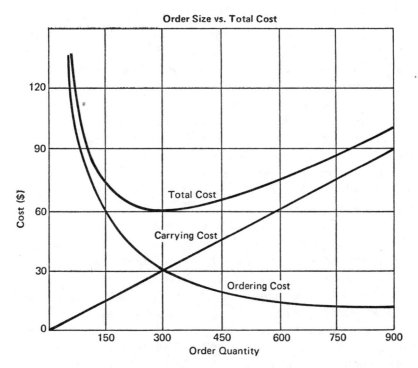

*Figure 33. Graph of EOQ Formula*

This is the EOQ formula, and Figure 33 shows it graphically. As order quantity increases, inventory carrying cost increases and ordering cost decreases. The total cost is lowest when the ordering cost and carrying cost are equal.

### Combining Runs through Common Set-ups

There are times when items go through a common set-up and have a "major-minor" set-up cost. It is possible to calculate an optimum lot size for a family of items assuming that they are all going to be run together.[1] The important thing, however, is to recognize the logic involved and to be sure that the practitioner is taking advantage of the economies that can result from running these items through a common set-up.

1. G. W. Plossl and O. W. Wight, *Production and Inventory Control: Principles and Techniques* (Englewood Cliffs, N.J.: Prentice-Hall, 1967), pp. 80–83.

This major-minor set-up problem occurs, for example, where screw machines are involved. A company making drill chucks might run one with a plain finish and one with a knurled finish. The major set-up to make the chuck having been accomplished, there is only a minor cost involved in adding or removing a knurling tool to switch from one chuck to the other. It is obviously desirable to run both of these items at the same time in order to reduce set-up time and increase productivity.

Most inventory systems will not order the two items simultaneously, and in practice the typical foreman will try to build up a backlog of work behind him so that he can try to combine some set-ups. This is not a very satisfactory way to do it. And it is far better to have the inventory system recognizing the economy of running families of items together. To accomplish this, one basic principle needs to be recognized: *WHEN a reorder is placed THIS time depends on the QUANTITY of the order LAST time.*

In other words, when the items going through a common set-up are ordered independently, they will tend to need to be reordered at random rather than at the same time. Items in a common family group, for example, should have their order quantities calculated so that the current lot size plus the amount on hand for each item in the family group is in an *equivalent time supply.* If the amount on hand and on order represents a four-months supply of one item, then the next item should be run in a quantity that would make its total inventory on hand and on order equivalent to approximately four-months supply. The items are not likely to require reordering at exactly the same time, but they should come close.

In practice this is a fairly simple thing to implement. The foreman can usually tell what items run through common set-ups (if anything he is likely to overdo this—it is important to separate the vital from the trivial) and these items can be noted in the inventory record so that they can be reviewed simultaneously by the planner. This is a particularly good approach to implement when set-up capacity is a problem. It will almost always generate a substantial increase in productivity and will usually decrease inventory investment if done well. Since more than one item will be run through the major set-up, smaller individual lot sizes can be used. This is easy to do for starting operations, but it is difficult to do for intermediate operations, since it is difficult to make several jobs arrive at intermediate operations at the same time. Fortunately, many of the high set-up costs in operations in many manufacturing facilities are starting operations.

*Lot Sizes for Dependent Demand Items*

When people first started to use the economic order quantity calculations, they ran into a very serious problem, and many of them are still wrestling with it: when the lot sizes for subassemblies are calculated independently of the assembly, they will not match up. As a result the theoretically *economic* lot sizes do not turn out to be very economical at all. Suppose, for example, that there is an assembly that is made in lot sizes of 500. One component's EOQ is 350, and another component's is 800. It is easy to see that there will be plenty of residual inventory around that does not really do anything.

The problem is a very simple one: *the square root EOQ calculation assumes constant usage and independent demand. For components in particular, the usage is erratic and usually comes in substantial lumps generated by the lot sizes at higher levels.*

There is, however, a lot-size calculation that can be made for this type of item. The approach is called *discrete lot sizing*. The least-total-cost approach to discrete lot sizing is shown in Figure 34. The second column shows the quantity required each week. The third column shows the cumulative lot size that would result from combining the requirements out through period six. If the requirements for weeks two and three were combined, for example, then the cumulative lot size would be 2200 units, and 2000 units would be carried in inventory for one extra week. The inventory carrying costs would be $40 (2000 × $5 × 0.004), and this would not quite balance the set-up cost of $50. By combining the requirements for weeks two, three, and four, and making them together, the

| Week | Amount Required | Cumula-tive Lot Size | Excess Inventory | Weeks Carried | Carrying Cost Per Period | Cumula-tive | Set-up Cost |
|------|------|------|------|------|------|------|------|
| 2 | 200 | 200 | | 0 | 0 | 0 | |
| 3 | 2000 | 2200 | 2000 | 1 | $40 | $ 40 | $50 |
| 4 | 300 | 2500 | 300 | 2 | $12 | $ 52 | $50 |
| 5 | 100 | 2600 | 100 | 3 | $ 6 | $ 58 | $50 |
| 6 | 1000 | 3600 | 1000 | 4 | $80 | $138 | $50 |

Set-up Cost = $50
Unit Cost = $5
Inventory Cost = $0.004 Per Week

*Figure 34. Discrete Lot Sizing—Least Total Cost*

cumulative inventory cost comes closest to balancing the set-up costs. Note that the logic is identical to the square-root EOQ: balancing the costs of ordering vs. the cost of inventory.

This is a useful approach that is frequently called *part period balancing*. It can be greatly sophisticated and the theoreticians have had a wonderful time making up more complex algorithms for lot size calculations. The manager should always remember, however, that the lot size calculation is an approximation at best. Requirements will change, since they are usually based on some kind of forecast and forecasts tend to be wrong. The unit costs used are usually only accurate within 15–20 percent, the set-up cost is usually only an estimate, and the inventory carrying cost is a guess. It is amusing to see how a mathematician can take an approximation, an estimate, and a guess and come out with an answer precise to three decimal places. In practice it is best not to complicate this type of calculation. The precision that seems to result is spurious and in the final analysis people will have to use the results. They will not use them intelligently if they do not understand the computations.

For this reason, another approximation that works quite well for determining economic lot sizes where requirements are discrete is called the period order quantity (POQ). This calculation starts by taking the standard square-root EOQ calculation and figuring an economic lot size. But, since it is recognized that during the year demand will not be constant, this lot size is converted into time periods. An item that has an annual demand of 50,000 units, for example, might have a calculated lot size of 10,000 units. This is really equivalent to a ten-week supply. The POQ approach then converts the square-root EOQ calculation, which is easy to work with, into a number of periods, and each lot size then is the sum of the net requirements for that number of periods out into the future. It is a simple approximation, and because it works in terms the planner is used to working with—number of weeks supply—it tends to work out quite well in practice.

It is important to be very careful with any dynamic lot sizing technique that recalculates lot sizes each time the MRP report is run. It can easily optimize the lot size at one level in the product structure and generate needless reschedules at the lower level.

Consider a subassembly that had a planned order with a lot size of 1000 last week. That planned order generated a requirement of 1000 for a lower-level screw machine part and an order for it was released. The following week, because of some additional requirements, the dynamic lot sizing calculation is refigured for the subassembly and it calculates a lot size of 1050. At the lower level, the screw machine part has already been run, and if the system were followed, an emergency order to run 50 additional would now be generated, or, worse, the added requirement for 50 might be converted to a larger lot size and released on an emergency basis.

Dynamic lot sizing techniques can be used effectively, but it is very important to recognize that when they are used in higher levels of the product structure they can cause added expense at the lower levels. A good rule to follow: never change a lot size inside the cumulative lead time for lower levels in the product structure without first checking to see what its effect will be.

### The Significance of EOQ

There are real savings to be made from calculating economic order quantities, but in most companies this is not one of the first things they need to tackle. They probably have some lot sizes today that work reasonably well. Unless the company makes a one-piece product to order, their most serious problem will most likely be keeping priorities valid with a formal system. It is folly to calculate economic lot sizes, and try to solve the "how much" problem before solving the "when" problem. When people do calculate economic lot sizes before solving their priority planning problems, they usually do not manufacture the item in the quantities planned anyway, since they are continually rushing smaller quantities through to cover shortages.

Economic order quantities can be a profitable tool to use after the priority planning system is functioning. When EOQ is used, people must use it as a management tool, not as a magic mathematical formula. The formula assumes that inventory and ordering costs change in direct proportion to the lot sizes that will be used. In practice this is almost never true. As a consequence, lot sizes computed for individual items do not really "optimize." These lot sizes must be considered in aggregate in order to predict the results that can be attained and assign responsibility for achieving these results.

# 12 | Aggregate Inventory Management

## Inventory Functions

There are only a few basic reasons for having inventory. These functions must be understood if inventory is to be analyzed to determine how much inventory is really required. The four basic functions are:

1. *The lot size inventory.* Because most companies tend to manufacture items in lots rather than at exactly the rate they are used, inventory in excess of immediate requirements will be carried.
2. *Fluctuation inventory.* These inventories exist because demand or supply fluctuates. Safety stock is fluctuation inventory. Another example of fluctuation inventory is the work in process queue that exists ahead of work centers in the factory.
3. *Anticipation inventory.* These are the inventories that are built in anticipation of future demand. Anticipation inventory might take the form of an inventory buildup during a slack season to keep the work force stable while providing for demand during the peak season. Inventory buildups ahead of a vacation, to anticipate strikes, and to provide initial inventories of new products and promotion items are also anticipation inventory.
4. *Transportation inventory.* These inventories exist because materials are moved from place to place. A company with a warehouse on the West Coast and a plant on the East Coast would normally have considerable amounts of inventory in transit between the plant and the warehouse. If the typical time for rail shipment across the country were two weeks, on the average there would be a two-weeks supply of inventory in transit.

176

While inventory investment ties up money that could be invested in other areas, it does, when properly managed, generate a payback. Each of the inventory functions mentioned above has its tradeoff:

1. *Lot size inventory.* The larger the lot, the fewer the replenishment orders that must be placed during the year. Smaller lots generate tradeoff costs in terms of increased ordering costs which then take two primary forms:

   A. Set-up cost in the factory. When a machine is being changed over or set up to make a particular product, it is not producing. The larger the lot sizes, the fewer the set-ups that will be required, but, of course, the higher the inventory. The smaller the lot sizes, the lower the inventory, but the higher the ordering costs.

   B. Purchase order costs. These costs are less easy to identify than set-up costs, but they definitely do exist. The greater the number of purchase orders placed, the larger the purchasing staff will have to be, more incoming inspection time will be required to put material away, etc. Usually purchasing departments see the effect of manufacturing set-up costs at the vendor in the form of a vendor discount schedule that reflects the higher unit costs for smaller order quantities. Once again, the larger the lot size the greater the discount; the higher the inventory investment, the lower the unit cost.

2. *Fluctuation inventory.* The greater the fluctuation in demand, the higher the safety stock that will have to be carried to give a particular level of customer service. Higher safety stocks, properly applied, *can* mean better service. Lower safety stocks often mean lower service. By the same token, the more fluctuation there is in the flow of work to a given work center, the larger the amount of queue that must be carried ahead of that work center to protect against running out of work. It is important to recognize that work-in-process queue can be manipulated using MRP and a dispatch list, thus dramatically reducing the need for safety stocks.

   In reality, few companies do anything to measure the variation in the flow of work into work centers, and thus they have no idea what the right level of queue is. When they do not know how much they need, they tend to carry more than they need in some places and less in others.

3. *Anticipation inventory.* The tradeoffs here involve the inventory investment versus changes in production rate. When there is seasonal demand, the

highest level of anticipation inventory will have to be carried if no changes in production rate are made. If production rates are changed to respond to demand, more costs of changing production—hiring, training, layoff, and so on—will be incurred. Another consideration is the amount of capacity available. A company that decides to build inventory ahead of its peak season because they want to operate at a level rate can operate with a lower capacity than a company that tries to change production rates two or three times during the year to meet these changes in demand. On one hand, building anticipation inventory and then depleting it enables a company to operate with the least possible hiring, training, and layoff costs (as well as other costs like quality problems involving training new people). On the other hand, building anticipation inventory ties up inventory dollars.

4. *Transportation inventory.* In general, the more expensive forms of transportation tend to take the least amount of time. Considering the choice of a transportation method, such as air freight versus ocean freight, the added transportation inventory required for ocean freight (as well as the extra safety stock required because of a longer replenishment lead time—due to the fact that forecast error tends to increase as lead time increases), should be taken into consideration.

These, then, are some of the basic functions of inventory and their tradeoffs. With an understanding of these functions, the manager can be in a position to require that some—or all—of his inventories be analyzed and justified. Some of the techniques for making this kind of an analysis are worth examining in more depth.

### Aggregate Lot Size Analysis

The economic ordering quantity *concept* is sound. There is a need to balance ordering costs and inventory carrying costs to come up with an economical lot size. Unfortunately, the mathematics often tends to obscure the practical problems involved, and this has led many a practitioner astray. An informal survey run by the author over a number of years indicates that about 80 percent of the production and inventory management practitioners have used EOQ at one time or another. When asked if they have seen any results—good or bad—only 20 percent said that they could detect any change at all! This means that the rest of them calculated

EOQs with the naive faith that they were doing something good, that somehow the calculation of economic lot sizes was the right thing to do, even if no discernible benefits resulted. This, of course, is pure nonsense.

In checking further, however, of those people who *did* detect some change in inventory levels or ordering costs, twice as many saw a bad result as saw good. In other words, more often than not, inventory increased when they were looking for a decrease. Or ordering cost increased when they had hoped it would decrease.

The problem really can be stated quite simply: most people tend to view the EOQ formula mathematically rather than from a management point of view. Looking back at Figure 33, anyone who understands the operation of a factory can see some assumptions inherent in the EOQ formula that simply are not valid in practice. Inventory carrying costs do not, for example, increase proportionately as the inventory investment increases.

Practitioners have recognized for a long time that out-of-pocket costs should be used in calculating the economic lot size. Unfortunately, even this does not solve the problem. Think of the size of the actual out-of-pocket costs to be incurred each time a purchase order is placed. They certainly are not very substantial. It is easy to come up with ridiculously low figures when only out-of-pocket costs are considered. The point simply is that more precise costs will not solve the real problems involved in using economic ordering quantity practically.

In order to use EOQ successfully, a few key points should be recognized:

1. In the real world, inventory costs and ordering costs are *not* linear.
2. Any results from the use of EOQ will occur because of the *aggregate* inventory or ordering costs that result, not because of any individual lot size. Just because each lot size is economical does not mean that the aggregate result will be economical or even practical.
3. Good results do not happen in the real world unless someone is assigned the responsibility to make them happen. Costs, on the other hand, can be increased very easily.

Space cost is an excellent example of a nonlinear cost. Virtually everything ever written about inventory carrying cost states that a cost must be assigned for space. Surely we cannot add up all the costs of warehousing and then assume that a 20 percent reduction in inventory, for example, will reduce these costs 20 percent.

What are the out-of-pocket costs that will actually be saved by this inventory reduction? They certainly are hard to identify specifically. Yet there could be substantial savings—if the warehouse were overcrowded and the inventory reduction reduced excess material handling costs, or if outside storage space were being rented and the inventory reduction eliminated the need for it.

The answer to this apparent dilemma is to look at the proposed new lot sizes *in aggregate,* predict what the change in overall inventory level will be due to these new lot sizes, and determine where savings—or increased costs—will occur.

The real results from better lot sizing will come because of their *aggregate* effect. The confidence that many people have—especially those whose understanding of EOQ is more mathematical than practical—is misplaced. It is possible in many situations to have all the individual elements correct yet have the result turn out wrong.

Consider, for example, a manufacturing engineer who is deciding what process to use to make a new part. He is trying to choose the most economical machine to run a particular job on. He reviews each individual job and assigns it where he thinks it should best run. Six months later there is a huge buildup of work behind one of the newer, more efficient machines, and nobody can understand why (except, perhaps, the foreman who has probably seen this happen many times before).

The real problem is very simple: the manufacturing engineer has considered each job individually without ever checking to see how the aggregate work load against this efficient machine would be affected. He has assigned far too many jobs to the most efficient machine and other less efficient machinery is now standing idle while production is bottled up behind his favorite work center.

This manufacturing engineer should have made a preliminary assignment of each job to the optimum machine, but then he should have checked to determine if there was capacity available. If not, the decision goes to management to judge whether to buy another machine right away. If they choose *not* to, because of limited funds, limited space, the fact that the machine is new and really on a trial basis, or a million other reasons that could exist in the real world of manufacturing, he should then make a second assignment of the job to a machine where capacity *is* available for the time being. These jobs should be reviewed frequently to present the decision to management so that they can regularly reevaluate whether or not another new machine should be purchased.

It is exactly this kind of problem that the practitioner runs into with EOQ. He usually calculates each lot size carefully, *but without checking on the total effect the new lot sizes will have.* It may very well be that the EOQs tell him to order smaller lot sizes than he has been ordering. The new lot sizes for the screw machine department may cause production to fall off because there simply is not enough total capacity available to handle the running time needed to make his annual parts requirements plus the additional set-up time required by the smaller lot sizes. The total annual running time plus set-up time *must be something less than the total available capacity.*

Many practitioners have calculated economic lot sizes for corrugated cartons, for example, where attractive discount schedules make larger lot sizes look very economical. Many have wound up storing corrugated cartons in the yard because the "economic lot sizes" simply were not practical in the real world and they exceeded their available storage space.

The third point above is worth thinking about also. Imagine what would happen in the purchasing department—or any other department for that matter—if larger lot sizes resulted in fewer reorders. This should result in less work load for the purchasing people. But Parkinson's very reliable law[1] tells us that work will expand to fill the time available. The purchasing people are not likely to step forward and suggest that their work force be reduced. In fact, they are not likely to recognize that their work *load* has been reduced in any way.

On the other hand, suppose that the number of requisitions to be processed *is increased.* Chances are great that they *will* notice the increased work load and check to find out why it is happening. The increased number of purchase requisitions will be used to justify adding more people.

The way to get results from EOQ is fairly straightforward:

1. Identify a group of items, like all corrugated cartons, or all screw machine parts, where there are likely to be substantial benefits from calculating economic order quantities.

---

1. C. Northcote Parkinson, *Parkinson's Law* (Boston: Houghton Mifflin Company, 1962).

2. Calculate all the EOQs for these items, convert them to dollars, total them up, and divide the answer by two. The result is the approximate total average lot size investment that will result from the new ordering quantities.

3. Divide the new individual lot sizes into the forecasts of annual requirements, estimate how many reorders will be required, convert this to set-up hours, number of purchase requisitions, dollars, or some other meaningful figure, again totalling the result.

4. Go through exactly the same process as described in steps 2 and 3 above for the *present* lot sizes (many practitioners will claim that they do not have any present lot sizes, but the inventory records can be used to determine what lot sizes have been used in the past).

5. Compare the aggregate lot-size inventory that would be generated by the present lot sizes with the lot-size inventory that should result from the new lot sizes. Compare aggregate set-up hours, purchase requisitions, or other measures of the total number of orders to be placed for the current lot sizes and the new lot sizes. Are the results going to be desirable and beneficial?

6. In the event that the new lot sizes will generate a larger lot-size inventory than is desirable, increase the inventory carrying cost that is used in the formula. This will reduce the lot sizes to a more practical level. *The inventory carrying cost should be used as a control in the EOQ formula.* Because of the stepped relationship of inventory costs and ordering costs in the real world, the inventory carrying cost used in the formula must frequently be adjusted to make the aggregate lot-size inventory, and the consequent aggregate ordering cost, fall into a range that will generate practical, profitable results.

7. Assign the responsibility to somebody to make sure these results *do happen.* If reduction in the work force in purchasing is expected, the purchasing agent should sign off on this and make it happen when the reduced flow of purchase requisitions actually occurs. If a reduction in set-up costs is anticipated, perhaps one of the set-up men can be promoted to foreman and the plant can operate with fewer set-up men. It is the plant manager's responsibility to be sure that this happens. Parkinson's Law tells us that it is easier to get bad results than good, and if these anticipated results are not spelled out and the responsibility for attaining them assigned to people, the chances of getting good results are very slim.

*The Higgins Company makes a line of expensive cutlery, including butcher knives, cleavers, etc. Because of pressure from corporate headquarters, the plant manager of the cutlery division decided that the manufacturing lot sizes should be reviewed. New lot sizes were calculated and compared with the old lot sizes that were in use. They indicated that the present lot sizes were far too large. The plant manager requested that a number of alternatives be explored. He was shown that the lot size inventory could be reduced about 15 percent without increasing his current set-up costs (this happens in practice because the economic order quantity formula establishes a better lot size relationship among the items to be produced. High annual dollar usage items with low set-up costs get small lot sizes, while low annual dollar usage items with high set-up costs get large lot sizes). This was not anywhere near the range of inventory reduction he wanted. He then had to explore the impact that increasing the total set-up hours in the plant would have on production, particularly in some of the tight capacity areas. It was determined that a reduction of 40 percent in the lot size inventory would be practical, and thus these economic ordering quantities were put into use. One of the corporate auditors, Harold Foster, later verified that substantial inventory reduction had occurred, but Harold was disturbed. He noted that the plant had gone on a four-day week and he claimed that the inventory reduction was not due to the new lot sizes, but was due to the shorter work week.*

Of course, the moral of the story of the Higgins Company is very simple: Calculating new lot sizes will not do anything. Inventory only goes down when you produce less than you use. The new lot sizes at the Higgins Company only told them *what it was possible to do:* specific action had to be taken to achieve that goal. At Higgins the inventory really came down because of the reduced production rate, but the recalculated lot sizes showed the management how much inventory *could* be reduced.

The theme that needs to be emphasized is very simple: the economic order quantity *mathematics* do not produce results; they should not be used with the assumption that good things will automatically result. This tool needs to be used by managers who know how to bridge the gap between theory and profitable practice.

As with the corrugated cartons discussed above, there are many items that have a very attractive discount schedule. Once a practical economic order quantity has been determined, the practitioner can decide whether or not to take the discount by calculating the extra inventory that would be required for the larger lot size and comparing it against the discount saving and the reduced number of orders. Once again a caution is in order: *each individual discount may look attractive, but the total result can be disastrous.* The aggregate effects of the new lot sizes should be calculated before implementing them on any large scale.

The aggregate lot-size calculations are easier to make using the square-root EOQ than with discrete lot sizing techniques that are often used in MRP. Aggregate lot-size calculations for discrete lot-sizing applications can be made using an MRP program as a simulator and trying different lot sizes. A simpler approach is to make the aggregate analysis using the square-root EOQ calculations and then convert these EOQ's to the period order quantities described in Chapter 11. The results will be a reasonable approximation that will probably be as accurate as extensive simulations that *appear* to be more precise.

Until MRP is working, lot sizing is not the major problem most companies should address. One missing component can cause a high inventory investment because the other components *are* in inventory, waiting. The quickest, most effective way to reduce inventories and improve service is better priority planning and control.

Once the priority planning and control *is* working, and components are being scheduled properly, the lot sizes will be the major cause of component inventory investment. When lot sizes *are* calculated, the manager should insist that aggregate analyses be done. This will insure that results can be generated and—just as important—avoid nasty surprises that often result when people apply lot-size techniques with blind faith.

### Aggregate Safety Stock Inventories

The statistical techniques for calculating safety stock for *independent* demand items were discussed in Chapter 10. There are computer programs available that can be used to make aggregate analyses to determine what levels of safety stock are required to give desired levels of service.

It is important, however, to recognize that:

1. Safety stocks tend to dilute priorities.
2. Priority planning can respond to both increases *and* decreases in demand, thus dramatically reducing the required safety stock investment.

Aggregate safety stock estimates should be based on safety stock over the *shortest*—not the *average*—lead time. Safety stock must be used very sparingly. A little can help, but the classical inventory theory assumes that it thus follows that a lot is better. Safety stock causes overstated priorities. If priorities are overstated very much or get confused because of safety stocks, service will go *down*—not up.

We have learned that the psychology of safety stocks is often a more significant factor than the statistics.

The service versus investment tradeoff for *dependent* demand items is a reasonably straightforward calculation. When MRP is being used, uncertainty exists only at the master schedule level. Forecast error measurement can be used to determine how many of a particular assembly or subassembly to overplan.

Safety stocks for dependent demand items can be *planned* at the master schedule level; where they are carried is a matter of timing. If an extra ten units of a subassembly are planned in the master schedule and they are allowed to move into the current time period, the inventory investment will actually be in subassemblies or final assemblies (depending on whether the master schedule is stated in terms of subassemblies or assemblies). If the overplanned quantity is planned further out in the future and not allowed to move into the current period, the safety stock investment will actually be carried as lower-level subassemblies, fabricated parts, or raw materials. It all depends on timing in the master schedule.

The service versus inventory investment relationships is really a tradeoff between the time to react and the investment required. A very meaningful analysis of overplanning to determine the amount of inventory investment required for a product family as a marketing hedge can be performed.

Fluctuation inventories on the shop floor—work in process queues—can be analyzed quite easily. Queue exists because of the fluctuation in input to a work center. Measuring the fluctuation in input can give a reasonable idea of the amount that is really justified. If the fluctuation in input can be reduced, as it often can by smoothing out input to a starting work center for example, the need for queue is reduced. The amount of queue, once established, can be built into scheduling rules like those used in Chapter 5. Few companies have established what queue levels they actually require; thus in the absence of a formal capacity planning and control system, shop queues tend to expand to fill the available space.

*Analyzing Anticipation and Transportation Inventories*

The lot-size inventory plus the safety-stock inventory constitute the base inventory. This is the ideal level of inventory that would exist in a company that simply bought and sold inventory and stored it in one location. They would be able to ignore anticipation and transportation inventories.

In a manufacturing company, anticipation inventories are a real and normal consideration. The base inventory is the *lowest level* of inventory in production plans such as those shown in Figures 7 and 14. Inventory being built above the base level in order to level production is anticipation inventory.

Production planning really precedes master scheduling. During the production planning phase, strategic management decisions about inventory investment—and its tradeoffs—must be made. In most companies several alternate production plans will be made as various strategies are reviewed.

Transportation inventory is fairly easy to quantify. It is simply equal to the usage in dollars over the transportation time. Significant amounts of transportation inventory exist primarily where branch warehouse shipments are involved, or where shipments to and from overseas locations are involved, and this computation and its tradeoffs are straightforward.

Aggregate inventory analysis is not a precise science. The ability of a company to respond to changes in priority, for example, can dramatically reduce its requirements for safety stock. This ability is *not* something that can be quantified easily.

Nevertheless, some estimates of the aggregate levels of inventory required are well worth developing. They can be used more effectively than industry averages, for example, in setting realistic inventory investment objectives. The manager, while he should not be misled into believing these computations are precise, should take advantage of these significant tools for aggregate inventory analysis.

## Costing Out the Plan

MRP has evolved into an effective simulation of the flow of material in a company. Properly managed it will represent what is really happening —and going to happen.

Back in the days when companies had a formal priority planning system that did not function properly, they tried to get aggregate dollar inventory reports. They failed. The typical purchase commitment report failed for the same reason that the machine load report failed. The formal priority planning system did not work, and consequently there were many, many late orders that were not really needed. The purchase commitment report showed these late orders costed out. As a consequence, it always indicated that more dollars were coming in during the current period than actually did come in.

With the ability to have a formal priority planning system that really works, MRP or the time phased order point can now be costed out, and realistic aggregate dollar figures will result.

The MRP format shows the current inventory on hand for each component. It also shows the scheduled receipts and planned orders. These scheduled receipts and planned orders can be extended by the standard cost, as can the current inventory position, to show the amount on hand and the amount that is coming in. Then the requirements, which are also time phased, can be extended by the standard cost to show the amount that is going out. The result is an inventory input/output report that is very useful indeed. Figure 35 shows this kind of report. The components in the small pump product line have been coded in the computer inventory record. The planned inventory balance for raw material has been projected for January, February, and March, in dollars. Planned input to this inventory has also been calculated. This comes right from the costed-out MRP which shows—by product line in total dollars—how much material will be received week by week and month by month. Planned output from

Small Pumps—Product Class 001
(Thousands of Dollars)

| | | Jan. | Feb. | Mar. |
|---|---|---|---|---|
| Inv. Bal. (Raw Mat.) | Plan | 250 | 270 | 280 |
| | Actual | 275 | | |
| | Dev. | +25 | | |
| Input (Purch.) | Plan | 140 | 160 | 170 |
| | Actual | 175 | | |
| | Dev. | +35 | | |
| Output (Fab.) | Plan | 120 | 140 | 160 |
| | Actual | 130 | | |
| | Dev. | +10 | | |

*Figure 35. Aggregate Inventory Flow*

raw material into fabrication is, of course, another by-product of a costed out MRP. The output is simply the time phased requirements for raw material.

This type of aggregate report is highly recommended. Most people in production and inventory management do not focus enough of their attention on dollars. Aggregate inventory reports can be a natural by-product of a formal production and inventory control system that works. With aggregate inventory information like this, inventory levels can be projected and the actual results can be tracked to make sure that they are happening. This can also be an effective tool to indicate when the master schedule is overstated.

Aggregate reports on new products can be particularly useful. Frequently, companies invest staggering amounts of inventory dollars in inventory to support new products, and do not seem to recognize that they have done it. By coding the inventory file so that new products can easily be summarized in dollars, this investment can be identified.

Aggregate inventory reports give the production and inventory management man some good handles on overall dollar investment. If he sees inventory building up at a greater than planned rate, he can go back to the master schedule and revise it. He will find that there is a normal distribution of product lines. There will be a "vital few and trivial many." By concentrating his attention on the dollar activity in the high dollar-volume product lines, he will be able to have better control over the aggregate level of inventory investment.

It is interesting to see how financial information can easily be a by-product of a formal production and inventory management system that really works. This undoubtedly indicates a closer working relationship between financial people and production and inventory management people in the future. It also offers the manager some hope that he will be able to get at least a few of his financial reports on a more timely basis when they are a by-product of production and inventory management information, which *must* operate on a timely basis rather than as a historical record-keeping function.

### Inventory: A Limited Resource

Time and again, companies get into serious difficulties because their managers fail to understand the very basic principles of inventory management. A responsible manufacturing executive should understand the implications of some of the policy decisions he faces, and how they affect inventories, service, and costs.

Decisions to add new products, purchase components overseas, and add distribution points can have a dramatic effect on inventory. In other areas, *lack* of decisions on things, like keeping product proliferation under control, assigning responsibilities properly for things like the accuracy of inventory transactions and maintaining basic documentation, like bills of material for products, can cause equally serious problems.

One of the sad spectacles of the early years of the computer age has been a fascination with techniques and a tendency to forget basic management principles. None of these techniques is so spectacular that it can work outside of the framework of a sound management operating policy.

Perhaps one of the most basic concepts that seems to be misunderstood as much as any other in a manufacturing company is the concept of limited resources. Yet this is the very name of the business game. All of the resources that most businessmen have to deal with are limited. They have a limited market, they have limited talents among the personnel, they have limited money to work with, limited machine capacity and capabilities, and it is the task of the businessman to do the best job he can in employing these resources to generate the most benefit for the organization.

It sounds like a fundamental concept, yet in practice it is ignored all too often. Consider the typical company's approach to the service parts problem. When parts are used both in current production and for service, there will always be the problem of allocating inventory most effectively. There will always be some parts that are in short supply. Then the important question is whether to use these to meet the assembly schedule or to handle service requirements. A great many companies attempt to handle this problem by separating the responsibility for service parts inventory and assembly parts inventory even though many of these parts are exactly the same. Usually the service parts inventory man has no control over production, but instead reports to somebody in marketing, sales, or the field service department. The responsibility for supplying parts to the assembly line is usually given to the production control manager. Obviously, these two people have been put in positions where they must compete against each other. Inevitably, conflicts arise, and sooner or later somebody responsible for service parts comes up with the idea that there should be a separate service parts inventory. Theoretically "untouchable" by manufacturing people.

This, of course, is going to mean an increase in inventory investment. Here is an example of one of the forecast characteristics discussed in the last chapter: *forecast error tends to be greater for individual items than it does for groups of items.* When a single inventory of parts is carried both for parts and for service and assembly requirements, the forecast error made in predicting assembly requirements tends to cancel somewhat the forecast errors made in predicting service parts requirements. Thus, the same level of inventory will give a higher level of service than it does when individual inventories are maintained.

This is a beautiful example of the *formal system* trying to do something that simply is not in the best interests of the company. The result is inevitable: an *informal system* will slowly develop that tries to get around the problems of the formal system.

There inevitably comes a day when the assembly schedule is not going to be met for lack of a part that is sitting in ample supply in the service parts inventory. Some of the service parts will then be physically transported back to the assembly department to be used to meet the assembly schedule.

This one instance is not going to cause any serious problems to the service people, but after it happens time and again, the assembly people may tend to rely more and more on getting parts out of the service inventory and, of course, service people, when they do run into a shortage, will often tend to blame it on the fact that "their parts" are being taken by assembly people.

The next step that sounds so logical is to physically remove the service parts inventory to a separate building in another town. Usually the company winds up hiring a fleet of trucks to shuttle back and forth, taking assembly parts over to cover real back-order problems in the service department—and taking service parts back to manufacturing to cover assembly shortages.

The point is a very simple one: *inventory is a limited resource that must be used in the best overall interests of the company.* Trying to compartmentalize responsibility for inventory ignores this basic truth. When management does not understand that the name of the game is handling limited resources, it is no wonder that the people out in the firing line get frustrated and confused. The service parts people have their rationale: "*If you do not supply service parts, pretty soon we will not have customers!"* The assembly people have their rationale: *"If we do not meet the assembly schedule, we will not ship the product, we will not have customers, and we will not meet our monthly shipping budget!"*

The fact of the matter is that there is truth to both arguments. It would be far better to give one man the responsibility for all inventory and to measure him both on service performance and assembly performance. It would be important also to teach him that inventory is a limited resource and that whenever we are dealing with limited resources, we inevitably come up against the situation where the choices are not good and bad, but instead, bad and worse. It does not take a great deal of intelligence to sort out good choices from bad choices, but it takes a lot of sound business judgment to identify the least worst choice.

There are many other areas where this concept of limited resources tends to be ignored. Consider the typical branch warehouse inventory control system. More often than not, the branch warehouse people themselves have been given the responsibility for ordering the material they need. Back at the main plant, inventory is shipped directly to local customers and also to replenish branch warehouse demands. Typically, the inventory manager at the main location sees only stock replenishment orders from the branch warehouses, and if he has any idea of their inventory status, it is usually only current at the time the order was placed. He will almost always have some items that are in short supply.

In the real world there will always be forecast errors, scrap, rework, strikes, mistakes, and all the normal things that go on. How does he know how to allocate scarce inventory items? Typically, he is measured only on the customer service for those *customers* supplied out of the main location. To him all branch warehouse replenishment orders look the same, and most of them *are* to replenish stock. Therefore, he develops a priority system in practice (the *informal* system) that gives preference to customer orders over warehouse orders. But, of course, this is not *always* the right approach. Frequently, a warehouse replenishment order is needed to cover customer back-orders at the warehouse itself, rather than just to build warehouse inventory back up to its normal level.

Here again, somebody needs to be given the responsibility for allocating the limited resource, performance needs to be measured properly to motivate people to do the best overall job for the company, and more often than not, up-to-date information needs to be provided so that the right kind of decision can be made. Beyond that, it should be recognized that because of the forecast characteristics discussed previously, it would be better to concentrate inventory reserves at one location that could quickly handle any positive variations in demand by shipping the inventory quickly, rather than trying to build up inventory in all locations.

The fact that this very fundamental inventory concept is not recognized has been demonstrated time and again by companies trying to develop elaborate computer systems so that they can facilitate the expensive transshipment of material among warehouses when an item is in short supply. The important objective is to keep the inventory at a central distribution center or back at the main manufacturing center and maintain the inventory reserves in one location, rather than scattering them out among the warehouses. Then when there is a sudden upsurge in demand, inventory can be shipped once rather than shipped to a warehouse and then back-shipped to another warehouse.

When a business pickup occurs, field pressure is almost always exerted to build up branch stock levels. Until production rates are picked up, the best reaction would be to reduce the levels at the branches. If branch inventories are increased before capacity, and thus main location stock levels have been decreased, the result is bound to be much lower customer service than would occur if reserves were concentrated in one location.

Inventory management principles are most important for manufacturing management people to understand. While it is always difficult to put precise measures on such things as the amount of inventory reduction that would occur from combining two inventories into one, it is well for manufacturing people to at least know what general kind of results can be expected.

*At Lake Machine Company, business had increased over the last few years while inventory turnover had decreased. The president, Howard S., was extremely disturbed. He pointed out that this requirement for added investment in inventory after an already extraordinary investment in research and development was straining the company's financial resources. Analysis of the problem uncovered the following causes:*

*1. The product line has been increasing so that each year there are approximately 25 percent more inventory items. When the number of items going through a high set-up area like the screw machine department increases, either set-ups or lot-size inventory must increase. If twice as many different part numbers were run through this department, for example, the lot-size inventory would have to double to keep set-up costs the same.*

2. *More inventory items mean a higher percentage of safety stock, since forecasts are more accurate for large groups, but less accurate for small. Splitting the demand out over many items usually increases the amount of demand variability.*

3. *A new branch warehouse in Los Angeles generated a requirement for added safety stocks (splitting demands again) and increased transportation inventory.*

4. *Lake Machine has also started buying many parts from an Irish subsidiary to reduce manufacturing costs. The added shipping time has resulted in increased lead time and the need for greater safety stocks (forecast error increases as lead time increases), and increased investment in transportation inventories.*

*Howard's agitation increased as he realized that not one of the policy decisions— to add new products without deleting old, open a branch warehouse, or buy parts overseas—had been made with any recognition of its impact on inventory investment. He called together the marketing and engineering executives and explained what had happened, emphasizing that the production and inventory management people had been blamed for increased investment, when in fact management policy decisions had caused the problem. He then visited with the production and inventory management people and explained that he now understood their problem better. He also emphasized, however, that they must assume the responsibility for making reasonable estimates of the impact that contemplated policy decisions would have on inventory investment, ordering cost, and customer service in the future.*

Aggregate inventory management requires a conscious effort on the part of managers. It does not automatically result because all the "right" lot sizes and safety stocks are computed. Managers who recognize the functions that inventories perform and some fundamentals about inventory management can make a significant contribution to their companies' inventory management efforts.

# Part 7 | Management Responsibilities

# 13 | Developing and Implementing Successful Systems

### Replacing the Insidious Informal System with a "Standard" System

Making formal systems work requires that we know *what* should be done. Just as important—and even less understood—are the *who* and *how*. Since we are replacing an informal system with a formal one that can work, it is important to understand some unconventional approaches and why they work. First we must be able to distinguish the formal from the informal system.

In the good old days, the informal system often worked reasonably well. But in time the informal system began to degenerate. Product proliferation, the retirement of experienced people, the demand for better service and lower inventories, all militate against the informal system. There is hardly a company today that doesn't have some oldtimer who can tell you how it used to run in the good old days. He tends to forget that the product line was simpler and that there were far more experienced oldtimers like himself around who had the product and company knowledge that would enable them to operate with incomplete, incorrect, out-of-date information.

Many people point to the fact that we do not seem to be graduating the type of potential employees from school today who are interested in coming up the hard way, the way the oldtimers did. This may or may not be true, but even if they did have the motivation, they're up against an insurmountable obstacle in most companies. There's simply no way to roll back the clock.

197

*Arnold S. joined the Continental Transmitter Company in 1923. He worked in the maintenance department, later in the weld shop, and later as an assembler. Eventually, he was promoted to foreman of the assembly department. The last ten years before his retirement in 1969, he was general foreman of all the assembly departments.*

*Arnold knew the product inside out. When he joined the company, they only made one line of transmitters. Two years later, they added another line. Three years later, they got into mobile radio transmission equipment. During the forties, they worked on large radar systems. During the sixties, they got into the development of telemetry equipment for the space program.*

*Arnold was able to absorb a lot of the product knowledge because it came along over a substantial period of time. He ran his departments with an iron hand. He looked at the schedules and at least once a week he would visually check the "floor stock" to support these schedules. He insisted that the expediters keep him supplied and could easily recognize from his daily plant tour when key parts were not moving through the fabrication shops to support his schedules.*

*On the other hand, the formal system consisted of ordering parts to support these schedules once a quarter! Theoretically, they were all supposed to be on hand at the beginning of the next quarter to support the assembly schedules. Of course, it never worked out this way, and the real system was the system of expediting from parts shortages.*

*Two years after Arnold's retirement, the president of the company was extremely concerned about the rising inventory, the poor customer service, increased costs of overtime, and the fact that the business just was not running as profitably as it had. When the obvious shortcomings in his formal system were explained, his reply was, "That may well be true, but we never used to have these kinds of problems." It never occurred to him that the loss of Arnold had seriously impaired the company's performance. He had replaced Arnold with one of his brightest young men, but somehow things never got back to where they were in the good old days.*

The informal system is doomed in most companies. It degenerates year after year until the day comes when somebody wakes up and realizes that the business simply cannot be run this way anymore. Perhaps the fact that a competitor *does* get the tools to run his business better helps to cause the rude awakening.

When computers first came along, a lot of new techniques were given great publicity and a number of old techniques were taken out of moth-balls. Techniques like PERT, linear programming, critical ratio, exponential smoothing, statistical inventory control, and so on, each were given great fanfare and publicity and hailed as the panacea for many of the ills of industry. Each of these techniques had its brief hour in the limelight and eventually fell into its proper perspective as just one of the many techniques that are available that can be helpful, but are not the vital few.

Many companies adopted these techniques, frequently taking them out of context and trying to build an entire system around them. For the most part, the systems were not successful and died before they got off the ground. In a few cases, they worked better than the old system. In most instances, these systems eventually degenerated.

Real progress began to be made when we recognized that production and inventory management starts with a formal priority planning system that works. The modern time phased material requirements planning technique—along with its close relative, the time phased order point—has become the standard industry technique for priority planning.

In spite of the fact that this technique has been around for a number of years and has gained increasing acceptance—with an almost explosive increase in application in the last few years—people still ask if this is not another flash in the pan. The answer to that is *no!* MRP is here, it is here to stay, and anything that supersedes it will be a refinement, not a serious change in direction in the opinions of the top professionals today. The reason for this is very simple: MRP is a formal system that does what the informal system always tried to do.

Consider the order point calculation by comparison. When used to order dependent demand material, it simply cannot put the right priority on the replenishment order, since it is looking at each item independently. *But even when used to order independent demand material, it puts a due date on the order, but does not then keep this due date up to date in line with current needs.* Improving this system by refining it with statistical calculations is not likely to generate any significant improvements. Someone will still be using an informal system to try to find out what the real needs are and to try and find out what the real shortages are. MRP is simply a formal way of predicting shortages ahead of time.

For years, companies really did not seem to make a lot of progress applying computer systems in manufacturing. Last year's showcase installation often became this year's "don't mention it in public" example of a systems disaster. Strides forward really began to be made when standard tools of the trade got identified and standard approaches to manufacturing control systems started to become widely adopted.

While the practitioner who has seldom seen any company other than his own often falls back on that ultimate parochialism, "Our company is different, our problems are unique," this simply is not true. The products are different. The problems tend to be similar and often identical.

So most manufacturing companies can benefit by using standard systems. This does not mean that a company with no priority planning problems needs to use MRP. It does mean that there are only a limited number of tools available that the practitioner and systems designer should choose from, rather than trying to invent new ones.

The justification for standard systems is overwhelming. They take less development time, they are tried and proven and there are usually computer software packages available to implement them. Professional education about these systems is readily available. Using standard approaches makes it possible to compare experiences with others and learn from their use of the tools. Standard techniques dramatically increase the odds for systems continuity; uniquely designed systems very seldom outlast their designer's tenure. Probably the most important aspect of standard systems is that with them it is easier to get people thinking about *using* the system rather than wasting their efforts debating about the system itself. Standard systems are depersonalized, utilitarian tools to do the job.

Practically none of the companies that has ever installed a standard, modern, time phased MRP technique has ever discarded it. There is a very good reason for this. *Every system gets challenged at some time.* Someone resentful of the fact that running the business still takes a lot of effort, and hoping for a panacea somewhere, questions that the current system is the best one. Someone being required to perform questions not only the information coming out of the system, but also the system itself. At that time, the best insurance a system can have is that it is a standard system— "If it works in other companies, why doesn't it work here?"

Long ago, the financial people recognized standard cost as a fairly universal technique. Today when the standard cost system breaks down, the professional financial man does not try to throw out the standard cost system. He tries to find out what his company is doing wrong and why it does not work better for them. We are finally attaining this level of professionalism in production and inventory management, and the standard system has made a dramatic contribution.

The breakdown of the informal system is almost inevitable in companies that have any growth, increase in product complexity, or suffer from the loss of the knowledge of experienced key employees who retire. The formal system can give a company a competitive edge today; tomorrow it will be essential for survival. The more standard that formal system is, the better it will be.

### Involvement and Education

People with experience in developing and installing systems almost universally agree that user involvement and user education are essential if a system is to succeed. They are likely to be more emphatic about this if their experience resulted from failure rather than success. Involvement and education are key words in any post mortem for an unsuccessful system.

Actually, however, the words are ill-understood and do not convey the real significance of the user's role. A man can be involved in a system-development effort *without accepting the responsibility for the success of the system,* and this is what the user really has to do. We should stop using the word involvement. We must require that the user accept the responsibility for success, since only he can make it produce results.

This means that the user must understand the system. It means that he must know how to participate intelligently in the system design. And this implies education. The steps in developing a system have frequently been defined as:

1. A systems study.
2. The systems design.
3. Programming the system, etc.

Education is usually fit into this sequence somewhere around step 3. That may very well be the right place for *training*. With a manufacturing control system, it simply is not the right place for *education. Education must precede intelligent participation in the systems study.*

We simply cannot assume that a user who has never worked with a formal system that really functioned for him, and who probably does not really understand the standard tools of the trade, will know what to ask for when the systems man asks him "what do you need?" He can hardly be expected to accept the responsibility for the success of the system when he does not fully understand the techniques that are being included in the system or understand the problems of making the transition from an informal system to a formal system.

### The Computer System Is a "C" Item

People with limited experience with computer systems usually tend to see the computer system itself as all-important. They put all their efforts into designing a system that is intended to be as close to perfect as it can be. They read about all of the techniques that are discussed in the technical journals and then try to include the latest and best techniques in the system. Then they install it, and somehow it does not seem to work.

Later they find that the engineer who never had to supply up-to-date bill of material information for the informal system simply does not understand why he needs to today. This seems to him like annoying clerical work: "And why do those expediters need it anyway?" They frequently find that the marketing man who always told the manufacturing people that he was going to sell a lot more than he really expected to (in the hopes that they would make about half as much) continues to do the same; the result is a badly overstated master schedule, overstated priorities, and a breakdown of the formal system.

They sometimes find that the assembly foreman who used to be a hero because he could steal parts out of the stockroom without making out requisitions and bothering with all the rest of the red tape still operates the same old way. Yet he is also one of the chief critics of the inaccuracy of the new computer system! They find that the stockroom foreman, who never did care much about paperwork, often does not really pay any more attention to the transactions that are supposed to accompany the movement of material than he used to.

Then the systems people get together and try to decide what has gone wrong. They often conclude that the problem was simply that management did not enforce discipline. This, of course, is usually patent nonsense! A system that was not designed primarily to be useful to the users will not be used. If it was designed with the idea that they were insignificant, that they were unimportant, that all they had to do was follow instructions, *it will not work*. Too often systems are designed with the naive idea that the *system* does the job, rather than the recognition that the system is simply a set of tools for *people* to use.

Too many times the way people work on computer systems is an excellent example of Parkinson's law of triviality, which states that people will devote their attention to subjects in inverse proportion to their contribution to the business. In inventory management, we learn that a *C* item is a low-value component. Low-value components are necessary. Without them the product cannot be put together, but the control efforts should not be devoted to the low-value components. It should be exerted on the high-value components.

The computer part of the system is the *C* item. The people part of the system is the *A* item. All a computer system can do is put information in front of people; their intelligent use of this information is what makes a system work.

*The Cleveland Machine Company was having problems with their inventory management system. It had been developed by a highly educated young man who was a recent business school graduate with a degree in computer sciences. It was a highly sophisticated system with all the bells and whistles. Before it went on the air, it had been written up in a number of technical journals as a great example of the latest sophisticated technology. After it went on the air, it was a disaster. None of the operating people seemed to like it. None of them had any confidence in it. Each of them could point to a number of fiascos that were the fault of "the system." The young man who designed it had moved on to corporate headquarters and was out of reach of the division management.*

*The division management were highly critical of the system and placed a great deal of the blame on the computer manufacturer. They called in a representative from the computer company and asked him to look into their problems. Since most of the problems seemed to fall into the category of inventory management, he asked to talk to the inventory manager. He was told that there was none. When he asked who the individual was who was responsible for managing the inventory, the response was, "The computer is supposed to do that"!*

*In another multidivision company, the executive vice president sent a letter to his manufacturing services director. He pointed out that division x had a highly successful computer system for production and inventory management. He suggested that this system be installed in all the divisions. The director of manu-*

*facturing services replied—quite correctly—that they would be better off to use*
*standard systems in all of their divisions rather than a home-brewed system that*
*happened to work in one division, and that it would be most important to move*
*the people from the successful division when the computer program was moved*
*in order to get really improved operating results:*

In the early days of computer systems, they were glamorized un-
realistically. Today we see them as tools. The young boy who would like
to play golf cannot wait for the day when he can afford a set of golf clubs.
He watches his favorite pro and is firmly convinced that a set of golf clubs
like the pro uses will certainly work well in his hands. The day comes when
he has his opportunity to try the clubs and he rapidly realizes that the
skill is not in the tools at all. The skill is in the hands of the user. The tools
are the *C* item, the user is the *A* item.

### *The Frivolity of Sophistication*

Sophistication has become a national preoccupation. Perhaps a lot
of the reason for this is the intellectual appeal of sophisticated techniques.
Even though these techniques are not being widely used, they tend to be
taught in colleges. Part of the problem, of course, is the system in academia.
Promotion comes to the man who publishes, it comes to the man who
develops advanced ideas. As a result, we frequently see techniques of little
significance—like linear programming—refined, rerefined, and mountains
of literature written on a subject that really has very limited application.

Sophistication, however, seems to many people to be an important
objective. What they fail to realize is that the people—the *operating* people:
foremen, planners, expediters—are not interested in sophisticated techniques. They want simple tools that will help them to do their job with a
little less effort and more results for the effort they expend. The very sophistication that appeals to some academic, consulting, and computer
systems people alienates those users who will have to make the system
work.

Two lessons about computer systems seem particularly significant
today.

1. Unless the systems outputs can be used with 100 percent reliability
   under all circumstances, the success of the system will depend on the
   user

2. A user will not assume the responsibility for the results of a system he cannot understand.

A simple, straightforward system (assuming it is sound production and inventory management and not just some home-brewed reinvention of the wheel) will give great results, *if people understand it.* Every additional bit of sophistication jeopardizes that understanding. We badly need to learn how to separate the vital from the trivial in systems design. We badly need to develop a systems value-analysis approach.

### People: The Key to Systems Success

The systems people are already sold on systems. The data-processing people are already sold on systems. The operating people, who probably have seen a number of abortive attempts at such follies as the "totally integrated management information system," are skeptical. They need to be sold, they need to be educated. But they do not need to be educated about a bunch of computer technology that is not significant to them. They do not need to be taught the mechanics of techniques that probably should not be included in the system anyway, but make good reading in textbooks and technical journals.

In selling to these people, it is well to remember that frequently the foreman has only a passing interest in inventory reduction. If he can be shown how a formal system *can predict shortages* sooner, and thus reduce the expediting chaos that he has to live with, he will be a lot more likely to support it. MRP is not complex or sophisticated. Any foreman knows what shortage lists are and how they are generated. He also knows that now we learn about shortages *too late. Predicting* shortages is usually something he can understand and want; that's MRP.

The lesson is a very simple one: *it is the people on the firing line who make any system work.* The system must be something they understand and it must be sold to them in their terms, or it is not very likely to work. Systems do not run businesses, people do.

*In the mid-1960s we experienced the great Northeast power blackout. The Northeast power grid had been set up so that each of the electric utilities was interconnected—and controlled by a computer system. One night there was a fail-ure at a power generating station. Immediately the computer switched to another power generating station, causing an overload that generated a failure there. It immediately switched to another power generating station and in 45 seconds the entire Northeast (except for Maine) was without electricity. Central Maine Power kept their power all night because some human beings—seeing what was happening—disconnected them from the power grid!*

*The lesson is a very simple one. The human being understands the intent of the system. The computer processes data in vast quantities, but like a high-speed idiot. It performs its assigned chores faithfully. Right or wrong.*

The computer technician frequently seeks to automate everything. He often has disdain for the people, yet practical experience repeatedly teaches us that it is the *people* that the computer system must be designed to serve.

*On April 11, 1970, Apollo 13 took off for the moon. Two days later, an explosion in the service module damaged the main power supply and cut off the oxygen for the crew. A major crisis had developed. The world held its breath while the men worked their way around the problem and brought Apollo 13 safely back to earth on April 17.*

*Apollo 13 was the closest we came to a major inflight disaster. It was frightening to contemplate men circling in space unable to get back to earth. But they did come back. And there were two lessons for other men in the computer age:*

1. *It was men—not a preprogrammed computer system—that flew that ship back. It was their ingenuity and wits that overcame unforeseen major problems.*
2. *There is little chance that men would have been able to fly that ship back without the aid of computer systems both on board the ship and at Mission Control.*

Intelligent design and implementation of computer systems starts with an intelligent philosophy of computer systems; *the best computer systems are those that are designed to enhance—not to supplant—capabilities of human beings.*

Those who understand the informal system environment that currently exists in most manufacturing companies recognize that the real challenge isn't in developing the system itself. Fairly standard sets of tools exist today. The real challenge is in getting an organization to make the transition from the world of the informal system to a successful formal system.

### Developing the System

Before any system development takes place, an education program should start. This education program should be aimed at teaching users the standard tools of the trade so that they will not reinvent the wheel.

As the education program progresses, it should spread out from the key users to some of the people in peripheral areas like the foreman, the stockroom people, engineers, and marketing people. The education program, of course, should be tailored to their needs, since they do not need to understand all the details of modern production and inventory management approaches. Usually the company will want to look outside for some assistance in education. Like anything, it is best done professionally. There is a great deal to be said for having the professional outsider reinforce the approaches that insiders want to take, especially when they are new. Somehow the expert role is best played by the outsider. People inside the company, then, can pick up the details of the education, reinforce the points, and relate them to specific company problems.

One of the most effective tools for inplant education is video-assisted instruction using video tapes, audio tapes, and written material. Classes can be run for as many people as should be educated. The classes are typically run on company time with two to three 2-hour sessions per week being the normal approach. One of the people from inside the company acts as the class coordinator and leads the very important discussion periods. The job of class coordinator is usually passed on to different people so that many of the students get the chance to be teacher the next time around. The video-assisted instruction approach is an economical, practical way to get to people without having them have to leave their company or take a lot of time away from the job. These courses can be tailored so that specific segments can be chosen to make up special shorter courses for top management people, marketing people, engineering people, and so on.

Education is a part of systems development that is almost always grossly underestimated. A good job done in this area will do much to avoid the common pitfalls of computer systems.

After many of the key users have been through the education program and it is continuing for others, they should study their problem and make a proposal for tailoring the standard tools of production and inventory management to their specific needs. They should specify the kinds of results they expect to get. An MRP system, for example, should be able to generate lower inventory, better customer service, increased productivity due to better availability of materials, and, as a consequence, lower costs. The potential users ought to talk to other people who have developed and installed this type of system to see what kind of results they have gotten.

They might very well be in a company where the informal system is still working reasonably well. One of the justifications for a formal system is to prevent having the company go out of control as experienced people retire and the problems get more complex. Under any circumstances, the proposal should include specific objectives. They may not be precise, but they should be estimated so that the payback is spelled out.

At this point, the computer programs will have to be tailored to come up with a specific system the users have requested. The developers will have to go through and specify some of the lot-sizing techniques they are going to use, how frequently the output will be seen, what kind of exception reports will be generated, etc. They need to provide inputs so that computer files can be loaded before the system can go on the air. Once again, these are the technical areas. They are fairly straightforward to handle. There are other areas that are more important that must get attention.

Some of the key areas that need to be addressed if a material requirements planning system is to function properly are:

1. Are the bills of material accurate and properly structured? Have provisions been made for handling engineering changes satisfactorily?
2. Does each item have a part number that is a unique identifier? A computer system must have this information if it is to function.
3. Are the inventory records—both on-hand and on-order—accurate? Has the responsibility for inventory transactions been assigned to people who have the tools to do the job properly?
4. Has the master schedule been designed? Who will be responsible for handling the master scheduling functions? Does everybody understand what a master schedule is and how significant its impact on the success of a modern production and inventory management system will be?

It is well understood by most people today, but it is worth repeating, that the users must take the initiative to get this type of system developed and installed. A user should head up the project team. It is also common knowledge that this must be a full-time job and he must be detached from any other activities. The day-to-day activities of running a production and inventory management function are always more compelling than the system-design activities. The man who wears both the doer and planner hats in theory never seems to get around to getting the planning done.

The head of the project team should be sure that the overall scope of the project is understood. Frequently, for example, people will expect that when MRP is installed the problems caused by lack of capacity planning will disappear. MRP is only the first step. It can function as a priority planning technique, but until the other tools are in place, the full benefits of this type of system will not be realized. Nevertheless, the system should be broken down into modules so that it can be developed and installed methodically and in segments that will give people the satisfaction of seeing something happen.

*Installing the System*

The actual installation of the system is also the responsibility of the user. He must recognize that there is considerable risk in changing the way a company goes about its business. He must recognize that his first responsibility is to keep things from getting worse while trying to make them better.

There are three approaches that have been used at one time or another for system installation:

1. *The cold-turkey method.* Using this method, the whole system is put on the air at once. The risks in doing this are obvious. The problems that are natural with any new system can become insurmountable, and the system not only stands a good chance of failure, it may very well seriously impair the company's operations.
2. *The parallel approach.* This is certainly the conservative approach and would appear on the surface to be a safe way to go. Unfortunately, it does not work out to be very practical. If a company has manual inventory records and decides to put them on the computer, running a

manual system and keeping the computer system going will require a lot of effort, probably more than people can handle. Parallel systems frequently result in the old system working and the new one not working because of the major effort required to keep two systems going, and the familiarity people have with the old system. There are many other instances where parallel systems are just plain absurd, anyway. Imagine a company using an order point system on components and switching it over to MRP. There is no way to compare the output from the two systems, since the old system is basically invalid anyway. The two systems will generate contradictory information and paralleling will prove nothing.

3. *The pilot approach.* This is by far the most satisfactory and most practical approach for installing a system. If inventory records are being put on the computer, for example, a small group of them should be put on the computer first and the results compared with the manual system. This running of parallel systems only seems to work practically on a pilot basis. If the MRP system is being put on the air, a product line should be put on first to check the system out and to see if people really understand how to use it. Then the other product lines can be put on.

There is considerable misunderstanding about pilot approaches, and quite a bit of resistance to them. Data-processing people often object vigorously because they feel that the major systems effort—developing the program—has been done, and there is no reason to go through the nuisance of trying to run a pilot system. They have failed to recognize that the important place where the system is either going to succeed or fail is in the hands of the people, and the pilot system is really a test of the ability of people to use the system.

Others claim that there is no way to isolate a product line in order to run an MRP pilot, citing the fact that there are many common components used in other product lines. This comment betrays a misunderstanding of the purpose of the pilot. It is not being run to see whether or not material comes through better using MRP, it is being run to see whether MRP *generates the right information* and whether people understand it.

If there are common parts used in other product lines, the results from MRP for those items can be ignored. The parts can be ordered using the old system. Those parts that are unique to the product line being piloted should, however, be watched very closely to make sure that the MRP system is really doing its job: *determining what the true need dates are.*

Note that the system is not supposed to get the material through the factory better or in from the vendors better during the pilot stage. It is being tested to see if it does its job of generating valid priorities and if people understand how to use it.

Once a pilot system has been on the air for a few weeks and people have confidence that there are no major bugs in the system, it is time to get that part of the system on the air across the board. Nothing is quite so demoralizing as continuing a pilot program for a long time when everybody recognizes that the system is sound and that this is only postponing the good results they all want.

In installing an MRP system, it should be remembered that one of the prime values of the system will be rescheduling. Some type of interim report—even if it only shows revised due dates by shop order—should be developed for transmitting these reschedules out to the shop floor until such time as a daily dispatch list has been developed. The full value of MRP will not be realized until the priority *control* technique is in place, and until the capacity planning and control systems have been developed and installed. An MRP system by itself only plans priorities. The dispatching system is needed to control shop priorities and capacity planning and control are needed to really make sure that there is sufficient capacity to execute the master schedule. The whole system cannot be installed at once, but once it has been started, it should be put into place very rapidly.

The computer end of this type of system used to be the big problem. Now that standard approaches have been identified, now that we recognize that there are many more similarities among manufacturing companies than differences, that is one of the simplest parts of the whole project. If the *A* area—the people area—is addressed properly, if the education job is done well, if the users take the initiative and the computer system is looked upon with understanding as a set of simple, straightforward, and extremely useful tools, there is no reason why any manufacturing company cannot make the transition from the chaos of the informal system into the world of the formal system where the production and inventory management function is truly a planning and control function rather than an order launching and expediting function.

# 14 | Managing Production and Inventories

### Systems Integrity: A Management Problem

Unfortunately, very few of today's manufacturing people have had experience using a formal production and inventory management system that really works. As a result, their sense of values is oriented toward those things that were important in the days of the informal system.

When the informal system was the real system, the accuracy of bills of material was not terribly critical. There was always good old Charlie, the expediter, who knew that the bills of material were not up-to-date and that part 17676 was obsoleted two years ago, replaced by part 17962. Whenever an assembly order was sent to the stockroom to have the part picked, he crossed out the old part number and wrote in the new part number. Good old Charlie had a lot of respect from his peers; the more time he spent in the shop and the less at his desk, the better they liked him.

Unfortunately, there are few companies today that can operate very well without a formal system. The product lines grow and get more sophisticated, while the experienced people (who might have been able to operate reasonably well with informal systems) are going. Today, with the advent of formal systems, the individual is less valuable than the team player. Team play made possible by a valid game plan—the formal system—may be less glamorous, but it generates better results.

A group of kids learning to play sandlot football will typically *all* run for the ball when the other team kicks off. It does not take them very long to learn that this is not a very effective way to play the game.

When they do start playing team ball, they play more successfully, and this is certainly true in handling the logistics of a manufacturing company. The formal system simply means that someone is going to be responsible for keeping inventory records right. Someone else is going to be responsible for ordering material and keeping the priorities up-to-date on open shop and purchase orders. Someone else is going to be responsible for using that material to make the product and get it out the door. The day when everybody was responsible for everything is over.

Engineering people, who in many companies did not do a timely job of maintaining bills of material, now must accept this responsibility. They need to recognize that the bills of material must now represent the way the product is really made. They need to work together with production and inventory management in planning and monitoring engineering changes. The engineering people are now a vital element in the team effort.

Marketing people must be shown what an MRP-based system is. They will have a better system for order acknowledgement, keeping delivery promises more faithfully and making conscious strategic decisions. They need to recognize, however, that when a rush job must be put into an already full master schedule, something has to happen. Either another job must be taken out, or more capacity obtained. Marketing people have a powerful tool in MRP. They also have some new responsibilities to step up to if it is to perform up to its potential.

Foremen who once worked to the hot lists and ignored schedules now need to believe in the schedules and capacity requirements. Experience, however, has shown that *if* the temptation to obfuscate the system with computer jargon and sophistication can be overcome, foremen usually *will* support this type of system enthusiastically. No one benefits more from a formal system that really works.

Management's job is to help pull these people together. To explain that the tools *do not* do the job, they only permit it to be done. They need to get them motivated to participate in a program to change the way the business is run.

The transition to a formal system is a real challenge, since our experience was all based on the informal system. How often some manager today says, "Accurate inventory records are great, but we've never had them and we always made money." Yet this is often the same man who cannot understand why the computer system does not produce the kind of results he wants. In the days of the informal system, relationships were vague and confused. How many managers, even today, can easily see the direct relationship between the accuracy of bills of material, for example, and the ability to hit the monthly shipping budget?

Inventory record accuracy is vital to any MRP-based system. Nothing is more indicative of the potential success of this type of system than management's willingness and ability to step up to, and solve, what is a serious problem in many companies today.

### Stores Control

For many years the literature in the field of production and inventory management was obsessed with order point systems. Oddly enough, the need for accurate inventory records was never[1] mentioned in this literature. This seems strange until one recognizes that the order point system was really just an *order launching* system. The more elegant order point computations—as well as the early computer-generated requirements planning systems—merely sophisticated the order launching. Since the informal "pull" system was the *real* system, the impact of these sophistications on operations was not great.

With MRP, inventory record accuracy takes on a new meaning. With MRP or the time phased order point, the factory and the vendors *will be scheduled based on the inventory records*. The effectiveness of this scheduling depends on accurate records.

There is a series of steps involved in developing real inventory record accuracy:

1. *Education.* Some staff people tend to think the management of a company is a simple hierarchy of one man giving orders to the man at the next level, and so on down the line. Unfortunately, it does not quite work this way. In practice, many of management's most impassioned directives are passively resisted in the factory. The real way to get enough people convinced that systems integrity is essential is to educate them to recognize the value of operating with a formal system and the vital contribution that accurate information can make. Most of the people in manufacturing and purchasing would like to get out of the crisis-to-crisis mode that is inevitable with the informal system.
2. *Assigning responsibility.* Inventory record accuracy requires handling inventory *transactions* accurately. The place where the inventory actually

---

1. I wanted to use the word "seldom" here, but, to my knowledge, "never" is accurate and "seldom" would not be.

*moves* is down in the stockroom. It is apparent, then, that the stockroom manager should be assigned the responsibility for being sure that an inventory transaction takes place when material moves in or out of the stockroom. He is on the firing line and he is the man who can do the job.

3. *Providing the tools.* The stockroom manager who is told that he must be responsible for a transaction occurring each time inventory moves will probably want to have a limited-access storage area. This is not to keep out the bad guys, but instead to keep out the *good guys!* The quality-control man who just wants to take a few parts out to check them, but does not bother to make out the transaction; the assembly supervisor who is too busy to get this month's shipments out to handle the paperwork properly; the engineer who feels that it is beneath his dignity to be bothered with paperwork; these are the real culprits.

Nowhere is the need for education more vital. Simply locking the stockroom will generate a negative attitude that management is just trying to make things tougher on the assembly people. They must be educated to recognize that the only way they are going to get a reliable supply of material is to have a reliable inventory record. The only way that this can happen is to assign the responsibility to somebody for keeping their records correctly. The money that the average person has in his bank account is his—it does not belong to the banker—but he would hardly trust a banker who did not require a withdrawal slip or a deposit slip every time money moved in or out of each bank account. Yet, in practice the need for accuracy in a bank is less than in a factory: *in a bank every component is interchangeable!*

4. *Measuring performance.* Cycle inventory counting, where a sample of the inventory items is counted and the inventory records reconciled—usually each day—not only helps to correct errors, but, more important, it can provide *an effective measure of inventory accuracy* on a regular basis. Tests for reasonableness can be built into a system. As material moves into a stockroom, for example, a computer program can check to be sure that the part number reported was a valid one, that it is being reported against the shop order or purchase order that was open, that the count is the same as the last operation, and so on.

5. *Correcting the causes of the problems.* Cycle inventory counting, for example, should not be used just to correct inventory records, or for that matter

just to provide a performance measure. Where errors do exist, the basic *causes* for these errors should be determined so that they can be corrected before more errors occur.

The job of providing the tools is sometimes difficult even when management wants to do it. Large components often cannot be stored in a storeroom but instead must be stored outside, for example. Nevertheless, the principle behind a storeroom is limited-access so that the responsibility for transaction integrity *can* be assigned. Some companies assign this to forklift truck drivers who must make out the transactions when they move material. This can work well for material that can only be moved by truck—as long as only certain trucks are allowed in the area where material is to be stored. The *principle* of limited access is far more significant than the *technique* of the locked stockroom.

Unfortunately, in many companies today, some major management policy decisions will have to be made about stores control. Many of today's factories, designed in the days of informal systems, have no provisions for controlled stores areas.

This may cost money, but the results are usually well worth it. And management should also ask, "If these problems are not solved, is our computer expenditure really justified?" Most companies today spend more than enough on their computer to provide an effective formal system, yet they really have the worst of both worlds: *they are paying the bill for a formal system and operating with an informal system.*

Inventory record accuracy revolves around people. Once again, we are back to management fundamentals: assigning responsibility, providing the tools, and measuring performance. Doing those fundamental, basic, common-sense things that have to be done if the system is really going to work.

### Engineering Change

In most companies, engineering change starts like a snowball and rolls on uncontrollably through the organization. Very few companies today would say that they control engineering change well, but that's really no surprise. Nothing can be controlled well unless it can be planned properly. In days gone by, when the formal system did not work, some companies even used order point on dependent demand items. In making an assembled product, for example, there would be absolutely no way with an order point system to evaluate when a particular component would be exhausted and another should be phased in. With an MRP-based system this can—and should—be planned.

There are essentially three categories of engineering change:

1. *Mandatory at once.* This type of change is sometimes categorized as engineering error, since it must be instituted immediately to correct a serious product fault. From a production and inventory management point of view this is the easiest type of engineering change to handle. It usually involves scrapping the superseded components and waiting for the new component to become available.

2. *Use up present stock.* This is the most common type of product-improvement or cost-reduction engineering change that calls for the new component to go into use when the supplies of the present component are exhausted. Material requirements planning facilitates this type of change. Some companies link the new component in the bill of material record in the computer to the component that it is replacing. They then change the lead time to zero and remove the lot-sizing rules from the component to be replaced, and put a lead time—and usually a lot size or lot-sizing rule—in the inventory record of the new component. This will cause requirements for the old component to drop directly through into the new component. It will be ordered, and its scheduled need date will be kept current. When the stock of the old component is used up, the inventory and product structure record for it are removed, and the new component is shown properly in the product's bill of material structure.

3. *Blocked changes.* Some companies, such as those making business machines where there are large numbers of maintenance people in the field, "block" their engineering changes so that when a significant one is put into effect a number of minor engineering changes take place simultaneously. This facilitates maintenance documentation. A field engineer can now be told that after a particular serial number, a series of changes is in effect up to another particular serial number. Once again MRP can be a most powerful tool in determining when the blocked change can be instituted most economically.

The critical part of instituting many engineering changes, especially when making an assembled product, is trying to balance out the matching components most economically and practically. If a new shaft with a keyway in it is replacing an old shaft with a keyway in it, there are times when it might be more economical to make a few more keys rather than to scrap a large number of shafts. In planning an engineering change, the time phased format of MRP can easily show when the current requirements will exhaust current supplies of superseded material to be replaced.

An MRP-based system is effective not only for planning an engineering change but also for monitoring it. The requirements will change; and projected material availability may change because of scrap, for example, thus changing the most desirable time for making the change effective.

Engineering change, because of the availability of techniques like MRP, is finally becoming a reasonably organized function in a few companies. These companies usually have a group with representatives from engineering and manufacturing—and sometimes even marketing and finance—who review all major engineering changes and plan the timing as well as project the costs of the major engineering changes. They then monitor the engineering change with the aid of the production and inventory management system, and also monitor its costs.

An MRP-based production and inventory management system is built on a sound foundation of accurate data. When it is managed properly it dramatically changes the job of production and inventory management.

### The Job of Production and Inventory Management

Yesterday's production and inventory management man did not have the tools to do the job properly. He could *not* handle the fundamental function of priority planning and keep his priorities up-to-date. He had to try to set priorities with the formal system and then use an informal system of expediting to get in some of the material that he really needed. His formal priority planning system obviously did not function very well, therefore purchasing people and manufacturing people recognized that in spite of the fact that he was constantly telling them that *they* were late, there were plenty of late jobs that he was not even looking for. Marketing people heard him complaining vehemently about poor forecasts, yet they often felt that this was buck-passing. They recognized that he could frequently get the factory to perform far better than he said they could perform—on a few items—if they just put enough pressure on. Overall, though, his performance seemed to be rather disappointing, since other items always slipped. Engineering people heard him complaining about lack of good data from them, yet they had little respect for a man whose prime activity was obviously firefighting.

The production and inventory management man was in a tough position. He simply did not have formal plans that would enable him to assign responsibility to other people so they could be held responsible for performing according to plan. He was constantly on the defensive. Frequently he developed a big chip on his shoulder from having to live in the environment of the informal system and the firefighting and finger-pointing that it generates.

When he has a formal system that *can* work properly, his job changes substantially. Instead of firefighting, fire prevention becomes the order of the day. His job has been defined as:

1. *Making plans* that other people can be held responsible for meeting.
2. *Monitoring* these plans to see that they are being met.
3. *Pointing out* where performance is not within the tolerance of the plan, and who needs to take corrective action to get back on plan, or what the consequences of not getting back on plan will be.

This is a new world for the production and inventory management man. In the past, whenever a job was not shipped on time, it was *his* fault. Why was the shipment missed? It might have been lack of engineering blueprints, it might have been lack of purchased material, it might have been lack of manufactured material, it might have been lack of proper tooling, but he was always to blame. Perhaps, ironically, *he deserved the blame* since he was incapable of *making the kinds of plans other people could be held responsible for meeting.* That is his prime responsibility. It is his job to get everybody playing to the same game plan and to point out deviations from the plan *in time* for corrective action to be taken.

What kind of man is needed for this new role of production and inventory management? Experience with informal production and inventory control systems of the past should be the least important consideration in choosing a man or developing one who is already in place. In either case, they will have to be educated to understand modern production and inventory management.

A good production and inventory management man should possess four fundamental characteristics:

1. *Perspective.* He should be able to back off, see the big picture, and point out what the problems are, what the alternatives are, and help the other managers to make plans that will enable the company to meet its objectives. He should also be able to sit back and identify those vital few problems that need to be called to management's attention when they cannot be solved at lower levels.

2. *Communication ability.* Many of today's production and inventory management people are basically expediters. They are hard-charging pushers who manage to get their shipments out month after month by energetic and often ingenious firefighting. The net result usually is that they have just as much firefighting to do the following month since the by-product of firefighting is to create havoc and more problems. The expediter, for example, who steals parts out of the stockroom without making out the proper paperwork because he "does not have time" has practically guaranteed that there will be a parts shortage in the near future. "Planning, monitoring, and pointing" requires a man who can *communicate* to get other people to do their jobs. It is a far cry from expediting.

3. *Objectivity.* Nowhere is there a greater requirement for objectivity than in production and inventory management. Here is the man who is trying to get other people to agree to ambitious plans and then frequently pointing out where they have missed them. He had better do this objectively and impersonally in order to get other people to work with him. The production and inventory manager who is constantly sharpshooting at marketing, purchasing, engineering, and plant supervision personnel can usually count the days before they will get fed up with him, and it must be remembered that they *do* outnumber him!

4. *Personal courage.* A good production and inventory management man is constantly pointing out to management what the alternatives are. Forcing them to face up to the least worst choice; even sometimes telling them that there are some things that *can't* be done; more often telling them how their plans *can* be accomplished, what needs to be done, what resources will be required, what sacrifices or additional costs will have to be incurred. People do not like to be forced to face up to prob-

lems ahead of time and it takes guts and confidence to perform this function properly.

The emphasis in production and inventory management has changed. With the proper use of the tools that are available today, the production and inventory management man is a planner and controller, not just a reactor.

### Separating the Vital Few from the Trivial Many

For many years, production and inventory management people have been aware of the so-called ABC inventory analysis technique. This is sometimes called the 80/20 rule. This technique involves ranking inventory items by annual dollars of usage so that the vital few items that constitute most of the inventory activity can be given the highest level of management attention, and the "trivial many" correspondingly less attention.

Many practitioners still think of the approach as primarily a method for sorting out the low-value hardware items for which a two bin or visual review system of inventory control would be more practical than posting inventory records. Today, with the computer, posting of inventory records is not expensive. Most companies show low-value items in their inventory records and do plan their requirements, even though they frequently disperse these items in bulk to the shop floor rather than counting out hardware items individually for each shop order.

Such inventory control techniques as the two bin system and visual review are less popular and certainly less justified than they once were, now that the computer is available. Nevertheless, the *principle* of separating the vital few is still as valid as it ever was. Aggregate inventory management requires management attention. Certainly management attention ought to be devoted to those inventory categories that generate the greatest number of dollars. Management attention is a limited resource even when the computer is available.

The principle of separating the vital few from the trivial many is just beginning to be recognized as an important aspect of systems design. Systems designers often try to incorporate every last possible degree of systems sophistication. In their naiveté they looked to the system to produce the results, unaware of the fact that the results are actually going to depend on how people handle the system. Today we recognize that system design must revolve around the users. If the system is not practical, simple, and transparent to the user, he probably will never learn to use it intelligently. Today we recognize that the vital few techniques that the computer can handle effectively that really matter are the ones that must be built into the computer system. The sophisticated trivia, such as fancy lot-sizing techniques based on data of dubious accuracy, should be left out. Any production and inventory management system involving the computer should be designed with a keen sense of value analysis, recognizing that no amount of system sophistication will make a system work if the people who must use it don't accept it and work with it vigorously.

The principle of separating the vital few from the trivial many is also an important part of the production and inventory manager's job. He should sit back at least once a week and try to identify those fundamental problems that are the most important ones facing management. In practice, this type of distillation of information is one of the most important functions that he can provide. Parkinson's law of triviality observes that people are easily distracted from the significant and waste their time on the trivial. The production and inventory manager must point out to management ahead of time where the problems are going to be and what has to be done to solve them. It is important to develop a sharp focus on the vital few. The effective production and inventory manager is constantly calling management's attention to the significant problems so that they either get solved or it becomes apparent which member of the team is not playing according to plan.

### Performance Measures

It is a truism that any function that has its performance measured generally tends to improve. There are a number of performance measures that are useful in production and inventory management:

1. *Inventory turnover* is usually calculated by dividing the sales (at cost) by the inventory. Frequently people will divide the inventory into the sales figure at selling price. This, of course, gives an exaggerated inventory turn figure, but does give figures that are often comparable with competition, since the inventory turnover for a competitor can be computed by looking at published reports giving his current inventory levels and

his sales. Very few companies publish figures showing cost of sales.

It should be noted that inventory turnover is only one measure of performance. A high inventory turnover rate at the cost of customer service and manufacturing expense is of dubious value. It should also be noted that it is extremely risky to compare inventory turnover rates company to company. One company may have its own foundry while another purchases castings. Another may carry finished inventory while another ships it directly to customers. One may have branch warehouses while another does not. It is far more rational to try to establish the proper inventory level for a company and use this as a norm than it is to set a target inventory level based on what others are doing—particularly since there is usually no practical way to evaluate what level of customer service their inventory turnover rate may be generating or the manufacturing cost they may be experiencing.

2. *Customer service* is relatively easy to measure in a make-to-stock plant. It is usually based on percentage of line items shipped. This is simply a tally of the number of items that have been shipped against customer's orders. If a customer order has ten items on it and nine are shipped, this order was shipped 90 percent complete. By tallying all of these customer orders, a daily or weekly performance indicator can be published. In a make-to-order plant, customer service can be measured by plotting the percentage of orders or dollars shipped as promised. It is worthwhile also to measure separately the number of re-promises met. Some companies measure separately the percentage of promises made that met the customer's requested delivery date.

3. *Overtime* is certainly a good measure of a company's ability to do effective capacity planning. Excessive overtime results when they cannot. Some overtime should be used to handle the random ups and downs in capacity requirements. A goal should be set for the amount of overtime that will be used, and this will probably have to be set empirically.

4. *Manufacturing costs* and idle time are other measures of production and inventory management effectiveness. Idle time, for lack of material in starting departments, is certainly an expense that should be charged to production and inventory management. Idle time in downstream operations should usually be charged to the upstream operations that did not perform on schedule. Manufacturing cost can be greatly influenced by the number of emergency machine set-ups that have to be made because of poor priority planning. Particularly in an assembly

operation, assembly cost can usually be greatly reduced by having all of the material available when an assembly order is issued.

5. *Departmental operating costs* are, of course, of concern to the production and inventory management department. The budget should be a flexible budget planned ahead of time. There are items in the budget that can be allowed to fluctuate with levels of activity. There are other items that should *not* be a function of the level of business activity. It is important to identify these, particularly since the temptation is so strong during a cost-cutting spree to economize in vital areas like data maintenance. Those people who are keeping bills of material up-to-date and accurate *are not expendable*. Managers used to living in the informal system environment tend to be prone to make cost reductions in areas that can now be disastrous. Unfortunately, their effects take some time to become apparent as the system slowly degenerates. A formal system requires accurate information—*all the time.*

Performance measures, then, are essential. They are essential particularly as a new system is going on the air. It is important to have benchmarks to know how things *were* in order to measure the progress that has been made.

It is important also to keep performance measures simple. Overly complex performance indexes that try to measure everything in one or two numbers should be avoided. They usually make sense only to the man who constructed the numbers. There are no performance measures that are perfect. Customer service in a make-to-stock plant, for example, could involve the amount of delay in getting back-ordered items into stock again, the importance of the customer being served, and so forth.

No measure will take everything into account. It is more important to have simple, understandable measures rather than all-inclusive measures. Above all, performance measures must be set so that people will understand the goals they are working toward and be able to see how well they are performing against these goals.

### Organization

It is interesting to observe how the traditional production and inventory management organization grew up around the inadequacies of the formal system. It is common to see a division between "production control" and "inventory control." The inventory control organization used to be the order launching group. This was the group that worked with the formal system. The production control group was the expediting group. This was the group that made the informal system work—at least well enough to keep the company going.

When a formal system that *does* work is available, the old form of organization does not make a great deal of sense. The inventory control group is no longer an order launching group, they are the priority planning group. They are not only responsible for putting the proper due dates on orders when they are issued, but also responsible for keeping these dates correct. By the same token, these same people have the information available to them for capacity planning, since it is a by-product of MRP. It would be more rational, then, to have a *central planning* group responsible for priority planning and capacity planning, and a *shop planning* group responsible for capacity control and priority control.

One of the key members of any modern production and inventory management organization is going to be the master scheduler. His is a most responsible job, calling people's attention to the alternatives they face, making the best possible decisions in the master schedule that will blend getting maximum performance out of the company while keeping priorities realistic. His is the responsibility for maintaining the credibility of the priority plan. He should report directly to the production and inventory control manager. He should be the man who is most likely to succeed the manager of the department.

One of the organizational forms that is currently in vogue is materials management. The idea behind the materials management concept is to incorporate all of the functions involved with materials—production control, inventory control, materials handling, stockrooms, traffic, and purchasing—under one individual, who would then coordinate all of these functions to get the best overall results for the company. The justification for this form of organization is that it should foster better communications and cooperation among all of these functions which often tend to encourage independent operation and conflict with each other under traditional forms of organization.

If there is conflict, it is an indication that people do not understand the objectives they are working toward. When the purchasing man, for example, is so concerned with keeping the cost of material down that he chooses poor vendors who cannot deliver, he is not working toward overall company objectives. This is caused, not by an organization problem, but because the priority plan as it exists today is not realistic enough for anybody to measure purchasing performance against it. There may be some temporary advantage, then, from forcing the purchasing man to work more closely with the production and inventory control man, because they have a common boss and cannot resort to buck-passing. But this does not address the major problem. The major problem is getting formal systems that can be used to generate plans that people can be held responsible for meeting.

Materials management? Nothing particularly wrong with it. It is a reasonable organizational form that has worked well in some companies and poorly in others. When the span of control of the plant manager or general manager has become too great, it is quite reasonable to establish a materials manager who handles purchasing, traffic, and so forth, in addition to production and inventory control. Under other circumstances it is hard to justify the addition of an extra level of management. This is especially true since most companies who adopt the materials management organization form are usually trying to solve a problem that was generated by lack of a formal system that could be used to establish realistic objectives.

It is worth thinking, too, about management by objectives. This makes a lot of sense in most companies. While we too often look upon it as a new management gimmick, it is simply a common-sense way of making sure that the objectives of the company are passed down through the levels of the organization and well understood by those people who have to meet them. But consider, once again, the impact of the lack of a formal production and inventory management system that worked. How can one possibly institute a management-by-objectives approach when formal plans are not realistic? No foreman can be measured on his ability to perform against an unrealistic schedule. Quite simply, then, a formal production and inventory management system must be made to work before management-by-objectives can be made to work very well in areas like purchasing and manufacturing.

The formal system, too, when it is made to work properly, will provide the basis for a management-by-objectives approach that will eliminate most of the symptoms that materials management as an organizational form is attempting to cure. There is nothing wrong with materials management as long as people do not try to use reorganization as a solution to problems that are not really organizational problems at all.

*Learning to Manage with a Formal System*

The formal system sometimes sounds like something highly structured, rigid, and inflexible. In fact, it is not. It is simply a way of getting everybody playing the same game to the same game plan. Certainly a better production and inventory management system can generate results, such as lower inventories, better service, and reduced manufacturing costs. But more importantly it can enable a group of people to get better results in responding to changes in business level, introducing new products, and in general keeping the company going in the direction it should be going. A team can always play a better competitive game than a group of individuals whose activities are poorly coordinated.

It must be remembered how the informal system generated buckpassing and defensiveness. Nothing destroyed the team spirit as much as the informal system. That kind of spirit has to be rebuilt, and people have to be educated to regard their chief competition as the competitor rather than the teammates. To a good many of the people in the typical manufacturing company the most unreasonable person in the world is the other guy down the hall, the marketing man, the manufacturing man, the man in engineering, purchasing or production control. It is management's job to focus people's attention on the competition outside rather than the competition inside.

The informal system also generated a credibility gap. Priority plans could never be realistic. Capacity plans, therefore, were never realistic. The typical reaction of the production control man who found that the shop could not deliver on time was to add a week to the lead time. The reaction of the shop was to deliver everything late because they knew there was plenty of fat built into the system. These same people, facing a world where a formal system *can* tell them the truth, have a real challenge in learning to use the formal system to do that. They will often want to overstate the master schedules, to overstate lead times, to build in too much safety stock, and to do all the things that seemed to them to be of help when all they had to work with was an informal system. These defensive measures did not help very much then, but with the availability of a formal system that really can work, they can be disastrous.

The system itself will not generate truthful information. People can use it to generate defensive information and create a credibility gap. The result is easy to predict: the informal system is waiting in the wings. Expediting and firefighting can easily become the order of the day once again.

The reaction of one general manager after visiting a few companies that have formal production and inventory management systems that really work was interesting. He was not surprised to see their inventories lower, their service better, their manufacturing costs down. What did impress him the most was *morale.* The formal system is much more satisfying to work with since it can produce results rather than frustration.

The production and inventory management system generates the basic information that must be used to run a manufacturing company. Without a sound formal system that works, the performance of other functions in the organization will be seriously impaired.

*Marketing performance* without responsive manufacturing support is extremely frustrating. When companies have both the ability to plan and control their manufacturing operations as well as good marketing, they have a distinct competitive advantage.

*Financial reports* are frequently seriously altered when inventory discrepancies occur. Financial people have always been strong proponents of more accurate inventory records. The operating people, however, will only put in the efforts to keep these records right when they actually use them to run their operations.

*Foremen and purchasing* people freed from the chaos and confusion of the informal system are in a better position to do their jobs more professionally. Few foremen have expediting in their job description, but today many must do it to survive. The result is that much of the work they *should* be doing does not get done.

Production and inventory management is not the only important function in a manufacturing company. But it is difficult to get the best performance from the other functions when manufacturing control is weak.[2]

The impact of the formal system is dramatic. The results are not automatic nor do they all come at once. As people develop their skills in using a formal system, the potential for payback seems limitless based on experience to date.

That impersonal electronic device, the computer, has made it possible to process information so that people can work together far more

2. "Good foremen are completely demoralized if their departments' schedules are continually falling apart because of bad production control and scheduling." "What Do You Expect From Foremen?" *Industry Week* (March 5, 1973).

effectively as a team. And in a world where most people have to work for a living, perhaps the most important benefit is not necessarily the economic one as much as the personal satisfaction that can come from a far less frustrating way of doing the job.

It is interesting to reflect on the computer's impact on production and inventory management. Mechanizing the payroll did not change the way the company was managed to any significant degree. Mechanizing the inventory records alone had little effect.

We have known how to compute the trajectory of a space ship for years, but before the computer this type of computation could not be done fast enough to be able to use the results to steer the ship. Similarly, in manufacturing, we have known for years how to calculate parts requirements and machine loads even manually. The computer, however, opened up a whole new way to manage a manufacturing business, because we could now generate this information fast enough to really plan and control the formal system.

The means for having formal production and inventory management systems that really work is here today. Some companies have succeeded in developing this type of system and in running their business better as a result. In those companies the challenge to management will be to keep their systems running well and in learning to realize even more of the potential payback. In other companies the challenge to management will be to make the transition from the informal system to a formal system that can be used to manage far more effectively. The responsibility lies, not with the computer technicians, but right where it always has been—with management.

# Appendix A: Questions for the Student

## Chapter 1

1. Cite some examples of informal systems in manufacturing companies other than the ones mentioned in the chapter.
2. Since informal systems have been used for so long and are the real systems in so many companies, why not continue with them?
3. "Priority planning" is a new term in the field of production and inventory management. There are no references to it in the older textbooks and articles on the subject. Why has this term come into use in recent years?
4. It has been said that the informal system tends to encourage "buck-passing." Think this through and try to explain why.
5. Priority planning has been called a keystone to production and inventory management. Explain this.
6. Why do you suppose companies with priority planning problems are often concerned about "scheduling" or priority *control*, and address their solutions to these areas rather than to the real root of the problem?

## Chapter 2

1. For years, inventory control people used the terms "on hand" and "on order." With the advent of time phased material requirements planning (MRP), the terms "projected available balance," "scheduled receipt," and "planned order release" have come into use. What is the significance of these terms? Why have they replaced "on hand" and "on order"?

2. It has been said that the planned order release concept is one of the very powerful technical aspects of MRP. Why?
3. When MRP first came along, it was primarily used for inventory ordering. It was only in recent years that people began to see it as a technique for priority planning. Explain this statement differentiating between inventory ordering and priority planning.
4. The current technology of MRP calls for no greater than weekly time periods and at least weekly recalculations. In years gone by, people used monthly time periods and frequently recalculated monthly. Why does the current technology demand a more precise approach to MRP?
5. A manufacturing company indicates that they are interested in using the MRP technique. It is always important to know whether they really have the type of problem that MRP would solve. How would you go about determining this?

### Chapter 3

1. For years, the textbooks on inventory management concentrated their attention on the calculations of economic order quantity and precise safety stock calculations. Why do you suppose they emphasized these points?
2. Today there is far less emphasis on the precision of safety stock calculation in practice. What has changed to make this occur?
3. The time phased order point concept is a relatively recent one. Why was the time phased order point not used much until very recently?
4. What are the advantages of the time phased order point versus the order point in its traditional format? Where would statistical safety stock calculations still be important today?

### Chapter 4

1 Much of the earlier literature written on MRP completely ignores the subject of the master schedule. The later literature emphasizes it heavily. Why?
2. The sales forecast is not a master schedule. Explain this statement.
3. Why, in practice, do people usually tend to overstate the master schedule? Why is this likely to cause problems?
4. The master schedule is the logical place to check to see when a customer order can be delivered. Explain this statement.

5. It has been said that the master scheduler's job is a good one for the future general manager of the company. Do you agree? Justify your statement.

### Chapter 5

1. Describe scheduling in a few words.
2. Describe loading in a few words. How is it different from scheduling?
3. What information would you require in order to make a machine load?
4. Describe the finite loading approach. To what do you attribute the fact that it has had a great deal of treatment in the literature and has great theoretical appeal, yet it has had very little successful application?
5. Machine loading seldom seemed to work very well in the past. Why?

### Chapter 6

1. Why do we talk about capacity planning today rather than machine loading? What is the significant difference?
2. It is important to separate the planning and control of priorities from the planning and control of capacity. Justify this statement.
3. Describe briefly how you would determine if there were enough capacity available to handle a master schedule.
4. When would a production plan be a good tool to use in conjunction with a master schedule? Is a production plan really a capacity plan?
5. When there are capacity limitations in the plant and the capacity to meet the master schedule is not available, what are the other alternatives?

### Chapter 7

1. There is very little discussion of capacity control in any of the literature on production and inventory management. Why do you suppose this is?
2. We used to be very concerned with keeping lead times to a minimum in order to have better control over priority. There is far less concern about this today. Why?
3. The input/output technique is a good capacity control device. It is easy to see why we want to know what the actual output was compared with the planned output. Why bother with the planned *input* and actual *input*?

4. Why does work normally tend to expand to fill the space available on the factory floor? Why do some companies feel that high levels of visible backlog tend to keep productivity up?
5. What is the biggest challenge involved in reducing queues out in the factory?
6. Describe the *informal* capacity planning system.

### Chapter 8

1. During the decade of the sixties, there was a great deal of emphasis placed on job shop simulation and sophisticated priority techniques. Many companies felt that they had their inventory control systems functioning satisfactorily, but that they really needed to improve their scheduling. Why did they take this approach? Was it correct or incorrect? Explain.
2. Shop floor control was a popular starting point in systems development for many companies. Do you think this is the right place to start installing a production and inventory management system? When should the shop floor control system be installed? Explain your reasoning.
3. The daily dispatch list has become a fairly standard tool of production and inventory management. Is there any need for it to be daily? What impact will computer technology have on future approaches to dispatching, in your opinion?
4. The responsibility of the shop planner has changed. Explain how it has changed.
5. The expediter was a standard fixture in production and inventory management systems for years. How is the role of the shop planner in a modern production and inventory management system different?

### Chapter 9

1. The materials management concept has become quite popular. Normally, this would involve combining, among others, the production and inventory control and purchasing functions. Do you think this is a good idea? What major problems is materials management addressing? Are there prerequisites to making materials management work?
2. The informal system encouraged buck-passing between the purchasing

department and production and inventory management. Explain why.

3. It is quite possible that many of the highly successful purchasing people of the past will not be as successful in the future working with a formal system. Justify this statement.

4. There is a high degree of correlation between those companies that feel that their vendor performance is satisfactory and the quality of their formal production and inventory management systems. Why?

5. Research question: Contact a manufacturing company and find out what percent of their manufacturing cost is material versus labor.

## Chapter 10

1. In spite of the development of many elegant forecasting formulas in the literature, most companies tend to use very simple techniques in practice. Can you explain this?

2. Some years back, a thesis was written pointing out that after much simulation comparing the results of exponential smoothing and a moving average, the exponential smoothing did not give noticeably better results. Does this seem logical?

3. Where did the name "exponential smoothing" come from? Do the necessary research to find out.

4. List three ways you think a practitioner could use the MAD calculation in practice.

5. Explain the calculation of a tracking signal in simple terms as if you had to tell an inventory clerk what it was and why it was important.

6. The general foreman of a manufacturing company complains that he is not given enough information to plan with. When asked what he wants, he says that he'd like to see the shop orders for the next three months. Do you think he really needs these shop orders? Would it be a good idea to give them to him? Can you think of an alternative approach you might want to suggest to him? Write your answer as if it were a letter explaining your approach to him.

## Chapter 11

1. The economic order quantity concept (EOQ) is one of the oldest mathematical techniques in the field of production and inventory management. Not very many companies, however, are using it extensively today. Why is this?

2. During the fifties, the economic order quantity calculation was in almost total eclipse. It only came back into prominence in the sixties. Why?
3. In what type of a manufacturing company would economic order quantities be a major concern that should be addressed rather quickly in order to get real systems improvements? In what type of company would it be well to postpone any precise calculation of lot sizes until other systems deficiencies were corrected?
4. A consultant has come in and sold the company on the idea of economic order quantities at the branch warehouses. These branch warehouses order from a distribution warehouse at the main plant. The consultant has suggested that a $10 ordering cost be used for these economic order quantity calculations. How would you go about determining what the real ordering cost was? Can you think of any problems that economic order quantities might cause back at the main plant and potentially at the branch warehouses? Do you have any ideas on a valid approach to lot sizing for branch warehouses?
5. A company has just calculated new order quantities, but they have not implemented them yet. They are using an inventory carrying cost of 21.5 percent. They have asked you two questions, (1) "Will the inventory go up or down?" and (2) "Are we using the right inventory carrying cost?" What information would you gather and how would you determine rational answers to these questions?

### Chapter 12

1. What is the significance of aggregate inventory management?
2. The aggregate inventory management concept has interesting implications for our traditional views of accounting. Do you think that accounting's role in the company is likely to change as a result? Explain.
3. In many companies, executives from marketing, finance, and manufacturing get involved in serious controversy over inventory policy. What causes this? If you were the general manager of the company, what would you do to get all of these functions working more toward overall company goals?
4. You have been asked to analyze the stores inventory and account for the current levels of inventory investment. How would you go about this?

5. List some reasons why "costing out the material requirements plan" could be worthwhile for a company. How is this approach different and why should it work better than the conventional "purchase commitment" report? If it would help, get a copy of a purchase commitment report from a local company.

## Chapter 13

1. In the early years of the computer age, it was assumed that only a computer expert could design a computer system. Think through and try to list a few of the misconceptions people had about computer systems that would make them feel this way.
2. Most users did not like and would not use computer systems very effectively. Put yourself in the position of an experienced person using a manual system. Why do you suppose they reacted badly?
3. The computer "system" became an obsession in the 1960s. Much was written about the "management information system" or "total system." Why do you suppose very few companies are interested in these concepts any longer? Explain.
4. The 1960s has been described as "the age of naive sophistication." Explain this statement.
5. The manager of a small company that has not previously used a computer is now ready to make the move. Write a few paragraphs explaining to the president how he should view computer systems and what his role will be.

## Chapter 14

1. The inventory records in a typical manufacturing company are inaccurate by their own admission. Why have these companies been able to survive without this accuracy? Why has management not considered it important to have accurate inventory records in the past?
2. Locking up the stockroom is one of the approaches many companies have used to try to get better control over inventory transactions. A company making a very bulky product stores most of their material out in the yard. They feel that it would be impractical to put it all inside a stockroom area. How would you suggest they go about trying to get record integrity?

3. A manufacturing company is about to launch on a "management-by-objectives" program. What are a few of the things you would check before endorsing this approach?

4. The production and inventory management man in many companies is quite frustrated. One of the common complaints is, "We have all of the responsibility and none of the authority." Do you really think this is a problem? How would you respond to this kind of comment? Write a few brief paragraphs.

5. The big challenge in putting a computer system into manufacturing companies is in making the transition from an informal system to a formal system. Explain this statement, giving specific examples.

# Appendix B: Case Studies

### Case Study 1: The Croft Receiver Company

You are the new general manager who has just moved into this position at the Croft Receiver Company, having been brought in from a smaller plant in the South. The problems at the Croft Receiver Company are many. Inventories are very high, customer service is so poor that your phone is ringing a good deal of the time with calls from irate customers. The business plan spells out a shipping budget but the best Croft has been able to do in the last three months is to ship about 75 percent of the budget.

Croft makes portable receivers for citizens' band radios and similar equipment. A small percentage of it is made-to-stock, but most of it is made-to-order. It is really custom assembled since most of the modules are fairly standard. The difference between one receiver and another might be just a small number of frequency-sensitive components. Croft's sales run around $20 million a year. They've been a good profit generator over the past years, but since April of this year, disaster has followed upon disaster.

It all started about two years ago when the corporate auditors were highly critical of the low rate of inventory turnover (1.7 turns at cost). They recommended the installation of a new inventory management system. A number of consulting firms were called in to bid on the job. The consultant that wound up designing the system had a slight edge right from the beginning since one of his firm's principals sits on the Board of Directors of Croft's parent corporation.

The old production and inventory management system consisted of manual inventory records that were posted by a battery of clerks. As

239

an order came in, they would "reserve" the components required for it and order any needed components. This system did have plenty of flaws. There was no time phasing and it was essentially an order point system where the reservation simply served to generate orders sooner. These were deducted from the inventory which meant that the order point would be reached sooner.

The system the consultant installed was very much the same type of system, only transferred to a computer and embellished with techniques like exponential smoothing and the mean absolute deviation used for calculation of the order point. Some of the production and inventory management people had read about MRP and were anxious to install it, but the engineering department said that the bills of material were not in any shape to put on a computer and that it would take several years before they could be corrected. The consultant had pointed out that because of the great product variety customer orders could not really be forecast and that order points on components would probably work as well or better.

The young man who was sent in by the consulting firm didn't seem particularly experienced in any area except systems. He could draw flow charts at a furious pace and seemed to know all the latest buzz words. He never went down to talk with the foremen in the shop and, in fact, made it very clear that this system was intended to get control *away* from *them* and that they would have to follow instructions to the letter when the computer reports started to come out. He made recommendations that resulted in transferring three of the oldest inventory clerks and giving retirement to two expediters.

It was this consultant who also insisted that the system be installed across the board. He said that this offered the advantage that people would have to sink or swim.

The system went on the air April 1 across the board, and by April 15, shipments had virtually stopped. One of the interesting features of the system as designed was that each assembly order that went into the computer reserved its components but *could not be released* until all components were available. It wasn't very long before there were many assembly orders in the system and none of them could be released. Since the earliest one had reserved the available components, the next one found fewer components available, and so on. There was no provision in the system to remove these orders without completely rebuilding the files. And with things in such a hectic state, this was hardly a desirable project to get started on.

The plant superintendent was the man of the hour when everything collapsed. He stepped forward, brought his foremen in to work early in the morning and kept them late at night. They pulled material out of the stockroom against customer orders, found out what the real shortages were, expedited material and finally got shipments out the door. They were not going out at the budgeted rate, but at least *something* was happening.

One of the people you talked to when you came on board was the materials manager. You asked him how he could have let this happen. While he was extremely upset by what had happened, his point was that he felt there was no way a large reputable consulting firm could have failed so badly. He had virtually delegated the responsibility to them for developing a system and, quite frankly, their representative had taken the initiative.

Recently, the consulting firm recommended that the materials manager be fired. They felt that he had not backed the system 100 percent and had been quick to let the foremen come in and go back to their manual methods for working around the system. They felt that the system simply had not been given a fair trial.

As the new general manager, you have a number of problems that you are facing. The division is paying twenty-eight thousand dollars a month for the computer and the activities that support it. This system is certainly no better than the manual system and, in many cases, seems to be worse. What do you think the chances are of reconstructing the old informal system? It is obvious that this is what really worked, since the manual system couldn't do a very effective job of putting proper priorities on components. On the other hand, should the present computer system be discarded in favor of a sound one? In short, the problem is to go backward or go forward—standing still is not a sound choice.

Should you keep the materials manager or fire him? What should you do about the consulting firm?

Since you have quite a bit of background in the production and inventory management area, sketch out the kind of system you think Croft Receiver requires. Justify why it would work better than the manual approach they have been using or the computer approach they have installed. Also give them some recommendations for working with a consultant in case they ever have to do that again.

**Case Study 2: The Dewey Stapler Company**

January 5, 1974

From: Martin Crane, Sales Manager

To: Allen Grace, President

Dear Allen:

Well, it has been a very disappointing year. We've missed our quota by 10 or 15 percent in virtually every district and this is the year I had such high hopes for. When we decided to open up four branch warehouses rather than shipping from our central location only, I was convinced that this would give us better customer service. The last of the warehouses was opened up last May, just before our peak summer season, so perhaps some of the problem is just not having enough experience with branch warehouses. But I think it goes deeper than that.

Our warehouse men are authorized to keep a one-month supply of inventory on hand. While I know you feel strongly that the substantial increase in inventory we had during the year was due to the warehouse program, I can't see why it requires any more inventory to keep a month's supply on hand in four branches and a main location than it did to keep a month's supply on hand back at the main location. A month's supply is a month's supply no matter how you look at it.

To my way of thinking, the real problem is customer service. Our salesmen are demoralized. They simply can't get the stock shipped out of the warehouses because the warehouses don't have it on hand. Forty percent of our customer orders, of course, are still being shipped out of the main location. Our warehouse people tell me that these customer orders get preference and their stock replenishment orders are pushed aside.

Allen, we've got to solve this problem. There's no sense in having a sales force if we can't have the stock to back them up. I propose the plant location be required to ship warehouse stocking orders just the same as they ship customer orders. They should treat the warehouses like a customer. In fact, the warehouses are their *biggest* customer and should be serviced accordingly. I propose also that the one-month inventory guideline be removed. Let the warehouse men stock whatever they think they need to support the salesmen. I would volunteer to have my district managers sit with the branch warehouse people to give them some idea of what they should really be ordering.

Allen, this branch warehouse program has been as big a disappointment to me as it has to you. I know you're concerned about the fact that inventories have been going up, but I frankly attribute that to poor management back at the plant. And, quite honestly, Allen, I don't think that people at the plant realize our problems out here in the field and are giving us the kind of support we need. Without it, we have no chance of making the sales quota. Instead of selling, I'm spending most of my time playing chaplain to a bunch of demoralized salesmen.

Sincerely,

Martin

From:   Robert Ellers, Inventory Manager

To:       Allen Grace, President

Dear Mr. Grace:

You asked me what my plans were to respond to Martin Crane's letter of January 5. I don't know where to start. This warehouse program has really torn us apart.

We thought that when branch warehouses were added, we would simply have to split some of the stock we had among the warehouses. Instead, we've had to build up the inventory very substantially. We don't get any plans from the warehouses at all. All we see is orders. We have no idea what their inventory position is when we get the orders and we only get them two to three weeks before we have to ship them. Then comes the moment of truth. We have a shortage on a particular item. Here's a customer order and also a warehouse stock replenishment order. Does the warehouse really need it? We know the customer does. In practice, I must admit we wind up waiting until the warehouse screams although we know we may very well be hurting customer service at the branch warehouses.

Mr. Grace, I'm more worried about *this* year than I was about last. Some of the warehouses that had been on the air since year before last showed a disturbing tendency to keep their inventories low during the off-season so that they could boast about their inventory turnover. Then during the peak season, they expect me to turn the faucet on back at the plant. We don't have enough storage space at the plant to build up the inventory required during the off-season in order to keep people working at a steady rate. We need this inventory buildup in order to give good service during the peak season. I've been told repeatedly by plant management that we must keep people working at a steady rate.

All this squabbling about inventory levels prompts me to suggest an approach. We normally would manufacture in a lot size that would be equivalent to about a three-month's supply. When we do that, why don't I just ship a three-month's supply out to each branch warehouse, and then we won't have to bother worrying about them until the next lot is manufactured. Then they can't complain that they're not getting their fair share.

One of the disturbing elements that you may not have heard about is that Frank, our Traffic Manager, has now suggested that we ship to the West Coast warehouses by sea. This would mean going through the Panama Canal and would substantially increase our lead time and reduce our flexibility. He says, "Flexibility is like motherhood. I'm talking a fifty-thousand-dollar savings in transportation costs, and if you guys have to work a little harder to make that happen, so be it."

Mr. Grace, I really am almost at my wit's end. Perhaps one of the things we ought to consider would be a computer system for tying all of the warehouses together so we could cover a shortage at one warehouse by shipping from another warehouse. Last September, I checked on items that were out of stock in the Atlanta warehouse and I found that virtually everyone of them was in adequate supply throughout the system; i.e., we either had them in Dallas, Los Angeles, Chicago, or back at the main plant. This type of computer system would be expensive, but perhaps this is the answer to our service problems.

Sincerely,

Robert Ellers

The Dewey Stapler Company has some very serious problems. There are a number of misconceptions about inventory management in the company that need to be corrected. Take the position of a consultant being called in by Allen Grace, the President. You have enough information in these letters to give him some very helpful recommendations.

### Case Study 3: Kadee Kitchens Company

Kadee Kitchens makes a wide variety of products. They started out making garbage disposal units, then dishwashers, and now a good deal of their business is in prefabricated custom kitchens. They make the counter tops with built-in ovens, the sink units, etc. Most of these are made to customer order and, frequently, some of the components, like the ovens, are purchased from outside appliance manufacturers. The following series of letters from Harold Stone, their new Manufacturing Vice President, to J. Leveritt Lull, their President, is self-explanatory.

October 5, 1973

J. Leveritt Lull:

It's really great to be with a division like Kadee. There are plenty of problems, but there's no question in my mind that we can solve them. Frankly, J. L., I see the same problems that I saw over at the Fallow Forge Division. Over at Fallow, as you know, we're making forgings primarily for the machine tool industry. Every bit of it was make-to-order so we didn't have the luxury of making some things to stock as you do here at Kadee. At Fallow, they weren't getting shipments out on time and we simply made people work to the schedule and got a very dramatic improvement. I guess you know about my past record so I won't bore you by bragging about the good results we had at Fallow!

I've been down to talk to the assembly foremen here and asked them why it's so difficult to get the shipments out every month. They tell me that the problem is parts shortages. I've been to ask the production control people and they've shown me their expedite lists and, quite honestly, most of the parts on those expedite lists, whether they come from our shops or from our vendors, are late. Here's the same old problem. People simply won't work to the schedules. With 68 percent of the parts late in the shop, it's no wonder that we are having trouble getting the shipments out on time. In fact, it's something of a miracle that we're only 15 percent behind schedule shipping assemblies!

The system that I want to install is called centralized dispatching. With this, we'll have data-collection terminals out on the shop floor and the operators will use these terminals to clock on and off each job. In the central dispatch area, we'll have output punches and timecard racks with a card for each operation lined up behind the work center. The dispatchers in the central location will get the work lined up in the proper priority by operation schedule date (this shows on the copy of a shop order that they get at central dispatching), and then they will call out to the shop floor two or three times a day and talk to the assistant foreman or floor dispatcher in some of the larger departments who will line the dispatch cards up in identical timecard racks at the floor dispatch station where we have the data-collection terminal.

We anticipate that it will take us four to five months to install this system by going "all out." I expect that the cost will run about thirty-six thousand dollars for systems design and installation (this includes programming by our computer staff to get reports showing us the percentage of late orders by work center department, vendor, etc.). Once we're on the air, the rental for the terminals will be twenty-six hundred dollars a month, but this will be partially offset by the number of keypunch operators we can save. There is a good chance we may get rid of several timekeepers also.

My system will give us a very precise control over the work-in-process. I wouldn't be surprised at all to see a reduction in work-in-process as a result. The objective, however, is to make people work to the dates on the orders so that we hit our schedule so that we get our shipments out on time.

By the way, J. L., one unpleasant thing that I'm going to have to do, and I know I have your backing, but thought that I should mention it to you anyway, concerns Freddie Alton. He has been with the company for many, many years, but as a production control manager, he simply doesn't fill the bill, in my opinion. He's a great "firefighter." Many shipments do go out the door because Freddie knows how to get one of his buddies in the model shop to drill an extra hole in another part and replace a part that was scrapped. But, frankly, Freddie is the most unsystematic guy you have ever met. He has shown no interest in the new system and I just wanted to let you know that as of December 1 he will be transferred to the estimating department.

July 17, 1974

J. Leveritt Lull:

I wanted this to be on your desk as soon as you got back from vacation. Last Monday, when we started up after the July 4 plant shutdown, we had what I call a wildcat strike, although the union prefers not to call it that. We had everything pretty well settled by Thursday, but it was a most harrowing experience. When the shop floor system went on the air, that seemed to precipitate the whole thing. Some of the shop people even poured coffee in the data collection terminals. I think one of the real unspoken issues was the problem of "kitties." As you know, with our incentive system, there is always the chance that one of the machine operators will have a bad day. As a consequence, they usually save a few jobs over from the previous days to help even things out. These "kitties" are intolerable with the kind of system that we are trying to make work; we must have work reported as it *is done*! We probably should have faced up to this issue before trying to install my system.

I've talked with our industrial engineering people and the union representatives and we feel that some adjustments can be built into our incentive system to give the operators a little more security. While this may cost a little more, we obviously need to do it if we're going to have any kind of a control system in the factory.

One thing I must admit, J. L., you kept emphasizing the need to educate people so that they understood what we were doing, and much as we felt we were doing that job, I don't think we did it well enough or explained it sufficiently to the shop people. I guess if I had to do it the next time around, we would have a couple of foremen install this shop floor system and we would explain it more thoroughly to the union stewards.

By the way, we've decided to add a few more shop dispatchers and to make the timekeepers we planned to get rid of into shop dispatchers since we've found that the amount of communication between the shop floor and the central dispatching group is a lot greater than we ever anticipated it would be.

Harold

September 14, 1974

J. Leveritt Lull:

I just wanted to tell you that I thought your comments at the staff meeting this morning were extremely unfair. I don't think we've had our system on the air long enough to see results and so I think it's far too early for you to make the kind of judgment that you made in front of the entire staff group.

Harold

February 21, 1975

J. Leveritt Lull:

I found our discussion in the hall today very disturbing. You're correct in stating that shipments have been down and that our backlog is building up. You are also correct in stating that our customer service level is not as good as it was at this time last year. I must admit also that inventories have started to climb. But I think that this is *the good sign*. Right now, 78 percent of all our stock parts are on hand in the stockroom. Last year at this time only 56 percent were on hand.

Frankly, J. L., this has been a most difficult experience for me. I've been trying to install a system with very little cooperation from anyone except the data-processing people and I think it's only fair for you to recognize that your lack of confidence in the system is probably one of the biggest problems I've faced. It's common knowledge in the shop that you'd like to have this system thrown out, that you feel it's costing too much money and that you are convinced that it's the reason we haven't met our shipping budget for the last several months. I can't agree with that. It seems apparent to me that getting people to work to the schedule is the most important task we have around here. It may take us time to see the results, but we need a little more time and a more positive attitude from everyone if we're going to achieve these goals.

Speaking of a positive attitude, J. L., I'm going to be presenting you some plans for reorganization very shortly. I think we have some poor attitudes in the production and inventory control area and there are people in the shop who, frankly, haven't given me the kind of support that I need.

Harold

What do you suppose the real production and inventory control problems are at Kadee Kitchens? Where would you look to verify these conclusions? What would you look for? What evidence have you seen in Harold's letters that supports your conclusions? Should this system be discarded? What are your recommendations for a future course of action at Kadee Kitchens?

# Appendix C: Classical Cliché and Nostrums

Until recently, production and inventory management was never a real discipline. Very few people who got into it had any specific education in the field. (Probably even if they had, with the type of education that was available in this field over the years, they would not have been any better off!) The result was that the typical production and inventory control person learned his own company's approach, which was usually some sort of a home-brewed system almost always built around the limitations of manual systems. Because there were oldtimers around who knew how to make an informal system work, things generally were not too bad for many years. But then they became worse and worse as an ever-increasingly complex product line and greater demands of the business made it more difficult to run with informal systems.

As a consequence, most manufacturing companies have run into problems in the production and inventory management area in recent years. It is extremely likely that they have been able to identify only the symptoms rather than the real diseases. Listed below are many of the common cliches that are used by sincere, hard-working people who are trying to get at the root of the problem. Since they have been used over and over again by many companies, it is worth passing on the experience of others.

### Category 1: Perennial Favorites

*"We're different—we're a job shop."* Most people tend to get a very parochial view of their own problems and tend to think they are unique. Virtually every manufacturing company can be defined as a job shop from some point of view. While products are extremely different, the logistics of

250

manufacturing tend to be very similar from company to company. As a consequence, the solutions to the problems tend to be very similar too.

*"It would be great to have a new system, but we could really work our present system a lot better."* This is one of the great all-time half-truths. It's important to define *which* system is being referenced here. Most companies would be in serious trouble if they ran their formal system a lot better than they are running it now, since that one does not really count! Making people work to due dates that are not right would not accomplish much. If any quick-and-dirty approaches have to be used, the emphasis should be put on temporarily improving the *informal* system. Experience has shown that there are no shortcuts to getting substantial systems improvements without the right kind of tools to work with. Many companies have wasted a lot of effort in trying to get short-term results, and a year later they are usually no better off than they were. If this effort had been put into developing better systems at the start, better results could be forthcoming in less than a year. This does not mean that while new systems are being developed and installed, operating people can relax. It does mean that they need to work the *informal system* harder until such time as the formal system is sound.

*"Let's hire a consultant to cure our problems."* It would be nice to be able to subcontract management. Unfortunately, consultants should play the role of educator and catalyst and should not take the initiative away from the users in developing a system. Most large consulting firms find it difficult to play the role of catalyst since they make their money by renting out people. The more people for the longer time, the more money they make. This is often at odds with the best interests of the client. The company that thinks that a consultant can accept the responsibility for developing a system for them simply does not understand that systems are tools for people, tools that people must understand themselves if they are to use them intelligently. On the other hand, there are companies that will never use a consultant. They tend to be very insular and spend a lot of time reinventing the wheel. A little consulting can be the catalyst that makes the difference; a lot of it almost inevitably spells failure.

*"Let's reorganize!"* Too often, reorganization is an attempt to get people to do a better job of working toward the company objectives. If this is the problem, then better objective setting and a formal system that can be used to measure performance would be far more likely to generate a satisfactory, lasting solution.

*"Let's cut the inventory by 10 percent across the board."* While everyone deplores this type of action, there is no question that it usually does result in an inventory reduction. Of course, it usually also results in a reduction in customer service soon after and the net effect is to then go on an inventory building spree to restore the service. If the level of inventory required to give customer service seems too high, the chances are that the people in production and inventory management do not have the right tools or do not know how to use them. It is more than likely that they do not even know what the right tools would be. An education program so that they know what the standard tools of the trade have become would be a good place to start. Then the development of an effective system that could enable management to really have a handle on inventory investment and get a better return on their inventory investment could follow.

## Category 2: From the production point of view

*"Our expediters do pretty well at getting some of the jobs through, but they just can't get all of them through—we need more expediters."* Expediting is a self-perpetuating function. People start with red tags and when they have red tags on everything, they start using green tags to identify the *real* rush jobs. Expediters try to follow up the jobs that are really hot, but of course they don't insure that all of the jobs get out the door on time, and to them it seems that a few more hands would cure the problems. A few more hands working in *manufacturing*, however, is more likely to solve the problem. Expediters do not cut chips. They do not make anything. They may, through some exhortations, occasionally convince a foreman to work overtime or do something else that will add to the capacity temporarily. But the real problem is lack of a real, good priority planning and capacity planning function. All the expediting in the world will not make up for this lack.

*"Let's pull the material out of the stockroom four weeks before it's needed."* "Staging" or "accumulating" material is the ancient technique for finding out what the manufacturing shortages are. Unfortunately, it never pinpoints the shortages soon enough and there is always someone who thinks the answer is to pull material further in advance to try to find out earlier what the shortages are. The result, however, is longer shortage lists, which just compound confusion with commotion. Staging material will not do a good job of showing what the *relative* priorities are, and, of course, it

tends to be a very inflexible system. MRP on the computer is really a technique for *projecting* what the shortages are going to be months in advance, and using this information to order and reschedule material. The advantage the computer has in doing this is the fact that it can recompute these priorities regularly. It's pretty difficult to put the staged material back in the stockroom every week and pull it all over again as needs change.

"*Let's print out a list of late orders and force purchasing and manufacturing to work on these.*" When the formal priority planning system has broken down, it tends to give the impression that it is really working fine if only people would follow it. A formal priority planning system that does not work generates lots of orders that are not needed. As a result, these orders wind up being late in the shop. When they finally are needed and turn up on a shortage list, the expediter looks at the shortage list and sees that all the jobs on it are late. He does not notice that most of the other work in the factory is late, too, and that he is expediting only a very small portion of the late jobs. His natural conclusion is that "if people would only work to the schedule, everything would be fine."

"*We don't pay our stockroom people enough to do a good job of handling inventory transactions.*" It may very well be that the wrong people are in the stockroom, but pay usually has little to do with it. The teller in the bank is not particularly well paid, but someone told him the day he came on board that management wanted the records kept right and that this was his responsibility. Accurate inventory records start with the accuracy of stockroom transactions. An improvement in this area starts with management letting it be known that they really think that this is important.

"*Our inventory control system isn't perfect, but it isn't really all that bad. We really need to work on capacity planning and shop floor control.*" Here again, the breakdown of the formal priority planning system tends to make it look like a shop floor control system would help by forcing people to work to the dates on the orders. Some production control people conclude that since there are so many orders that are late in the shop, they really need a machine loading system to make sure that adequate capacity is available. Unfortunately, neither of these areas can be improved very significantly until there is a priority planning system that generates valid need dates and keeps them valid. *The truth will out on the firing line.* When order due dates are late, but they are not really needed, no amount of systems effort in the capacity planning or priority control area will make up for the deficiencies in the priority planning function

*"If we just had a little more lead time, we could get everything out on time."*
Lead time inflation is a classical pitfall for manufacturing people. Increasing the lead time generates orders sooner, increases the backlog, which adds to the lead time. With an effective MRP system, an increasing backlog of open shop and purchase orders is not too serious a problem. The increased orders will be put in their proper time frame and if the master schedule is handled properly, they will be constantly reevaluated and kept in their proper time frames. Unfortunately, most companies do not have a good MRP based system and increasing their lead time will very seriously aggravate their priority problems.

### Category 3: From the systems/data processing point of view

*"We don't have anybody in manufacturing who really knows enough to develop successful systems. We'll have to do it for them."* Any company that doesn't have people who could develop successful systems in their manufacturing organization has little chance of having anybody capable of using good systems. Systems developed by anyone other than the user inevitably fail. It *is* true that users generally don't know enough to even know what kind of system to ask for, but they should be given the proper education so that they *will* know what the standard tools of the trade are and will be able to take the initiative in developing these tools.

*"We need to write up the procedures for the present system and document it."* Since the present system is usually a formal system that doesn't really work, this is an exercise in futility. Writing up the procedures in the hopes that this will get people to work to the system ignores the basic, fundamental issue: *the formal systems in production and inventory control usually were irrelevant.* It was the informal systems that were used by the people on the firing line.

*"Our people don't understand much about computers. We must send them off to computer school."* Teaching manufacturing people computer languages like COBOL, FORTRAN, and teaching them octal, hexadecimal, how many bits will fit on a disc drive, and other useless information does little to enhance their ability to participate intelligently in the development of effective computer-based systems. They need to be taught *the applications*, not to be awed with a bunch of technical trivia that means nothing to them.

*"What we really need is finite loading."* This is a technique that is particularly appealing to technically oriented people. It is highly sophisticated,

very, very complex, and chews up vast amounts of computer time. Functionally, it is a technique for recalculating priorities to make them fit into available capacity. *No company should ever* put in finite loading before they have MRP and capacity planning. Obviously, if they do not have a valid priority planning function, there is no sense in remassaging these priorities. On the other hand, if they do not know what capacity they really need, it could be disastrous to start fitting orders around the capacity that is available. The finite loading approach has dubious value under any circumstances, but certainly is *not* the place to start.

*"The reason our systems do not work is that management does not enforce discipline."* There has been far too much attention paid to the technical side of systems and far too little paid to the people side of systems. Production and inventory management systems are tools that people have to use. No amount of discipline will force people to use tools that don't make sense to them. This is one of the reasons that oversophisticated systems inevitably fail to work.

# Appendix D: Diagnosing Production and Inventory Control Problems

There are many problems that can keep a production and inventory management system from functioning satisfactorily. People usually do not know how to diagnose these problems properly and, in fact, frequently suggest solutions to the problems that are likely to aggravate them even worse (see Appendix C). The best way to diagnose the real production and inventory management problems is to use the framework of priority and capacity planning and control that has been used throughout this book.

The following checklist is not intended to be comprehensive, but is intended to indicate the most likely cause of production and inventory management problems. Keep in mind that priority planning is a prerequisite. Without a formal priority planning system that works, there is no chance of having capacity planning that is credible, and obviously no chance of a formal capacity or priority control system that truly functions. Few companies had manual systems that generated a valid priority plan. Mechanized versions of these systems usually perpetuated the problem. As a consequence, this is the first and most likely place to look for problems, even though the symptoms may seem to be in other areas. The following diagnostic checklist should prove helpful to the executive trying to diagnose his own problems:

1. *Does the formal priority planning system really work?*
   A. Can the shop and vendors actually work to the formal priority planning system, or do they have "due dates" which are superseded by "shortage lists" which are superseded by "hot jobs"?

256

Typical symptoms of a priority planning system that does not work are:

1) Material is pulled from the stockroom before it is needed and "accumulated" to determine what the shortages are. This type of accumulation is expensive, confusing, can generate false shortages, and is extremely unresponsive to reschedule changes. (How do you put all the material back on the shelf when a particular order is rescheduled to a later date?) Companies resort to accumulation when their formal priority planning system does not function and also use it because they do not believe their inventory records.

2) Expediters spend most of their time writing out hot lists.

3) There are many late orders in the purchasing department and in the shop and only *some* of these are being expedited.

B. Check for these causes:

1) Is an order point system being used on dependent demand items? There is *no way* that this can generate priorities that are legitimate.

2) If MRP is being used, is it at least a weekly recalculation in time periods no greater than one week? If it is not, there is no chance that the MRP system will actually act as a priority planning system. It may very well *order* material, but it cannot possibly be sensitive enough to keep the priorities correct on material that is already on order.

3) Assuming that a properly designed MRP system is being used, if it does not function satisfactorily as a priority planning system, make sure that the master schedule is realistic, that it is not overstated, that material is rescheduled when it is not actually needed, etc. Make sure that inventory records are as accurate as they can possibly be. Check the accuracy of bills of material and the structure of the bills of material. If the product is modular, are the bills of material modular?

2. *Does the formal capacity planning system work?*

The chances are, in the typical company, that capacity planning may *look* like a problem area when, in fact, it is the priority planning that is the problem. In the event that there is a large "past due" in the capacity plan and that shop people do not believe it, the most likely problem is that the formal priority planning system does not work. It could also be overstated lead times or it *could* be a genuine capacity problem.

A good point to check is what percentage of the components in process are late vs. what percentage of the assemblies are late in a company making an assembled product. A small percentage of late components could make a lot of assemblies late. In most companies, the fact that a large percentage of the components are late and a small percentage of the assemblies are really late is a dead giveaway that the priority planning system is not functioning properly. If it has been determined that the priority planning input is correct and the problem really appears to be in the capacity planning area, then check:

A. Are *planned orders* from MRP or the time phased order point being introduced into the capacity plan? In the event that this is a company making a one-piece product, some type of capacity forecast separate from the materials forecast may be required. This can frequently be done by having some type of "models" of the product and simply forecasting incoming business in terms of a few categories of these models. Remember that capacity plans must stretch out far enough into the future for shop people to be able to take action; otherwise, they will simply react to backlogs. By definition this will mean that backlogs will have to become very large before capacity will be changed.

B. Are the operating people using the capacity plan properly? Supervisors, foremen, superintendents, manufacturing managers, plant managers, and even manufacturing vice presidents usually got their manufacturing experience in a world where the informal system was the only one that worked at all. They frequently find it difficult to adjust quickly to capacity planning information that is meaningful. Almost every company that has installed a good production and inventory control system finds that the first substantial increase in business catches the operating people off guard. They have numbers that really tell them what should be done, yet they react too slowly to them because they simply do not believe the numbers.

3. *Does the capacity control system function properly?*

Assuming that the priority planning system has been examined and is working satisfactorily and that the capacity planning system is working satisfactorily, the most likely problem with capacity control is that it simply does not exist at all. In the classical approaches to production and inventory control, capacity control was nonexistent. A capacity control system should show a leveled, practical capacity plan by work center at least two or three months out into the future, and it should then monitor actual output against this plan. The input/output format is recommended because it does focus attention on backlogs and tends to show clearly whether or not work is available at a given work center. Nevertheless, output control alone has been used satisfactorily as a capacity control device.

4. *Is the priority control system the problem?*

Once again, the chances are that the priority planning system is the problem area. In practice, for every 100 companies that start working on their priority control system, 99 of them really have a problem in priority planning. Nevertheless, priority control problems could exist. Check the following:

A. Assuming that the priority planning system is being updated at least weekly using either MRP or the time phased order point, are these updated priorities being conveyed to the shop floor via a daily dispatch list? Daily is recommended so that the dispatch list will show where the jobs actually are.

B. Is it a simple, straightforward dispatch list designed to support people's activities rather than one that has complex scheduling algorithms that are supposed to replace human judgment? The best type of priority control system blends the computer's ability to update the pure priorities with the human ability to cope with the real-world problems of a factory, like machine breakdowns, scrap, absenteeism, broken tooling, and the like.

C. Do people support it? In a few instances, perfectly valid priority control systems have not functioned properly because the systems were imposed on shop people rather than sold to them as a tool to help them. In the final analysis, priority control—doing the right jobs at the right time—is the responsibility of the foreman. Providing him with the proper information to accomplish this objective is the responsibility of the production and inventory management department. Foremen need to be educated and shown the advantages of a formal priority control system over the confusion of the informal expediting system. They need to be involved and assigned the responsibility for making this type of system work, rather than seeing it as one more interesting intellectual exercise for the computer/systems people.

Frequently, systems that are not successful have no significant technical flaws. It is a mistake to believe that systems will work properly just because they are good systems. If the users do not understand them and want them, no system is good enough to produce results by itself.

# Glossary

A comprehensive dictionary of production control, inventory control, data processing, and related terms is available from the American Production and Inventory Control Society: Suite 504 Watergate Building, 2600 Virginia Avenue, N.W., Washington, D.C. 20037.

**ABC classification.** A list of the items in inventory ranked by annual usage in dollars. The result shows that a small percentage of the items (20 percent for example) will usually represent the bulk of the dollars. Usually three categories of items are chosen. The high value or *A* items are ordered frequently and given close attention while the low value or *C* items are usually ordered less frequently, kept in larger supplies, and thus require less attention. Also called the 80/20 rule, or distribution by value.

**Accumulation.** See Staging.

**Adaptive smoothing.** A mathematical forecasting technique that uses exponential and particularly trigonometric functions to describe sales patterns. It has not proved to be particularly useful in practice since for all its mathematical sophistication, it still has the weakness of all statistical forecasting techniques in that it assumes that the future will be like the past.

**Aggregate inventory management.** Managing the inventory investment in total dollars; costing out the MRP to project total dollar inventory investment by product line; making lot size or safety stock decisions, for example, based on the aggregate inventory investment compared with the aggregate ordering cost that would result.

**Allocation.** In an MRP system an allocated item is one for which a picking order has been released to the stockroom but not yet sent out of the stockroom. It is an "uncashed stockroom requisition."

261

**Alpha factor.** The weighting factor that is applied against the most recent sales data to compute the exponential smoothing average.

**Anticipation inventory.** Inventory built ahead of requirements to level production, for new product introduction, to support a promotion program, etc.

**Available inventory.** See Projected available balance.

**Back order.** When a required item is not in inventory, an order created to withdraw it when it becomes available is called a back order.

**Backward scheduling.** Establishing schedule dates for operations or groups of operations using scheduling rules and working back from the required due date.

**Beta factor.** An exponent used to adjust the MAD when the forecast interval over which the MAD was computed is different from the lead time interval.

**Bill of materials.** A listing of the components required to manufacture a product. A bill of materials is similar to a parts list except that it usually shows the product structure, i.e., it would show that raw material is used to make fabricated components, the fabricated components go into subassemblies, the subassemblies then go into an assembly, etc.

**Blanket order.** A long-term commitment to a vendor for material against which short-term releases will be generated to satisfy requirements.

**Buckets.** Data-processing slang for the time *periods* used in time phased MRP.

**Capacity control.** Monitoring actual output against plan for a work center or centers.

**Capacity requirements planning.** A time phased MRP not only releases orders, but it also generates planned orders that are used to create lower-level material requirements. Capacity requirements plans can be made then by taking into account the hours by work center by time period needed to produce both the open shop orders and planned shop orders.

**Capacity planning.** See Capacity requirements planning.

**Central dispatching.** A dispatching function that places groups of dispatchers in one central location where they determine the priority of jobs and relay this information to the shop floor. Feedback from the shop floor, usually via intercoms or data-collection terminals to the central location, keeps the dispatchers up-to-date on job progress.

**Central planner.** A production and inventory management person who usually works in an office with the material requirements plans and the capacity requirements plans.

**Component inventory.** The word component embraces any inventory item that is used to make another, thus a raw material, a part, or subassembly can be a component of another product.

**Critical ratio.** A dynamic priority technique originally conceived in an environment of order point inventory control. The idea was to review the inventory and the progress of the job periodically, usually weekly, and to revise the priority accordingly. As it became more and more apparent that order point inventory control was an obsolescent technique, critical ratio was adapted to be used with MRP. It expresses the priorities that MRP regularly updates, in a ratio form.

**Cycle count.** Regular, usually daily, counts of items in stores. Typically a cycle count approach would count some items each day so that all items were counted at least once a year.

**Demand filter.** A technique for signaling any extraordinarily large demands. Usually a quantity that is a function of the mean absolute deviation is established, and if demand for any given period is greater than this quantity, an exception message is generated.

**Dependent demand.** Demand on an item is called dependent when it can be calculated from the need to manufacture or replenish inventory for a higher-level item. A part that goes into a subassembly has dependent demand. If it is also sold directly to customers as a service part, it also has independent demand. A raw material that is later converted into semifinished inventory is released and has dependent demand. The demand on the semifinished inventory is likely to be dependent demand unless that semifinished inventory is sold directly to customers. Dependent demand requirements should be *calculated* using techniques like MRP rather than *forecast* using order point techniques.

**Deterministic demand.** See Dependent demand.

**Discrete lot sizing.** Lot sizes in an MRP system that are equal to the requirements for one or more time periods.

**Dispatching.** The selection and assignment of jobs at an individual work center.

**Dispatch list.** A schedule for a work center usually generated by computer, usually issued daily, showing the priority sequence of jobs to be done at that work center.

**Distribution by value.** See ABC classification.

**Distribution requirements planning.** Material requirements planning (MRP) was originally developed as a way to order material to support assembly operations. After it had been in use for a number of years people began to recognize that distribution inventories also have levels. Branch warehouses draw inventory from a distribution center which in turn replenishes its inventory by ordering in lots from factories. Distribution requirements planning is simply the term given to MRP when it is used to properly time phase these dependent demands on finished goods inventory.

**Double smoothing.** Synonym for second order smoothing.

**Economic order quantity.** The mathematical computation for finding the least total cost lot size. The EOQ formula solves for the lot size where ordering cost and inventory carrying cost are equal.

**EOQ.** Economic order quantity.

**Exchange curves.** See Trade-off curves.

**Expediting.** Trying to get jobs rushed through the shop to cover shortages or to meet shipping requirements. Expediting is a bad word in most companies because the entire system has often degenerated into an expediting system. The expediter typically finds out what material is needed too late and thus is chronically causing disruptions in factory schedules.

**Explosion.** An extension of an assembly or subassembly bill of materials into the total of each of the components required to manufacture a given quantity of the assembly or subassembly.

**Explosion chart.** Matrix bill of materials.

**Exponential smoothing.** A rather pretentious name for a moving weighted average.

**Exposures.** Dividing the lot size into the annual usage determines how many times inventory will have to be replenished per year. Each of these replenishment periods "exposes" the inventory to the chance of a stock out, thus large lot sizes require less safety stock, small lot sizes require more.

**Extrinsic forecast.** A forecast based on external factors such as basing forecasts of automotive parts sales on automobile registrations.

**Finished goods inventory.** Product that is ready for shipment and is carried in inventory in anticipation of customer orders.

**Finite loading.** Conceptually the term means putting no more work into a factory than the factory can be expected to execute. This is a function of master scheduling. The specific term usually refers to a computer technique that involves automatic shop priority revision in order to level load operation by operation.

**Firm planned order.** In material requirements planning, a planned order explodes material requirements to lower levels and is rescheduled automatically, as opposed to a scheduled receipt, which does not explode material requirements since it is assumed that material was available when the order was issued (unless a back order for a particular component had to be created) and is *not* rescheduled automatically. Since the planned order at any level generates the requirements at the lower levels, it really acts as a master schedule. Good MRP requires that the master schedule be controlled very carefully to represent what is actually going to be done. Thus the firm planned order is a planned order that can be frozen in quantity and time so that it does not change without human intervention.

**First order smoothing.** See Exponential smoothing. The term first order merely differentiates the basic weighted moving average from the more sophisticated second order smoothing.

**Floating order point.** An order point that is recomputed on a regular basis usually using exponential smoothing to update the average demand figure and the mean absolute deviation to update forecast error.

**Fluctuation inventory.** Inventory carried as a buffer against fluctuating demand or flow. Safety stock and work in process queues are examples.

**Forward scheduling.** Using scheduling rules to determine the schedule dates for operations or a series of operations working forward from the start date, and thus generating a completion date.

**Gross requirements.** Material requirements that have not been reduced ("netted") by deducting the on-hand and on-order quantities.

**Indented bill of materials.** A bill of materials that is printed with the level "0" items usually shown in the left-most column, level-one components indented to the right, etc.

**Independent demand.** Demand for an inventory item is considered independent when it is unrelated to any higher-level item that the company manufactures or stocks. The demand for a service part that is shipped directly to customers would be considered independent. On the other hand, if that service part were shipped to a branch warehouse, the demand on the service part would be a function of branch warehouse replenishment and thus would be considered dependent. Generally, independent demand items are those that are carried in finished goods inventories, although not all finished goods items are necessarily independent demand items, because much of their demand might derive from branch warehouses, for example. Independent demand items can be replenished using stock replenishment systems like the order point, although today the time phased order point would probably be used.

**Infinite loading.** Showing the work behind work centers in the time periods required regardless of the capacity available to perform this work. The term infinite loading is considered to be obsolete today, although the specific computer programs used to do infinite loading, when they take into account planned orders as well as released orders, can now be used to perform the technique called capacity requirements planning. Infinite loading was a gross misnomer to start with, implying that a load could be put into a factory regardless of its availability to perform. The poor terminology obscured the fact that it is necessary to generate capacity requirements and compare these with available capacity before trying to adjust requirements to capacity.

**Input/output control.** A simple technique for capacity control where actual output is compared with planned output developed by capacity requirements planning. The input to a work center is also monitored to see if it corresponds with plans so that work centers will not be expected to generate output when material is not available.

**Intrinsic forecasts.** A forecast based on internal factors, such as an average, is called intrinsic.

**Inventory accounting.** Maintaining inventory balance records; what used to be called perpetual inventory records.

**Inventory control.** A rather nebulous term sometimes used to refer to *inventory accounting*, sometimes used to describe order point based replenishment systems as distinguished from MRP systems; properly used it means having the right material in inventory to meet needs. In an MRP-based system, inventory control is a by-product of priority planning.

**Inventory turnover.** See Turnover rate.

**Item master record.** A computer term for the inventory record.

**Lead time.** The time it takes to replenish an item in inventory. The overall lead time starts from the moment it is determined that the item needs to be replenished until the time that it is determined that it is back in inventory and once more available.

**Lead time offset.** Time phased MRP shows planned orders in their proper release time period based on the lead time. A planned order is created when the projected available balance goes below zero or safety stock; in other words, planned orders are offset by lead time from net requirements.

**Least total cost.** A discrete lot-sizing technique that compares the inventory carrying cost for a given lot size with the ordering cost and chooses the lot size where the carrying cost is most nearly equal to the set-up cost.

**Least unit cost.** An obsolete discrete lot-sizing technique that adds ordering cost and inventory carrying costs for each trial lot size and divides by the number of units in the lot size, picking the lot size with the lowest unit cost.

**Levels.** A bill of material must be properly structured to represent the way its product is made. In the United States, the final product is called the "0" level. The subassemblies, for example, that go into the final assembly, are at level 1, their components are at level 2, etc.

**Load center.** See Work center.

**Loading.** Measuring the backlog or "load" behind work centers. Loading has been superseded by capacity requirements planning, which puts the emphasis on forecasting capacity requirements rather than just adding up backlog.

**Loading to finite capacity.** See Finite loading.

**Loading to infinite capacity.** See Infinite loading.

**Lot-size inventory.** This is the inventory that exists because most items are made in lot sizes rather than at the same rate at which they will be consumed. The average lot size inventory investment is approximately equal to one-half the lot size for independent demand items.

**MAD.** See Mean absolute deviation.

**Management science.** Synonym for operations research.

**Master production schedule.** See Master schedule.

**Master schedule.** The build schedule, stated in bill of material (or bill of material module) numbers, that drives the MRP—and consequently the capacity planning systems.

**Materials management.** This is an organizational concept that involves putting all of the functions concerned with the movement of materials, i.e., production control, inventory control, traffic, stores, materials handling, purchasing, etc., under one manager. The rationale is that this avoids conflicts among groups with different objectives.

**Materials planning.** Obsolescent term for MRP.

**Matrix bill of material.** A chart made up from the bills of material for a number of products in the same or similar families. It is arranged in a matrix with parts in columns and assemblies in rows (or vice versa) so that requirements for common components can be summarized conveniently.

**Mean absolute deviation.** This is an approximation to the standard deviation (MAD times 1.25 approximates the standard deviation). It is more convenient to work with since there is no square-root calculation involved. This makes it particularly convenient to update the MAD using techniques like exponential smoothing. The mean absolute deviation is calculated by averaging the difference between the forecast demand and the actual demand. "Mean" means average, "absolute" means regardless of whether the deviation was plus or minus, "deviation" refers to the difference between the forecast and the actual demand.

**Min/max system.** This is a stock replenishment system where the minimum is actually an order point. When stock reaches this minimum level, enough material is ordered to bring it up to the maximum, thus a minimum is an order point and the maximum is the order point plus the order quantity.

**Modular bill of material.** A bill of material used for master scheduling that expresses the material requirements for a product without showing the final configuration of the product. Modular bills of material for an automobile, for example, would list the engines, the transmissions, the body styles, the upholstery options, etc., rather than attempting to show the final configuration of a specific automobile. Modular bills of material are particularly useful for material requirements planning where the final configuration of the product is extremely difficult to forecast.

**MRP.** Material requirements planning.

**Material requirements planning.** Computers were used shortly after their introduction into manufacturing companies to explode material requirements or do "requirement generation." With the introduction of time phasing, these material requirements could be expressed in detail in specific time periods, usually weeks. By this time netting out gross requirements against on-hand and in-process inventory had become well-accepted technology. Modern MRP, therefore, is an approach for calculating material requirements not only to generate replenishment orders, but also to reschedule open orders to meet changing requirements. Today it is thought of more as a scheduling technique than an inventory ordering technique.

**Net change MRP.** Material requirements planning on a true exception basis. The net change concept specifies that a partial explosion will be triggered by a change in inventory or requirements or open order status. A scrap ticket, for example, reducing the quantity of material on order would generate a new net requirement, thus triggering a partial explosion down through the lower inventory levels of materials. The net change system is a transaction-driven system. While theoretically the net change system would be a continuous processing type of system, in practice net change is usually done in daily batch mode. See also Requirements alteration.

**Netting.** Deducting gross requirements from the amount on hand and on order in order to generate the true material needs or net requirements.

**Offset.** See Lead time offset.

**Operations research.** The attempt to use statistical and mathematical techniques to quantify business decisions. The techniques of statistical inventory control such as exponential smoothing, the use of techniques like the mean absolute deviation to quantify forecast error, and the use of simulation are all generally considered operations research techniques. Synonym is: management science.

**OR.** See Operations research.

**Order point.** A quantity that is established for reordering purposes. When the total stock on hand plus on order falls below the order point, a new supply is ordered. The order point is computed by extending the estimated demand over the replenishment lead time and adding a safety stock to account for forecast error.

**Part period balancing.** Another name for the least total cost lot sizing technique.

**Parts list.** A simple listing of the parts that go into an assembled product, usually without any product structuring shown.

**Pegging.** Showing what items at higher levels caused specific requirements in an MRP output report.

**Periodic visual review.** See Visual review.

**Period order quantity.** Time phased MRP makes it convenient to express order quantities in terms of time periods. MRP will then add up the net requirements for these time periods and convert them to a lot size that will reflect some of the requirements for this time period. The time period to be used in the period order quantity calculation can be determined using a standard economic order quantity formula based on total annual usage and then converting the lot size quantity into a lot size in terms of time periods. For example, an item with a 12,000-unit annual usage might have a 3,000-unit lot size as calculated by the square-root EOQ formula. This would mean that the item would be ordered four times a year, thus the period order quantity to be used with MRP would be 13.

**Physical inventory.** A count of the actual inventory on hand in order to reconcile it to the book figures. Usually this is done annually for auditing purposes to be sure that the financial records accurately reflect the assets of the company.

**Picking.** Collecting material from a stores area to satisfy a shop or customer order.

**PICS.** A set of concepts supported by some application programs developed by IBM. The acronym stands for production information and control system.

**Planned order.** In a time phased MRP system, "gross requirements" are deducted from the inventory on hand and on order (scheduled receipts) to project an available balance. When requirements exceed the amount on hand and on order, a negative balance or net requirement results. The net requirement is converted to a lot size if necessary, and is then offset by the lead time to create a planned order release. Planned orders at one level in the product structure become requirements at the lower level.

**Planned order release.** A planned order shown in the time period when it should be released (i.e., offset) in an MRP output report. A planned order release is really the net requirement lot sized and offset for lead time. Lower-level components must be on hand when the subassembly replenishment order is released, thus planned order releases at one level in the product structure generate material requirements in the proper time periods at lower levels.

**POQ.** See Period order quantity.

**Priority control.** Follow-up in manufacturing and purchasing to be sure the right jobs are being worked on and will be received on schedule.

**Priority planning.** When MRP was first developed, it was considered to be an ordering system. Then it became recognized that it could also handle rescheduling. Today, we recognize that the most serious deficiency we faced before the computer was available was the inability to schedule properly and that this was due to the fact that the inventory system launched orders while the production control system consisted primarily of expediting. As MRP saw more and more use in practice, it became evident that the real power of the technique was its ability not only to order material at the right time and to establish the correct due dates on the shop and purchase orders when they were issued, but also to keep these dates correct and in line with the latest requirements. The term priority planning was coined to describe this function.

**Probabilistic demand.** See Independent demand.

**Production plan.** Setting the level of manufacturing operations, usually by product group or in some other broad terms. Production plans are established in units, dollars, or hours, but the term is used to describe a general type of planning that is not as detailed as capacity requirements planning.

**Product structure.** The way materials go into the product during its manufacture. A typical product structure, for example, would show raw material being converted into fabricated components, components being put together to make subassemblies, subassemblies going into assemblies, etc.

**Projected available balance.** In an MRP output report, the amount on hand is projected into the future by deducting each period's requirements and adding scheduled receipts.

**Purchase order.** An order going to a vendor authorizing the vendor to deliver one or more items.

**Purchase requisition.** A document usually generated by production and/or inventory control personnel authorizing the purchasing department to issue a purchase order for material.

**Quick deck.** A technique for calculating gross material requirements down through all the levels of the product structure without netting requirements at any level. A crude technique dating back to the punched card era when true MRP was virtually impractical.

**Regeneration.** The oldest and most common form of MRP where the entire master schedule is periodically reexploded down through the bills of material, usually once a week, and netted out against on-hand and on-order inventory to determine what net requirements are. At the same time, open orders that are out of phase with requirements are noted so that they can be considered for rescheduling. Compare regeneration with net change and requirements alteration.

**Reorder point.** See Order point.

**Requirements.** See Gross requirements; Net requirements.

**Requirements alteration.** Another exception type approach to MRP where a change in requirements at any level of the product structure will trigger a partial explosion to lower levels. Note that requirements alteration, unlike net change, is not truly transaction driven. A change in the product structure, a scrap ticket affecting the quantity on an open order, or an inventory discrepancy would not trigger a partial explosion in a requirements alteration system, but would trigger a partial explosion in a net change.

**Requirements generation.** One of the many terms used to describe early approaches to MRP. Usually "requirements generation" implied that gross requirements for material were not netted against inventory to determine net requirements. Sometimes the term is used to describe the function of exploding net requirements through the bill of material to the lower component levels as one phase of level-by-level time phased MRP.

**Requirements planning.** Obsolescent terminology. See Material requirements planning or Capacity requirements planning.

**Reservation.** See Allocation.

**Reserve stock.** See Safety stock.

**Resource requirements planning.** When a master schedule is first being composed, a resource requirements plan is frequently made. In broad terms this compares the demand on some of the manufacturing facilities, engineering facilities, etc., with the availability of these resources in order to determine whether or not the master schedule is reasonable.

**ROP.** Reorder point.

**Routing.** A specification of the operations required to manufacture a product.

**RSFE.** Running sum of the forecast errors; See Tracking signal.

**Safety stock.** Stock replenishment systems are based on estimates of demand over lead time. Since demand in any particular lead time could exceed the estimates, extra inventory called safety stock is planned into the order point.

**Scheduled receipt.** An open shop or purchase order in an MRP output format. So called because the date the order is expected to be received is especially important since so much of the value of MRP derives from its rescheduling capability.

**Scheduling.** Establishing the timing for performing a task. There are various levels of scheduling within a manufacturing company. The master schedule establishes the overall logistics plan for supplying material to support production and sales. Material requirements are generated, and scheduled due dates are established for this material to support the master schedule. Shop orders may be broken down into more detailed schedules for each operation and desired completion (or start) dates for each of these operations established to show when they must be completed in order to get the shop order completed on time.

**Scientific inventory control.** This was the name given to the use of statistical techniques for computing safety stock and mathematical computations of economic order quantities.

**Second order smoothing.** A more sophisticated form of exponential smoothing that includes a smoothed "trend correction."

**Semi-finished inventory.** Inventory that is stored before some final operations which will convert it to different products. Builder's hardware, for example, is usually stored before the finishing operation so that it can be plated or painted to meet specific requirements.

**Shop order.** An order going to the factory authorizing manufacture of an item.

**Shop planner.** A production control person who works in the factory with dispatch lists and capacity control reports.

**Shortage list.** This is the list of material missing when the required material is staged; see Staging.

**Single smoothing.** Synonym for first order smoothing.

**Slack time priority rule.** Scheduling virtually always allows some time between operations. Subtracting the standard hours of set-up and running time from the total schedule time shows the slack time. Dividing the number of operations into this slack time gives a reasonably logical priority rule where the job with the least slack time per operation has the highest priority, etc.

**Staging.** When the formal priority planning system did not work, expediters pulled material from the stockroom to see which ones were missing to make the products on the master schedule. An expensive, confusing, obsolete practice. A synonym is accumulation.

**Stock chasing.** An obsolete yet still descriptive term for expediting.

**Time phased order point.** Material requirements planning for independent demand items where the independent forecast, rather than higher-level requirements, is put into the time periods.

**Time phasing.** A term frequently used as a synonym for MRP. Modern MRP systems are time phased into weekly time periods by definition, thus the term is obsolescent. Strictly speaking it refers to the practice of showing requirements, scheduled receipts, the projected available balance, and planned order releases in their proper time relationship to each other.

**Time series planning.** Synonym for MRP; obsolete terminology.

**Time shift.** A time phased MRP system is usually designed to eliminate the current time period when it is over. This would occur weekly in a system using weekly time periods. When the shift takes place, some planned orders will "mature," i.e., those with release dates in the time period that has now become current will need to be released. Scheduled receipts may move into the "past due" period, unreleased requirements may become past due, etc.

**Tracking signal.** A simple technique for determining whether a forecast is working well. The deviations from forecast are added together. Since the pluses will cancel out the minuses, this "running sum of the forecast errors" will be a very small number if the forecast is operating well. If sales are picking up rapidly and the forecast isn't tracking it properly, a large running sum of the forecast errors (RSFE) would result. Usually the mean absolute deviation is divided into the RSFE, and if this number exceeds a preestablished limit, an exception message is generated.

**Tradeoff curves.** A curve showing the amount of inventory required to give various levels of customer service or the amount of lot-size inventory that would be generated by a given number of orders. Sometimes called "exchange curves."

**Transportation inventory.** Inventory that exists because it must be transported. If it takes two weeks to ship inventory from one point to another an average two-week supply will be in transit.

**Turnover rate.** A performance measure that is most meaningful within a company rather than comparing a company's performance with other companies. The turnover rate is calculated by dividing the inventory investment into the annual cost of sales to see how many times the inventory "turns over" during the year. Frequently, turnover rate is calculated by dividing the inventory investment into the actual sales figure, which tends to give an inflated turnover rate.

**Two bin system.** A simple inventory control technique where a quantity of the item equivalent to its order point is sealed in one bin while the "free stock" is stored in another. When the free stock is exhausted, the sealed bin is opened and a reorder is generated. No inventory balance records are kept. Used primarily for low-value items with a steady, predictable demand.

**Visual review system.** A simple inventory control technique that involves periodically looking at the physical amount of inventory on hand and determining whether or not to reorder based on the level in a bin, the number of containers on hand, etc. No inventory records are posted. Used primarily for low-value hardware items with steady demand.

**Where used list.** An inverted bill of material that shows where each component is used at its higher level.

**Work center.** This is a group of machines or work stations or people who can perform similar operations. A number of presses of the same capacity that can take the same dies could be considered within one work center for capacity planning purposes.

# Bibliography

This is a very brief bibliography, not intended to be comprehensive at all, but only to point out a few books and articles that should be of particular significance to the student and executive. A comprehensive bibliography is published periodically by the American Production and Inventory Control Society, Inc. (APICS), Suite 504 Watergate Building, 2600 Virginia Avenue, N.W., Washington, D.C. 20037. It would be of interest to anyone who wishes further references.

### General Production and Inventory Control

Greene, James H. *Production and Inventory Control Handbook.* New York: McGraw-Hill, 1970.

> This book covers all facets of production and inventory control. A good deal of it was written by practitioners and, in general, it is down to earth and straightforward.

Plossl, G. W., and Wight, O. W. *Production and Inventory Control: Principles and Techniques.* Englewood Cliffs, N.J.: Prentice-Hall, 1967.

> This is the standard textbook and business reference in the field of production and inventory management. While some of the more recent topics like MRP are not covered in sufficient depth, they are given more coverage than in any other textbook available.

*COPICS Manuals* (Communications Oriented Production Information and Control System), IBM Corporation, Data Processing Division, 1133 Westchester Avenue, White Plains, N.Y. 10604, 1972.

> This is an eight-volume description of the elements of a modern computer-based production and inventory management system. It is available from IBM branch offices.

### Order Point Based Priority Planning

Independent demand "inventory control" systems were the only ones discussed in the literature for years. Most of what was written is highly mathematical with very little practical orientation. Independent demand inventory control topics are covered in the references listed above, but the following two references would be of interest to someone who wants to pursue the subject more deeply.

Brown, Robert Goodell. *Decision Rules for Inventory Management*. New York: Holt, Rinehart, and Winston, 1967.

> Brown is the authority on statistical inventory control and this is his most readable book. One must always remember that independent demand inventory systems are his primary interest, and the reader must be aware that he typically presents a world where all of the problems fit these solutions in spite of the fact that in the real world only a very small percentage of them do

Brown, Robert Goodell. *Management Decision for Production Operations* Hinsdale, Ill.: Dryden Press, 1971.

> In this book, Brown launches into many other areas as well as covering his favorite topics of statistical order point and economic order quantity. It is not a book on production and inventory management by any stretch of the imagination, but perhaps the title of section 5, "The Decision Analyst's Kitbag," best describes it. For someone who wants to have an idea of the operations research solutions and the problems that fit them, this is an excellent reference.

### MRP-Based Priority Planning

Thurston, Phillip H. "Requirements Planning for Inventory Control." *Harvard Business Review* (May–June, 1972).

APICS Special Report. *Material Requirements Planning by Computer*. Washington, D.C.: American Production and Inventory Control Society, 1971.

> This brief (86-page) booklet was a milestone in the field of production and inventory management. It drew out the knowledge of a number of companies who were the pioneering users of MRP. It summarizes their experience and shows their output reports.

Orlicky, Joseph A.; Plossl, G. W; and Wight, O W. "Material Requirements Planning Systems." IBM-sponsored publication, 1971, Form #G320-1170. (Subject: speeches by the authors at the 1970 APICS International Conference in Cincinnati.)

Chobanian, John A.; Garwood, Dave; Langenwalter, Daniel F.; Orlicky, Joseph A.; Plossl, George W.; Wight, Oliver W.; and Zimmermann, John C. "Structuring the Bill of Material." IBM-sponsored publication, 1973, Form #G320-1245. (Reprints of articles, papers, and book excerpts on the subject of bill of material structure.)

Wight, Oliver W. "Time Phasing." *Modern Materials Handling Magazine* (October 1971). (Subject: computer-based MRP.)


### Capacity Planning and Shop Control

Plossl, George W., and Wight, Oliver W. "Capacity Planning and Control." (Speeches given at the APICS International Conference in St. Louis, November 4, 1971.)

Goddard, Walter E. "How To Reduce and Control Lead Times." (Speech presented at the APICS International Conference in Cincinnati, October 9, 1970, and published in conference proceedings.)

"Which is Better—Red Tags or Critical Ratio?" *Newsletter*, Number 10, Oliver Wight, Inc., P. O. Box 435, Newbury, N.H. 03255.

"Input/Output Control in Perspective." Newsletter, Number 14, Oliver Wight, Inc., P. O. Box 435, Newbury, N.H. 03255.

"Input/Output Control." *Modern Materials Handling Magazine* (September 1970).

Wassweiler, William R. "MRP—The Key to Critical Ratio Effectiveness." *Production and Inventory Management Journal* (3rd Quarter 1972).

Garwood, Dave. "Delivery As Promised." *Production and Inventory Management Journal* (3rd Quarter 1971).


### Computer Systems

Orlicky, J. A. *The Successful Computer System.* New York: McGraw-Hill, 1969.

> This book presents a management approach to computer systems. It is thorough and gives the executive a good basic understanding of the computer and computer-based systems.

Wight, Oliver W. *The Executive's New Computer.* Reston, Va.: Reston Publishing Company, 1972.

> A very readable, somewhat iconoclastic look at the computer in the business world, pointing out the common pitfalls of computer systems and what needs to be done to avoid them.

*Unlocking the Computer's Profit Potential.* McKinsey & Company, Inc., 245 Park Avenue, New York, N.Y. 10017, 1968.

>This is a survey of companies using computers that draws some conclusions about their reasons for success and failure. It is updated periodically.

Dearden, John. "M.I.S. is a Mirage." *Harvard Business Review* (January–February 1972).

>A well-reasoned critique of the misguided attempts at a total management information system.

### Audiovisual Material

MRP Crusade Films.

>This is a series of eleven films on many of the significant aspects of MRP. The film series is sponsored by IBM, and the films were made available to APICS. Companies wishing to use these films should either contact the APICS National Office in Washington, D.C., or any IBM branch office.

Video-assisted instruction courses on production and inventory management and MRP are available from Advanced Systems, Inc., 1601 Tonne Road, Elk Grove Village, Ill. 60007.

# Index